LIBRARY OF SECOND TEMPLE STUDIES

97

formerly the Journal for the Study of the Pseudepigrapha Supplement Series

Editor
Lester L. Grabbe

Founding Editor
James H. Charlesworth

Editorial Board
Randall D. Chesnutt, Jan Willem van Henten, Judith M. Lieu,
Steven Mason, James R. Mueller, Loren T. Stuckenbruck,
James C. VanderKam

LEGAL EXEGESIS OF SCRIPTURE
IN THE WORKS OF JOSEPHUS

Michael Avioz

LONDON • NEW YORK • OXFORD • NEW DELHI • SYDNEY

T&T CLARK
Bloomsbury Publishing Plc
50 Bedford Square, London, WC1B 3DP, UK
1385 Broadway, New York, NY 10018, USA
29 Earlsfort Terrace, Dublin 2, Ireland

BLOOMSBURY, T&T CLARK and the T&T Clark logo
are trademarks of Bloomsbury Publishing Plc

First published in Great Britain 2021
This paperback edition published in 2022

© Michael Avioz, 2021

Michael Avioz has asserted his right under the Copyright, Designs and Patents Act, 1988, to be identified as the Author of this work.

All rights reserved. No part of this publication may be reproduced or transmitted in any form or by any means, electronic or mechanical, including photocopying, recording, or any information storage or retrieval system, without prior permission in writing from the publishers.

Bloomsbury Publishing Plc does not have any control over, or responsibility for, any third-party websites referred to or in this book. All internet addresses given in this book were correct at the time of going to press. The author and publisher regret any inconvenience caused if addresses have changed or sites have ceased to exist, but can accept no responsibility for any such changes.

A catalogue record for this book is available from the British Library.
A catalog record for this book is available from the Library of Congress.
Library of Congress Control Number: 2020942376

ISBN: HB: 978-0-5676-8115-7
PB: 978-0-5676-9695-3
ePDF: 978-0-5676-8116-4

Series: Library of Second Temple Studies, volume 97

Typeset by: Forthcoming Publications Ltd

To find out more about our authors and books visit www.bloomsbury.com and sign up for our newsletters.

Contents

Preface	vii
Abbreviations	ix
INTRODUCTION	1
Defining 'Halakha'	1
The Corpus	2
Earlier Studies	2
Methodology	5
Omissions	7
Note on Translations and Editions	8
Outline of the Remaining Chapters	8
Conclusion	9
Chapter 1	
THE LAWS OF EXODUS IN JOSEPHUS	10
Omissions	10
Passover (Exod. 12, Lev. 23.5-14, and Num. 28.16-25 //	
Ant. 2.311-19)	12
Tefillin (Exod. 13.9, 16)	14
The Ten Commandments	15
Slavery Laws	24
Three Capital Offenses (Exod. 21.12–17)	26
Infliction of Bodily Injury (Exod. 21.18-27)	26
Striking a Pregnant Woman (Exod. 21.22-23 // *Ant.* 4.278)	27
Animal Theft (Exod. 21.37–22.3 // *Ant.* 4.272)	28
Deposit Law (Exod. 23.4-5; Deut. 22.1-3 // *Ant.* 4.274)	29
The Prohibition of Sorcery (Exod. 21.17 // *Ant.* 4.279)	30
The Altar Law (Exod. 20.23)	31
Goring Ox (Exod. 21.28-36 // *Ant.* 4.281-82)	31
Conclusion	32
Chapter 2	
THE LAWS OF LEVITICUS IN JOSEPHUS' WRITINGS	33
The Structure of Leviticus	34
Laws of Leviticus in Josephus' Antiquities	34

The Starting Point of Leviticus	36
The Ending of Leviticus	36
Laws Omitted by Josephus	37
Sacrifices in Josephus (*Ant.* 3.224-57)	37
Animals Forbidden for Consumption (Lev. 11 and Deut. 14 // *Ant.* 3.259)	49
Prohibition on Eating Fat, an Impure Carcass, and Blood (Lev. 7.22-27; 11.24-47; 17.10-16; *Ant.* 3.260)	49
Childbirth (Lev. 12.2-8 // *Ant.* 3.269)	51
Homosexuality and Incest (Lev. 18 and 20 // *Ant.* 3.274-75)	52
Various Laws for Priests (Lev. 21–22 // *Ant.* 3.276-79)	53
Sabbatical Year (Lev. 25 // *Ant.* 3.280-85)	54
Votive Gifts (Lev. 27 // *Ant.* 4.71-73)	55
The Blasphemer (Lev. 24 // *Ant.* 4.202)	56
Mixture of Wool and Linen (Lev. 19.19 and Deut. 22.11 // *Ant.* 4.208)	56
Fruit of the Fourth Year (Lev. 19.23-25 // *Ant.* 4.226-27)	57
First Fruit of Trees (Lev. 19.23-25 // *Ant.* 4.227)	57
Conclusion	58

Chapter 3
THE LAWS OF THE BOOK OF NUMBERS IN JOSEPHUS 59
   Omissions 60
   The Census and Encamping of the Tribes
      (Num. 1–2 // *Ant.* 3.287-94) 63
   The Commissioning and Purification of the Levites
      (Num. 3.5-10; 8.5-26 // *Ant.* 3.258) 64
   Law of the Sotah (Num. 5.11-30 // *Ant.* 3.270-73) 70
   The Nazirite Law (Num. 6.1-21 // *Ant.* 4.72) 76
   Grain Offering Accompanying Sacrifices
      (Num. 15.4-10 // *Ant.* 3.234) 78
   The Red Heifer (Num. 19 // *Ant.* 3.262; 4.79-81) 78
   Zelophehad's Daughters (Num. 27 and 36 // *Ant.* 4.174-75) 79
   Regulation to Redeem a Firstborn Donkey (Num. 18.15 // *Ant.* 4.71) 80
   Laws of the Cities of Refuge
      (Exod. 21.12-14; Num. 35; Deut. 4; 19 // *Ant.* 4.172-73) 80
   Conclusion 81

Chapter 4
THE LAWS OF DEUTERONOMY IN JOSEPHUS 83
   Omissions 85
   The Holy City and the Temple (Deut. 12 // *Ant.* 4.200-201) 86
   Pilgrimage (Deut. 16.16 // *Ant.* 4.203-204) 87
   Second Tithe (Deut. 14.22-27 // *Ant.* 4.205) 87
   Harlot's Fee or a Dog's Price (Deut. 23.19 // *Ant.* 4.206) 87

Summoning the People (Hakhēl) and Studying Torah
 (Deut. 31.9-13 // *Ant.* 4.209-11)   88
Israel's Judicial System (Deut. 16.18–17.13 // *Ant.* 4.214-18)   88
Witnesses (Deut. 19.15-21 // *Ant.* 4.219)   89
Unsolved Murder (Deut. 21.10 // *Ant.* 4.220-22)   90
The Law of the King (Deut. 17.14-20 // *Ant.* 4.223-24)   92
Prohibition on Moving Boundary Markers
 (Deut. 19.14 // *Ant.* 4.225)   93
Various Laws of Charity and Tithes
 (Deut. 14, 24, 26 and Lev. 19 // *Ant.* 4.231-43)   93
Liturgical Declarations Recited When Bringing the First Fruits
 (Deut. 26 // *Ant.* 4.242-43)   96
Marital Laws (Deut. 22–25 // *Ant.* 4.244-59)   96
Levirate Marriage (Deut. 25.5-10 // *Ant.* 4.254-56)   99
The Law of a Captive Beautiful Woman
 (Deut. 21.10-14 // *Ant.* 4.257-59)   100
The Law of the Rebellious Son (Deut. 21.18-21 // *Ant.* 4.260-64)   101
Prohibition on Exposing Corpse after Hanging
 (Deut. 21.22-23 // *Ant.* 4.265)   105
Taking and Holding Distrained Property
 (Deut. 24.10-13 // *Ant.* 4.267-70)   106
Caring for the Blind (Deut. 27.14; Lev. 19.14 // *Ant.* 4.276)   107
Torts (Exod. 24.2; Lev. 24.19; Deut. 19.21 // *Ant.* 4.277-84)   107
Building a Parapet on the Roof (Deut. 22.8 // *Ant.* 4.284)   110
Timely Payment of Wages (Deut. 24.14-15 // *Ant.* 4.288)   110
Preventing Transgenerational Punishment
 (Deut. 24.16 // *Ant.* 4.289)   110
Castration (Deut. 23.2 // *Ant.* 4.290-91)   111
Laws of Warfare (Deut. 20–21; 23.10-15; 24.5 // *Ant.* 4.296-300)   112
Cross-Dressing (Deut. 22.5 // *Ant.* 4.301)   113
Eradicating Amalek (Exod. 17.8-16; Deut. 25.17 // *Ant.* 4.304)   113
Apostasy (Deut. 13 // *Ant.* 4.310)   114
Conclusion   114

Chapter 5
JUXTAPOSITION IN JOSEPHUS' REWRITING OF THE LAWS   116

Chapter 6
REASONS FOR THE COMMANDMENTS IN JOSEPHUS' WRITINGS   120
 Josephus – Between Interpretation and Apologetics   122
 The Sabbath Law   123
 The Law of Shemittah   123
 The Law for Interest on Loans   124
 Tefillin (*Ant.* 4.213)   125

Pledge (Deut. 24.10-13 // *Ant.* 4.267-70)	125
Kilayim (Mixed Species)	126
Levirate Marriages (*Ant.* 4.254)	127
Conclusion	128

Chapter 7
JOSEPHUS' PERSPECTIVE ON DEFINING MOSES
AS A LAWGIVER OR MEDIATOR 129
    Conclusion 131

Chapter 8
WAS JOSEPHUS INFLUENCED BY ROMAN LAW? 132
    Methodological Problems 135
    Conclusion 138

CONCLUSIONS 139

Bibliography	141
Index of References	159
Index of Authors	174

Preface

This book developed from my classes on Josephus delivered at Bar-Ilan University over the last decade. A few parts of this study were published elsewhere and have been reformulated, updated and adjusted for the current book. I would like to thank Harrasowitz Verlag for their permission to republish the section on the law of the rebellious son (*ZAR* 2017); Peeters for their consent to republish the section on the purification of the Levites in Josephus (*ETL* 2014); and de Gruyter, for their permission to republish my forthcoming work on the Sotah in the BZAW series.

I am very grateful to Bloomsbury Press for accepting to publish this book, and in particular to Sarah Blake and Dominic Mattos for helping to bring this study to its completion. Also, my thanks go to Dr. Michael Graham and Mr. Yoni Brukirer for their assistance in improving the English style.

Last but not least, I wish to thank Dr. Duncan Burns for his patience, good advice, and excellent copy-editing, which helped me a lot in preparing a manuscript of the highest standards.

ABBREVIATIONS

Note: The LCL translations of Josephus' writings are cited using the relevant translator's surname (e.g. Begg, Feldman, Thackeray, Whiston). Full publication information for the LCL volumes is supplied in the bibliography.

AOTC	Apollos Old Testament Commentary
AB	Anchor Bible
ABD	*Anchor Bible Dictionary*
AJSR	*Association for Jewish Studies Review*
BBR	*Bulletin for Biblical Research*
BETL	Bibliotheca Ephemeridum Theologicarum Lovaniensium
BibInt	*Biblical Interpretation*
BZAW	Beihefte zur ZAW
BZNW	Beihefte zur Zeitschrift für die neutestamentliche Wissenschaft
CBET	Contributions to Biblical Exegesis and Theology
CBQ	*Catholic Biblical Quarterly*
CQ	*Classical Quarterly*
CRINT	Compendia Rerum Iudaicarum ad Novum Testamentum
DJD	*Discoveries in the Judaean Desert*
ETL	*Ephemerides Theologicae Lovanienses*
FAT	Forschungen zum Alten Testament
FRLANT	Forschungen zur Religion und Literatur des Alten und Neuen Testaments
HCOT	Historical Commentary on the Old Testament
HTR	Harvard Theological Review
HUCA	*Hebrew Union College Annual*
JAAR	*Journal of the American Academy of Religion*
JAJ	*Journal of Ancient Judaism*
JBL	*Journal of Biblical Literature*
JJS	*Journal of Jewish Studies*
JPS	Jewish Publication Society
JQR	*Jewish Quarterly Review*
JSJ	*Journal for the Study of Judaism in the Persian, Hellenistic and Roman Period*
JSJSup	Journal for the Study of Judaism Supplement
JSOT	*Journal for the Study of the Old Testament*
JSOTSup	Journal for the Study of the Old Testament, Supplements Series
JSP	*Journal for the Study of the Pseudepigrapha*

JSPSup	Journal for the Study of the Pseudepigrapha, Supplements Series
JSQ	*Jewish Studies Quarterly*
LBHOTS	Library of Hebrew Bible/Old Testament Studies
LCL	Loeb Classical Library
LNTS	Library of New Testament Studies
NICOT	New International Commentary on the Old Testament
NovT	*Novum Testamentum*
NovTSup	Novum Testamentum, Supplements
NRSV	New Revised Standard Version
NTS	*New Testament Studies*
OBO	Orbis biblicus et orientalis
OTL	Old Testament Library Commentary Series
PEQ	*Palestine Exploration Quarterly*
RB	Revue Biblique
REJ	*Revue des Études Juives*
SBL	Society of Biblical Literature
SBLDS	SBL Dissertation Series
SCI	*Scripta Classica Israelica*
SCS	Septuagint and Cognate Studies
SJOT	*Scandinavian Journal of the Old Testament*
SPhiloA	*Studia Philonica Annual*
STDJ	Studies on the Texts of the Desert of Judah
TSAJ	Texts and Studies in Ancient Judaism
TZ	*Theologische Zeitschrift*
VT	*Vetus Testamentum*
VTSup	Vetus Testamentum Supplements Series
WBC	Word Biblical Commentary
WTJ	*Westminster Theological Journal*
WUNT	Wissenschaftliche Untersuchungen zum Neuen Testament
ZAW	*Zeitschrift für die alttestamentliche Wissenschaft*

INTRODUCTION

Flavius Josephus (37–100~ BCE) is generally known as a historian and as a military commander. Less known are his abilities as an exegete. In my recent book,[1] I tried to show how this component is revealed in Josephus' rewriting of the books of Samuel. I intend to continue this approach in the present work, this time examining legal exegesis (referred to by earlier scholars as the halakha) in Josephus' rewriting of the Torah.

I will focus on his retelling of the laws of the Torah in his works and compare it with tannaitic literature as well as other contemporary, Second Temple period sources. When there are similarities, are we to suppose earlier knowledge of a certain form of the tannaitic sources? When there are dissimilarities, do they stem from a different Vorlage? Do they reflect the 'early halakha'?[2] Did Josephus try to bridge the gap between Judaism and Hellenism in an apologetic manner? In other words, are the changes deliberate or accidental? Can they provide us with the realia of the Second Temple era?

Defining 'Halakha'

Halakha may be described as the tradition of formulated rules of conduct regulating life in Judaism.[3] Tomson adds that

> it has a literary, a legal and a social aspect: halakha is, besides midrash and aggada, one of the classic literary genres of Rabbinic literature; it is also a legal system which develops in comparable ways to other systems yet distinct from them; and it is the whole of traditional behavioural rules of the Jewish people.[4]

1. Avioz 2015.
2. Frankel and Geiger coined the term 'early halakha'. See Sussmann 1989–90: 13–14. It referred to the 'development of Jewish religious life and thought in the period between the conclusion of the Hebrew Bible and the first generations of the *Tannaim*'. See Teeter 2014: 28.
3. Safrai 1987.
4. Tomson 1990: 19.

As Schiffman[5] has pointed out, there is some anachronism in using the term 'halakha', which is taken from the rabbinic literature. This term was not yet fixed at the time of Josephus and thus Amihay and Jassen[6] preferred the term 'Jewish Law'.

The Corpus

Josephus' treatment of the biblical legal material is found in his *Antiquities* book 3 (§§224-86) and 4 (§§67-75, 199-301).[7] However, we need to further extend the scope to include narratives found outside the Pentateuch, where legal elements appear in biblical prose and in other literary genres. Likewise, there are relevant materials in Josephus' other works: e.g., *Ag. Ap.* 2.145-295;[8] and in *War* 6.423 and 426-27 there is a summary of the laws of the paschal sacrifice.

Josephus rewrites the book of Leviticus in the third and fourth books of his *Antiquities*; specifically in *Ant.* 3.90-286 and 4.196-301. *Antiquities* 3.224-86 follow Leviticus and Numbers; *Ant.* 4.196-301 largely draw upon Deuteronomy.

David Altshuler has observed that over 600 verses of biblical laws have no parallel in the *Antiquities*, despite Josephus' claim of completeness.[9]

Other Second Temple sources used in my research were composed or are preserved in various languages – Hebrew, Aramaic, Greek, and Latin. They include Philo, Josephus, Qumran, the New Testament, and rabbinic literature.

Earlier Studies

Scholars of the halakha usually worked with rabbinic literature in order to reconstruct the development of the halakha from its earliest phases. At first, the sources that were examined for that purpose included the Apocrypha, Pseudepigrapha, Philo,[10] Josephus, the New Testament, and rabbinic literature. With the discovery of the Dead Sea Scrolls, a great

---

5. Schiffman 2009: 115.
6. Amihay 2017: 7; Jassen 2014: 1 n. 1.
7. I will not deal with the laws prior to Moses (namely in Genesis). See Wadler 2018. Related to this issue is burial, where some details may be deemed 'law', while others may be defined as practice. On burial in Josephus, see Avioz 2014.
8. See Kasher 1996; Gerber 1997; Barclay 2007.
9. Altshuler 1982–83: 5.
10. See Ritter 1879.

advance in this field was made, since it enabled scholars to directly access Second Temple period evidence on how certain authors thought halakha should be practiced. The halakhic material includes the Temple Scroll, the Damascus Document, Miqṣat Ma'ase ha-Torah (MMT), and others.[11] Most scholars dealing with Qumran either left Josephus out of their studies or paid little attention to him.

Research on Jewish law in Josephus began in the nineteenth century with Tachauer, Olitzki, Weyl, Koehler, and others, whose works were reviewed by Feldman.[12] These works mainly focused on Josephus' sources for halakhic issues.[13] In the twentieth century, three major dissertations were written on this topic: Altshuler (1977), Goldenberg (1978), and Gallant (1988). To date, the most recent dissertation written on the halakha in Josephus is that of Nakman (2004).

Louis Feldman was a leading scholar on Josephus. Over a period of more than fifty years he published many important studies on Josephus. With regard to the halakha he wrote the notes in volumes 1-4 for the Brill Josephus Project.[14] However, these notes, important as they may be, cannot be regarded as a thorough analysis.

Feldman presents 36 cases where Josephus' legal position diverges from the plain meaning of the biblical text. In half of these cases, Josephus' view concurs with that of rabbinic halakha, and Feldman suggests that the other half reflect an 'earlier or alternate version of the Oral Torah'.[15] Feldman's conclusions should be taken with caution; these issues are considerably more complex than his simplistic solution suggests.

Feldman attributed many of Josephus' changes to his apologetic agenda. This is similar to Fraade's position: 'Josephus's reconstituting of biblical laws into a "constitution", however, fits well within a recurring apologetic

---

11. See Shemesh 2009: 2; 2010; Werman and Shemesh 2011. See also the numerous studies written by Schiffman; Jassen 2014; Amihay 2017.

12. Feldman 1989: 416–20. Other reviews can be found in Goldenberg 1978 and Nakman 2004.

13. See Kohler 1931: 69: '[Josephus] had before him an older priestly document, similar to that found in the so-called Zadokite Manifesto of Damascus...and, as he did in many other instances, embodied it in his work with occasional alterations, without mentioning his source'. Goldenberg (1978: 14) summarized the opinions of these scholars as to Josephus' sources: oral law, apology, ignorance, contemporaneous practical law, Josephus' own opinion, Roman law, Philo, Targum, written legal source, Josephus' intention to write a separate treatise on the laws, and Josephus' character.

14. Feldman 2000. See also his 1997 essay as well his 1989 annotated bibliography.

15. Noam (2011a) follows this line of thought. See also Schwartz 2014.

theme of Josephus's overall narrative history'.[16] A more nuanced attitude is required, paving the way for alternative explanations.

Even though Begg has written extensively on Josephus, he barely wrote on Jewish law in Josephus, and the only paper that relates to this topic is his study on Yom Kippur in Josephus.[17]

Other works have been devoted to specific legal issues in Josephus: in 2002 Collautti wrote a monograph on Passover in Josephus' writings, and in 1999 Doering wrote a chapter on Josephus in his monograph on the Sabbath.

David Nakman wrote his doctoral dissertation in 2004 on the halakha in Josephus' writings. His aim was to 'examine the scope and quality of the halakhic material in Josephus' works and explore how and to what extent it can be used in order to study the halakha prevalent in the Land of Israel in the first century CE'.[18] Regev and Nakman wrote an article in 2002 where they tried to examine Josephus' sectarian affiliations. Nakman has recently written that: 'By studying Josephus's halachic material, we can assess both his sectarian affiliations and his familiarity with the practices of those common Jews who did not belong to the sects'.[19]

The overall attitude of Nakman towards Josephus is negative. He interprets many differences between Josephus and the Hebrew Bible as Josephus' ignorance or sloppiness. Like Belkin and Feldman,[20] he too gives preference to the in-depth discussion of the rabbis over the supposed shallowness of Josephus. This can be seen in his comments on the ritual described in Deut. 21.1-9:

> Josephus describes the procedure [in Deut. 21.1-9] in great detail, and hardly omits anything from the MT. The details he added and the changes he entered are insignificant… In contrast, the rabbinic Sages read the Torah carefully and had many novelties.[21]

In contrast to these evaluations, I argue in turn that Josephus' exegetical project is by no means insignificant. If we regard the ancient scholar as not fluent in biblical Hebrew and having many questions on the biblical record, then Josephus' s additions and changes are very valuable.

---

16. Fraade 2011: 24.
17. Begg 2012.
18. Nakman 2004: 1.
19. Nakman 2016: 283.
20. Belkin 1970: 304; Feldman 2000: 294 n. 622; 2006: 381–411.
21. Nakman 2004: 144.

In most cases Nakman does not examine the biblical background of the laws, the difficulties in the biblical record, and the research published on these laws in recent years.[22] Such an examination would have led to a very different conclusion, especially in those cases where Josephus suggests an interpretation that is accepted by modern scholars. I concur with Mason who wrote that 'it seems bizarre to maintain that these deviations must be due to Josephus' imperfect knowledge, faulty memory, and tendentious reworking of the tradition'.[23]

There are various approaches among scholars regarding Josephus' testimony on halakhic matters. On the one hand, Abraham Schalit[24] has written: 'There is no reason to doubt the veracity of Josephus' words in *Life*, that he learned a great deal of Torah in his father's house and excelled in his acumen and proficiency'. Hadas-Lebel[25] also followed this line. On the other hand, Chanoch Albeck[26] has cautioned against the unconditional use of Philo and Josephus in studying the history of halakha. Josephus writes for a non-Jewish audience and aims to reconcile Judaism with Greco-Roman points of view. Both derive their statements from their own Scriptural exegesis, and may not represent the normative halakha of their day.[27]

Goldenberg[28] suggests that the near correspondences between Josephus and tannaitic sources might be explained by the existence of a written source of Jewish legal practices that was known to Josephus and later became part of the tannaitic writings. Yet, this conclusion is far-fetched since there are also many cases in which Josephus deviates from the tannaitic sources. Moreover, one cannot prove that Josephus relied on a written source; the similarity may be based on oral tradition as well.[29]

Methodology

Christina Termini rightly pointed out the many problems in dealing with the legal material in the Torah:

---

22. His constant use of charts limits the scope of discussion to a few words on omissions, additions and changes.
23. Mason 2009: 49.
24. Schalit 1944–63: XXXVI.
25. Hadas-Lebel 1993.
26. Albeck 1930.
27. See Schiffman 1975: 13.
28. Goldenberg 1978.
29. Cf. Nakman 2004: 52–7.

[T]he large number of precepts spread throughout the biblical text; the casuistic character of the formulation; the apparently incoherent alternations of cultic, ethnic, civil and penal laws; the numerous contradictions; and the even more frequent cases of partial restatement.[30]

To this we may add that the notion of 613 Mitzvot (laws) appears, first, in a non-legal passage of the Babylonian Talmud (*b. Mak.* 23b-24a).[31] There is a long-standing debate among Jewish halakhic authorities as to what constitutes a distinct commandment. This is very important when comparing Josephus to other commentators through the ages. It is not obvious that what Josephus counts as a law other sages and scholars viewed in the same way. This point was never addressed in the work of Nakman.

To complicate matters even further, there is no scholarly study that tries to identify all of the biblical laws. The reason for this lies in the fact that scholars do not agree on what can be deemed 'law' and what is not. Should Numbers 31 be identified as law? This situation adds more complexity to the attempt to collect all biblical laws and compare them to Josephus' rewriting, since there is no consensus as to what is a law in the Bible. I have tried to skirt this issue by consulting well-established commentaries on the books of Exodus to Deuteronomy to ensure that the units being compared are defined by at least some scholars as laws.

I will compare the laws in Exodus through Deuteronomy to their rewriting by Josephus. I will analyze changes between the biblical text and Josephus and compare the rewriting to other Second Temple sources. Likewise, the textual witnesses of the Old Testament will be consulted as well, especially the LXX.[32]

When analyzing a specific issue in Josephus we need to assemble all relevant sources. However, when consecutive verses are involved, the situation is much more complex. While Nakman sorted the laws of the Torah according to the assumed order of Josephus, I have decided to provide the reader with a super-commentary by Josephus of the Pentateuchal books. I will follow Josephus' order but at the same time coordinate it with the order of the MT whenever possible. When a law appears in several books, I will usually deal with the main source appearing in the MT.

---

30. Termini 2004: 1.
31. Herman 2016. For other problems inherent in biblical law that necessitated interpretation, see Bernstein 2013: 2:449.
32. See recently Avioz forthcoming b.

Introduction 7

My starting point in each chapter of this book are the biblical laws and the specific problems they entail. Then follows an attempt to explain the changes between the Bible and Josephus, with an eye on the relevant Second Temple sources. Other relevant passages in Josephus' works will also be examined.

Omissions

One of the well-known phenomena in Josephus' writings relates to omissions. This holds true for the rewriting of biblical laws as well. Omissions may be the result of several factors. Shaye Cohen[33] writes that

> Josephus freely omits whatever he does not need: long lists of Semitic names, incidents embarrassing (Reuben and Bilhah; Judah and Tamar; the golden calf; the complaint of Aaron and Miriam against Moses' wife) or difficult (the mention of Goliath in 2 Samuel 21.19)…and miracles. Some passages he just forgot (the pestilence of the Ten Plagues; the reign of Tola). He condenses technical material (the laws and rituals of the Pentateuch) and uninteresting details (the complications of the apportionment of Canaan among the tribes).

We may categorize the omissions as either intentional and unintentional, both of which may be related to:

1. Textual reasons: Josephus may preserve a divergent version, different from the MT, the LXX or both.
2. Apologetic concerns: the most famous omission by Josephus is the golden calf narrative (Exod. 32–34) – a narrative that presents Aaron in a problematic light, as well as Israel as idolatrous, immediately after the Decalogue and the theophany at Sinai.[34] Also relevant in this context is the omission of circumcision from several places. Here we may include personal, national, theological and ideological reasons for omissions.[35]
3. Complexity: The source may be too obscure and complicated for Josephus and omitting it may solve the problem (i.e. David and Goliath in 1 Sam. 17).

---

33. Cohen 2002: 37.
34. See Sterling 2018.
35. See Spilsbury 1996.

4. Irrelevance: Josephus did not find the whole Bible relevant to his aim of reconstructing the history of Israel. Josephus himself states in *Ant.* 9.242: 'This prophet prophesied many other things about Ninue in addition to these that I did not think it necessary to speak of, but have passed over in order not to seem tiresome to my readers'. He also avoids mentioning lists of names as in *Ant.* 2.176; *Ant.* 7.369; and 11.152 (Ezra). Finally, Josephus omits direct speech, as well as the biblical songs (i.e. Judg. 5).

With regards to unintentional omissions, one may relate them to sloppiness and negligence. In many cases, this is the line of thought taken by David Nakman in his dissertation on the halakha in Josephus.[36]

Generally speaking, Jason von Ehrenkrook advises the following in his book *Sculpting Idolatry in Flavian Rome (An)Iconic Rhetoric in the Writings of Flavius Josephus*:

> In the end, it is difficult to know what to make of this omission, and we should be cautious not to read too much into the silence…any attempt to answer such questions enters the realm of speculation.[37]

Note on Translations and Editions

The text of the MT follows the *BHS* and *Mikra'ot Gedolot Haketer*.[38] The English translation of the MT generally follows the NRSV. The LXX is according to Brooke-McLean.[39] Josephus' Greek text is based on Niese's edition, while the English is cited according to Brill's translation; when dealing with those books not yet translated by the Brill project, I will refer to the Loeb Classical Library. For the Hebrew texts from Qumran, I turn to Ulrich's and Parry-Dimant's editions.[40] Editions and translations of the rabbinic literature will be mentioned throughout the book.

Outline of the Remaining Chapters

In the next four chapters, I will examine Josephus' rewriting of the laws from Exodus to Deuteronomy. The remaining chapters contain my investigation of general issues in Josephus' rewriting of the laws: juxtaposition

---

36. Nakman 2004.
37. Ehrenkrook 2011: 83.
38. Cohen 1996, 2011, 2013a, 2013b.
39. Brooke and McLean 1909, 1911.
40. Ulrich 2010; Dimant and Parry 2015.

of the laws, reasons for the commandments, Moses as an intermediary or lawgiver, and the question of Roman influence upon Josephus' reshaping of the biblical laws. The book closes with a chapter on conclusions.

Conclusion

The purpose of this chapter has been to clarify the topic, assumptions, and methodology of the present study. Despite earlier studies written on Josephus' legal exegesis, there is still room for further inquiry. This monograph reexamines Josephus' rewriting of four of the books of the Pentateuch with a focus on their exegetical features. Since we have two source texts, they must both be examined. One cannot analyze Josephus' *Antiquities* 1–11 without a preliminary understanding of the Bible.

1

The Laws of Exodus in Josephus

This chapter deals with Josephus' retelling of the laws in the book of Exodus. The narrative of the Exodus from Egypt is a central theme in the collective memory of Israel's tradition. It reappears in the Apocrypha and Pseudepigrapha, Jewish-Hellenistic literature, ancient translations, Qumran, the New Testament, and in rabbinic literature.[1]

Scholars have divided Exodus into three parts: (1) the departure from Egypt (Exod. 1.1–15.21); (2) the journey from Egypt to Sinai (15.22–18.27); (3) Israel in Sinai: the Covenant and the Laws (chs. 19–40). The last third of the book contains instructions for building the tabernacle and their execution (chs. 25–31; 35–40).[2] The story of Moses is fundamental to the national story of the People of Israel.

The laws are scattered throughout various parts of Exodus: Passover (Exod. 12); redeeming a firstborn donkey (13.12-13); tefillin (phylacteries) (13.9); the sabbath (ch. 16); the Ten Commandments (ch. 20); the Covenant Code (chs. 21–24); and the laws regarding the construction of the tabernacle (chs. 25–40).

Omissions

Many attempts have been made to categorize the laws in Exodus, but they have proven unsuccessful. Josephus devotes *Ant.* 2.201–3.203 to the rewriting of Exodus. In the following table I present a comparison of Josephus and the biblical laws of Exodus.

---

1. See Dozeman, Evans, and Lohr 2014; Gärtner and Schmitz 2016.
2. Ska 2006: 27.

Masoretic Text (MT)	Josephus
Passover (Exod. 12)[3]	*Ant.* 2.311-13
Redeeming a firstborn donkey (Exod. 13)	*Ant.* 4.70-71[4]
Tefillin (Exod. 13)	*Ant.* 4.212-13
Sabbath (Exod. 16)	—
Ten Commandments (Exod. 20)	*Ant.* 3.91-92
Covenant Code: civil, criminal, social legislation, and cultic laws (Exod. 21–24)	*Ant.* 4.266-85
Laws regarding the building of the tabernacle (Exod. 25–40)	*Ant.* 3.100-203[5]

Josephus omits the reference to the Sabbath in his rewriting of Exodus 16. On the one hand, this cannot be explained by the assertion that this law was ordained prior to the giving of the Law at Sinai, since in this case one would have to explain the mention of tefillin in Exodus 13 in Josephus' rewriting. On the other hand, Exod. 16.23 states that the Sabbath was already given to Israel, while it is mentioned only in the Decalogue (Exod. 20). It is perhaps this difficulty that made Josephus skip the Sabbath episode.

Other omissions may be explained by Josephus' avoidance of repetitions and redundancies. Josephus does not rewrite the law of cities of refuge appearing in Exod. 21.13-14.[6] The reason for this omission may be that all laws of cities of refuge are assembled in *Ant.* 4.172-73, summarizing Exodus 21, Numbers 35, Deuteronomy 4, and Deuteronomy 19.

Josephus disregards the law of loans (Exod. 22.24-26; appearing also in Lev. 25.35-38; Deut. 23.20-21, and 24.10-13), since he refers to it in *Ant.* 4.266.

---

3. The rabbis (*Mek. Pes.* 1–3) regarded Exod. 12.1 as the basis for calculations of the lunar calendar. Josephus does not mention it here, but rather in 2.318; 3.240, 248; 4.78; 7.84. Philo (*Questions Exod.* 1.1) presents the Jewish calendar as distinctive from that of the non-Jews. Josephus does the opposite – he says that Nisan is equivalent to the Macedonian Xanthikos and to the Egyptian Pharmuthi (2.311). See Stern 2002: 110–11.

4. This law will be discussed in Chapter 3, on Numbers in Josephus.

5. Since this topic differs markedly from other biblical laws discussed in this book, it is not included in my analysis. See Robertson 1991; Norton 2011.

6. Despite this omission, Josephus rewrites the holding of the horns of the altar in 1 Kgs 1.50-52 and 1 Kgs 2.28.

Josephus omits all references to the prohibition 'You shall not boil a kid in its mother's milk' (Exod. 23.19; 34.26; Deut. 14.21).[7] The rabbis extended this law to include any mixing of meat and dairy products (*m. Ḥul.* 8.1). The explanation for this omission in Josephus may be that this prohibition was not widely accepted during the Second Temple period. Philo (*Virt.* 143-44) does mention the prohibition, but does not relate it to eating milk after meat. This prohibition is also missing at Qumran.[8]

Passover (Exod. 12, Lev. 23.5-14, and
Num. 28.16-25 // Ant. 2.311-19)

The first mention of Passover in the Torah is Exodus 12. It is a blend of law and narrative. God gives Moses and Aaron the Passover instructions, dealing with its timing, organization for each family, details related to the animal slaughtered, regulations regarding the Passover blood, and the preparation and eating of the meat and its leftovers. There are rewritten versions of this chapter in *Jubilees*, the Exagoge, Wisdom of Solomon, Philo, Pseudo-Philo, the New Testament, and rabbinic literature.[9]

Josephus rewrites Exodus 12 briefly in *Ant.* 2.311-14, 316-19. In *Ant.* 3.248-51 Josephus summarizes the laws of Passover found in Lev. 23.5-14 and Num. 28.16-25. He omits reference to the command to circumcise before Passover (Exod. 12.43-44). This omission may be related to his ambivalent view towards circumcision in *Antiquities* 1–11. Spilsbury has shown that this ambivalence is demonstrated by the omission of biblical narratives that include circumcision in Josephus' rewritings.[10]

Another omission is related to the details of the sacrifice (Exod. 12.3-11). While Josephus mentions the unleavened bread in his rewriting of Exodus 12, he refers to sacrifices later, at *Ant.* 3.248-49,[11] 14.21, and 20.106.

---

7. Nakman (2004) does not mention this omission. Exod. 34 is part of the golden calf narrative (Exod. 32–34) which was completely omitted. See Sterling 2018.

8. See Kraemer 2007: 37: 'In all probability, observant Jews did not cook young animals in the milk of their own mothers. But they ate meat prepared with dairy without compunction.' Cf. Werman and Shemesh 2009: 423–4; Van der Horst 2014: 21–9.

9. *m. Pes.* ch. 10. See Christopher 2018.

10. Spilsbury 1996.

11. Colautti 2002: 23.

He also omits Exod. 12.10, where it is commanded that the leftovers must be burned, but it is found in his rewriting of *Ant.* 3.248 ('with nothing of those [animals] that were sacrificed being preserved for the following day').

On the whole, we may surmise that Josephus counted on his earlier descriptions of Passover in *War*[12] and *Antiquities* 12–20. For example, he attests that the groups performing the eating of the lamb included no fewer than ten people (*War* 6.423), a detail relevant for the interpretation of Exodus 12 (cf. *t. Pes.* 4.15).

It is interesting to note that only here Josephus testifies: 'Hence still now, in accordance with the custom, we sacrifice thus' (*Ant.* 2.313). This is based on Exod. 12.14, 17, 42. In other laws, he avoids rewriting phrases such as 'it is a statute forever throughout your generations in all your settlements' (Lev. 23.12).[13]

As for the reason for celebrating Passover, Josephus (*Ant.* 3.316) explains: 'Having at their disposal nothing of the produce of the soil because of the desert, having kneaded wheat-flour and having baked it with only a short period of heating, they subsisted on the bread made from this; and they lived on this for thirty days'. A similar explanation is found in Philo, *Spec. Laws* 2.158. At first glance, Josephus seems to distinguish between the Passover sacrifice associated with the death of the first-born and the Exodus on the one hand and the unleavened bread associated with the Israelites' hurried baking on the other. However, according to *Ant.* 3.17 and 14.21 he seems to view them as one and the same.

In §317, Josephus mentions an eight-day festival, whereas the Torah mentions only seven. Some have maintained that Josephus speaks from the viewpoint of the Diaspora.[14] However, Philo mentions seven days (*Spec. Laws* 2.28, 156).

According to Balberg and Chavel,[15] Josephus transforms the domestic Passover ritual of Exodus 12 into a centralized ritual. They take their cue from the Greek φατριάς (*Ant.* 2.312), which they translate as 'tribes' (φατριάς) and gathered them [what?] together in one place. They maintain that 'Josephus adds this seemingly inconsequential detail exactly in order

---

12. On Passover in War, see Siggelkow-Berner 2011. In her view, Josephus used the festivals for apologetic purposes.
13. Bar-Kochva 1997: 391. He ascribes this omission to political reasons, namely the precarious situation of the Jews in the Roman Empire.
14. See the reference in Colautti 2002: 31. Cf. Nodet 1990: 124 n. 9.
15. Balberg and Chavel 2017: 330.

to liken the pesaḥ in Egypt to the centralized pesaḥ of the Jerusalem temple [sic?]'. However, this is a far-fetched conclusion. There is no hint that Josephus centralized the domestic ritual of Exodus 12. This Greek term was translated by Thackeray and Feldman as 'fraternities', a reasonable substitute for the Hebrew הבית (i.e., בית אב), instead of the LXX literal οἰκία.[16]

Josephus does not mention the details of חמץ, leavened bread. This is also true for other sources, such as Philo and Qumran.[17]

Tefillin (Exod. 13.9, 16)

Tefillin (phylacteries) are mentioned in Exod. 13.16 and Deut. 6.8; 11.18. The rabbis (e.g., b. Menaḥ. 34b–35a)[18] understood it as referring to 'a pair of small leather cases, whose parchment contents are inscribed... with four passages from the Torah (Exod. 13.1-10; 13.11-16; Deut. 6.4-9; 11.13-21)'.[19]

Josephus writes in *Ant.* 4.212-13:

> Twice each day, both at its beginning and when the time comes for turning to sleep, bear witness to God of the gifts that He granted them when they were delivered from the land of the Egyptians, since gratitude is proper by nature: it is given in return for those things that have already occurred and as a stimulus for what will be. They shall also inscribe on their doorways the greatest of the benefits that God has bestowed upon them, and each shall display them on his arms (βραχίοσιν); and as many things as are able to show forth the power of God and His good will towards them let them display on the head and the arm (βραχίων),[20] so that the favor of God with regard to them may be readily visible from all sides.

16. Feldman (2000: 221 n. 817) surmises that Josephus is alluding to the 'unit being in Athens a political subdivision of the Greek tribe (φυλή) and originally consisting of a noble family and its dependents who shared in the family cult'.

17. Werman and Shemesh (2009: 424) argue that the details of חמץ are not mentioned in Qumran since they were already known and widespread. Colautti (2002: 239) considers this as a possible solution to Josephus' silence as well. However, he offers another option: 'The theme of purity replaced it, considering the extreme weight FJ [=Flavius Josephus] attributes to that theme, especially in relation to Passover'.

18. For a comprehensive analysis of the rabbinic sources, see Cohn 2008.

19. Cohn 2008: 1.

20. On the inconsistency in the use of singular and plural forms (arms/arm), see Nodet 1997: 177.

Nakman[21] notes that 'Josephus therefore writes his words here in a very general and very inaccurate manner. Halakhic details are not important to him, but only the idea behind the law'. However, Cohn views things differently: Josephus does refer to the arm and head, rather than the 'hand' and 'between/before the eyes' as in the MT and Septuagint, 'thus demonstrating familiarity with an actual practice of the kind that the rabbis discuss'.[22] Josephus knows more than Philo (*Spec. Laws* 4.137-39), who does not mention the forehead.

In this regard, one may also mention the unusual interpretation of Rashbam (Rabbi Shmuel ben Meir, 1085–1158) regarding tefillin. Contrary to the rabbinic interpretation, he understands it metaphorically without hinting at the rabbinic understanding that these boxes should literally be placed on the arm and head. Could we argue that Rashbam was not familiar with this ritual? Probably not. The analogy from Rashbam may exemplify Josephus' method in dealing with biblical laws: to interpret them in order to understand their exact meaning and not to necessarily reconcile them with later practice.

The Ten Commandments

The Ten Commandments are recorded in Exodus 20 and Deuteronomy 5.[23] They have had significant 'moral, theological and literary influence upon world culture'.[24] These commandments raise many different questions: Should we divide them into several categories and how should they be divided? What makes the commandments unique among the other laws of the Bible? How should we settle the discrepancies between Exodus and Deuteronomy in their different presentations of the text? Did God speak all the words of the Decalogue himself or only the first two as found in rabbinic interpretation?[25]

---

21. Nakman 2004: 126 n. 18.
22. Cohn 2008: 109.
23. The numbering of the MT verses is also a point of variance: most Christian listings begin the commandments in v. 3, while the Jewish listing begins in v. 1. In Exod. 20 and Deut. 5, the sixth, seventh, eighth, and ninth commandments are recorded in some editions as one verse (Exod. 20.12 or 13; Deut. 5.17), but in other editions as four different verses (Exod. 20.13-16; Deut. 5.17-20). In Deuteronomy, the second commandment starts a new verse (5.7) in some editions, but in others it starts in the middle of 5.6. See Tov 2001: 5. I follow the Aleppo Codex.
24. Reventlow and Hoffman 2011: xi.
25. On the Decalogue, see the collections of B. Z. Segal 1986; Frevel et al. 2005; Reventlow and Hoffman 2011. See also DeRouchie 2013.

When dealing with the Ten Commandments in Josephus, one has to take his other references to these laws into account, either in other laws or narratives rewritten according to the Bible or in other extra-biblical sources.

The Title of the Commandments

The name עשרת הדברות is not mentioned in the Hebrew Bible and it is the rabbis who coined it (e.g., *y. Ber.* 1.5 3c). In the Pentateuch, they are termed עשרת הדברים (Exod. 34.28; Deut. 4.13; 10.4).[26] The LXX translated this term as δέκα λόγους, 'ten words' (LXX Exod. 34.28 and Deut. 10.4). Philo and Josephus followed this line and they too call the Ten Commandments δέκα λόγους (Philo, *Dec.* 154; Josephus, *Ant.* 3.90, 101, 138; 4.304; 8.104), in accordance with the biblical text.

The Division of the Tablets and the Order of the Commandments

There are various views regarding the division of the Ten Commandments. Were there two tablets containing five commandments each, or only one divided into two tables? Josephus maintained that five commandments were on each stone tablet (*Ant.* 3.101). This is also the view of Philo (*Dec.* 50).[27]

As for the order of the commandments, there are different traditions, especially regarding the order of the prohibitions against murder, adultery, and theft. Philo followed the order of the Decalogue according to the LXX, which differs from that of the MT. The LXX has two orders, one in Exodus and one in Deuteronomy. In Exodus, the LXX's order is adultery, theft, murder (LXX[B] Exod. 20.13-15). In Deuteronomy, the order is adultery, murder, theft (LXX[B] Deut. 5.17-19). The MT's order is supported by the Samaritan Pentateuch, the Peshitta (Exodus and Deuteronomy), several Qumran scrolls, and Josephus. The LXX's Exodus order is supported by the Nash Papyrus and Philo (*Dec.* 10.36; *Spec. Laws* 3.8).[28]

The order of the commandments in Josephus is almost identical to that of the MT. Only the sixth and seventh commandments have changed places. In Josephus' retelling, the people rejoice at the giving of the commandments (*Ant.* 3.93) and ask Moses to bring them laws (νόμοι)

---

26. See Gruber 1982.
27. For the rabbinic tradition, see *Mek. de R. Ishmael*, Yithro, Bahodesh 8 on Exod. 20.12-14; *y. Sheq.* 6.1.
28. See DeRouchie 2013: 95 n. 5, where a full list is given. See also Gurtner 2013: 376–80.

from God. Regarding these, Josephus indicates that he intends to write a separate work, and thus does not detail them here (*Ant.* 3.94; cf. *Ant.* 1.25, 29; 3.205, 223).[29] Unfortunately, he never accomplished this task.

The First Commandment

Like Philo, Josephus emphasizes monotheism in the first commandment, and it is reminiscent of the *Shema* (Deut. 6.4): 'The first saying teaches us that God is one and that it is necessary to worship him alone' (*Ant.* 3.91). Abraham was, according to Josephus, the first to recognize the belief in one God (*Ant.* 1.155-56).[30] Josephus does not specifically state that other gods are not to be worshipped. Nevertheless, he criticizes the Greeks for worshipping multiple gods while emphasizing the oneness of the Israelite God (*Ag. Ap.* 2.190-92, 238-54). The phrase 'God is one' also appears in *Ant.* 4.201 (cf. *Ant.* 1.155; 5.97, 112 and 8.343).

The Second Commandment

What is the second commandment? While some view the words 'I am YHWH your God' as the second commandment,[31] Josephus thinks that it is 'You shall not make for yourself an idol'. In his rewriting of the second commandment (*Ant.* 3.91), Josephus presents it as a prohibition against making an image of an animal in order to worship it.

Von Ehrenkrook[32] devoted a monograph to the difficulties inherent in this commandment, where he poses the following questions: What is the relationship between the various prohibitions beginning with לא in vv. 3-5? Is the prohibition against making and worshiping images (20.4-6) integral to or distinct from the prohibition against other gods (20.3)? What do the forbidden images represent? Are images of foreign gods in view here, namely the אלהים אחרים of 20.3?

Since this topic is vast and beyond the scope of this monograph, I will suffice with highlighting specific points. Josephus refers to the second commandment at least nineteen times throughout his writings, such as *Ag. Ap.* 2.190-92 and in his rewriting of the Solomon narrative (*Ant.* 8.195).[33]

---

29. See Barclay 2007: xxv.
30. See Spilsbury 1998: 59. See also Phua 2005: 69–76. See also Bruno 2013: 97–104.
31. See DeRouchie 2013.
32. Ehrenkrook 2011: 67–8.
33. See a full listing in Ehrenkrook 2011: 183–4.

Von Ehrenkrook relates to Josephus' rhetoric and apologetic rather than to exegetical concerns: to remove some of the anti-Jewish sentiment in Rome. Von Ehrenkrook argues that *Ant.* 3.91 prohibits only the making of images for the purpose of worship, while in his other writings Josephus speaks against making any figurative image for any purpose.

The Third Commandment: Misuse of God's Name

The third commandment is found in Exod. 20.6 and is rewritten in *Ant.* 3.91. There are various opinions regarding the intention of the third commandment: to avoid the use of magic, false oaths, and general misuse.[34] In Lev. 24.10-11 it includes cursing and swearing oaths by the divine name. Josephus seems to understand this commandment as a command against making false oaths.[35] According to Josephus (*War* 2.135), the Essenes avoid any oaths. However, Philo (*Dec.* 157) extends the law to everyone, not just a specific group. Philo (*Mos.* 2.208) views the offense of 'naming the name' as consisting of making 'the most holy and divine name an expletive'. Ben Sira (23.10) mentions the practice of using the name of God in swearing oaths. The Peshitta and Josephus (*Ant.* 3.91) support the third position, namely, that the third commandment prohibits the misuse of the Lord's name by using it thoughtlessly.

The Fourth Commandment: Sabbath

Josephus writes briefly: 'the fourth – to observe the seventh day by ceasing from all work' (*Ant.* 3.92). The most detailed description of the Sabbath practice can be found in rabbinic literature, and to some extent in some other second Temple literature.[36]

Josephus' short notice has been expanded in his many references to the Sabbath in the following places: *Ant.* 1.33;[37] 3.281 (Josephus' addition); 12.4, 274 ('for the law requires us to rest on that day' [Thackeray's translation]); 13.252 ('we are not permitted to march either on the Sabbath'); 14.63 (rest on the Sabbath day); 18.318, 359; *War* 2.456; *Ag. Ap.* 1.212; 2.174.

---

34. See Rooker 2010: 63–74.
35. See Coffin 1900; McDonough 1999: 87.
36. See Doering 1999.
37. Feldman (2000: 12 n. 56) claims that for Josephus 'the basis for observance of the Sabbath is *merely* imitatio Dei' (emphasis added). In contradistinction, other scholars argue that 'imitatio Dei' has a prominent place in the Hebrew Bible. See, e.g., Davies 1999.

The reason for stopping work on the Sabbath is, according to Josephus, that the Jews 'give every seventh day over to the study of our customs and our law, for we think it necessary to occupy ourselves, as with any other study, so with these through which we can avoid committing sins' (*Ant.* 16.43 [Thackeray's translation]).[38]

Weiss[39] claims that Josephus 'does not fail to refer to any memorable Sabbath practice or event'. Leviticus 24.8 notes that the twelve loaves of the bread of the Presence, which according to Exod. 25.30 were to be set 'on the table before me always', were in fact to be replaced with new ones every Sabbath. This detail is noted twice by Josephus, in *Ant.* 3.143 and 255. Likewise, Num. 28.3-10 specifies that, whereas the 'continual offering' consisted of the daily sacrifice of one lamb in the morning and another one in the evening, on the Sabbath two lambs were to be offered at each of the appointed times. Josephus records this detail in *Ant.* 3.237.

Nakman observes that Josephus omits many details regarding Sabbath practice. However, Josephus does not pay attention to every detail since it was not his goal. He was merely following the biblical text, where there is a paucity of sources regarding the Sabbath.[40] For instance, many prohibitions regarding the Sabbath are found in the prophetic literature,[41] a source from which Josephus in general drew a very limited amount of evidence. McKay is correct when she writes that 'there are no texts about regular Sabbath worship for the ordinary worshipper in the Hebrew Bible'.[42] Weiss[43] concludes that we have no reason to doubt Josephus' observance of the Sabbath practices.

Josephus' description of war on the Sabbath has fueled many scholarly discussions. However, since I am interested mainly in the biblical sources, this issue will remain outside the scope of my inquiry.[44]

The Fifth Commandment: Honoring Parents (Exod. 20.12; Deut. 5.16)

Josephus refers to the fifth commandment in *Ant.* 3.92: 'the fifth [commandment] – to honor parents'. He omits the reward for respecting parents, namely longevity.

---

38. For other references to Torah readings on the Sabbath, see den Hollander 2014: 303.
39. Weiss 1998: 368.
40. See McKay 1994: 15–18; Doering 1999: 18–22; Amit 2000: 24–40.
41. Hos. 2.13; Amos 8.5; Isa. 1.13-14; 56.2-7; 58.13; 66.23; Jer. 17.19-27; Ezek. 20.12-24; 22.8, 26; 23.38; 44.24; 45.17; 46.1-5, 12.
42. McKay 1994: 18.
43. Weiss 1998: 390.
44. See most recently Borchardt 2015, with earlier bibliography.

While Ben Sira (3.3-7) and the rabbis (*m. Pe'ah* 1.1)[45] emphasize the reward for honoring parents, Josephus dwells on the punishment. Perhaps he did not see the necessity for offering a reward for such an obvious law. Philo views matters similarly: in *Spec. Laws* 2.261 he writes: 'Let not him who honors his parents dutifully seek for any further advantage, for if he considers the matter he will find his reward in his own conduct'. Josephus elaborates more on honoring parents in *Against Apion*, where he writes:

> It ordered honor of parents, second to honoring God, and if anyone does not reciprocate the gifts he has received from them – however little he may fall short – it hands him over to be stoned. It gives instruction that the young should honor everyone who is older, since God is oldest. (*Ag. Ap.* 2.206)

Josephus alludes to this law in his retelling of the law of the rebellious son (*Ant.* 4.260-64)[46] and in his retelling of the Aqedah (Gen. 22; *Ant.* 1.222).[47] Kugel[48] deals with the difficulties inherent in this law: Why did the Torah mention this law at all? Commentators assumed that it had to carry further meaning. That is the reason for their view that honoring parents is second only to honoring God (*Ag. Ap.* 2.206). This idea also appears in Ben Sira (3.5) and in Philo (*Dec.* 165–66; *Spec. Laws* 2.226-27). Weinfeld[49] views Philo's and Josephus' positions as reflecting their Hellenistic environment.[50] However, this idea is already found in Leviticus 19 and thus most modern scholars view it as stemming from Scripture.[51] In addition, there are significant differences between the Greek and Hebrew sources, as Blidstein has shown.[52]

45. See the sources in Blidstein 1976.
46. See Blidstein 1976: 159 n. 6; Reeder 2012: 112.
47. Burke 2003: 56. Burke reviews the subject of parents and children in the Jewish sources, focusing on Philo, Pseudo-Phocylides, and Josephus. However, his review sees mostly the common elements between these sources, while failing to highlight the points of distinction.
48. Kugel 1998: 652.
49. Weinfeld 2001: 83.
50. Cf. Collins 1997: 62. This idea appears already in the Greek tradition: Diogenes Laertius (7.120); *Letter of Aristeas* 228; *Sibylline Oracles* 593–94; Pseudo-Phoclydes, line 8. See Balla 2005: 86–111. See also *b. Kid.* 30a.
51. Cf. Durham 1987: 291; Greenberg 1990: 112 n. 46; Hartley 1992: 312–13; Baker 2011. Tigay (2016: 1:232) writes: 'This commandment is the first after the commandments between man and God, for the honor of the parents corresponds to the honor that God himself deserves; thus the fifth commandment serves as a bridge between the two groups'.
52. Blidstein 1976: 1–8.

The Sixth Commandment: Murder

The sixth commandment, according to Josephus (*Ant.* 3.92), is 'to desist from murder (φόνου)';[53] Josephus does not specify whether the prohibition concerns intentional murder only. He is merely interested in the general principle, relegating any specific case to the larger biblical legal tradition (*Ant.* 4.172-73). As an example of the implementation of this law, we may mention *Ag. Ap.* 2.202:

> It [the law] gave orders to nurture all children, and prohibited women from causing the seed to miscarry and from destroying it. But if it were to become evident, she would be an infanticide, obliterating a soul and diminishing the [human] race.

Gorman explains that Josephus expanded the commandment 'you shall not kill' to include infanticide as well.[54]

The story of Cain and Abel (Gen. 4) anticipates the commandment not to kill. One can glean Josephus' views on murder from this text, namely, that it may be motivated by jealousy. Cain should have been severely punished but was not.

Genesis 9.6 is also connected to this commandment: 'Whoever sheds the blood of a human, by a human shall that person's blood be shed; for in his own image God made humankind'. Josephus rewrites it as follows:

> However, I counsel you to refrain from slaughter of humans and to keep yourselves pure from murder and to punish those who do some such thing, and to use all the other creatures for whatever purposes you wish and whatever cravings you have. For I have made you lords of all creatures on land and sea and as many as hover and have activity high up in the air, but without blood, for the soul is in it. (*Ant.* 1.102)

The Seventh Commandment: Adultery

The seventh commandment according to Josephus (*Ant.* 3.92) is 'not to commit adultery (μοιχεύω)'. This translation is similar to that in the LXX. Adultery appears in several places throughout his writings.[55] According to Josephus, the reason for this prohibition is the concern for the interests of both state and family that children be legitimate (*Ant.* 3.274). Josephus adds that a young man should not seek a married woman as his wife (*Ant.* 4.244; cf. *Ag. Ap.* 2.201). Those who commit adultery are exposed to the

---

53. Castelli (2018) prefers 'avoid'.
54. Gorman 1998: 43.
55. Loader 2011: 349.

death penalty (*Ant.* 3.474-75; *Ag. Ap.* 2.215).⁵⁶ When dealing with the punishment, Josephus follows the biblical record (Lev. 20.10-12; Deut. 22.22-23). Josephus illustrates this crime from the biblical narrative on several occasions (e.g., *Ant.* 1.164-65, 207-209; 2.41-44; 7.130-61).⁵⁷

The Eighth Commandment: Theft

Josephus (*Ant.* 3.92) follows the MT in prohibiting theft (κλοπή). This commandment is referred to in other biblical laws (Exod. 21.16; 22.1-3; Deut. 24.7). The biblical law differentiates between stealing property and kidnapping, albeit using the verb גנב in both cases.

Theft appears in Lev. 19.11. However, since Josephus omits almost all of Leviticus 19, we do not have access to his retelling of this chapter. Josephus narrates robbery made by the priests of the Second Temple (*Ant.* 20.206, 214). He does refer to Leviticus 19 in *Ag. Ap.* 2.216, where he writes that the punishment for theft is death. Scholars relate this statement to the apologetic nature of Josephus. In *Ag. Ap.* 2.208 Josephus writes 'he shall touch nothing belonging to others'.

According to Belkin,⁵⁸ Josephus sought to adopt a strict and extreme position in order to prove the supremacy of the laws of the Torah over the Greco-Roman laws, the latter being more lenient. However, the biblical law decrees death only in the case of kidnapping (Exod. 21.16; Deut. 24.7).⁵⁹ Josephus himself says in *Ant.* 4.271 that the punishment of thieves will be at least twice the payment of what was stolen. Kasher⁶⁰ thinks that this change suggests that Josephus followed Philo and deliberately resorted to an excessive interpretation, due to either apologetic or polemical purposes in order to praise the laws of the Torah.⁶¹

---

56. In the Aramaic targums, death and pestilence are cited as consequences of adultery. In Pseudo-Philo (44.10), death of the fruit of the womb of adulterers is mentioned as punishment. See Houtman 2000: 62.

57. Barclay 2007: 285 n. 809.

58. Belkin 1936: 15–18; Kasher 1996: 2:516.

59. Belkin 1936: 18; Jackson 1972: 200.

60. Kasher 1996: 2:516.

61. Barclay (2007: 294–5 n. 870) points out that the death penalty was mentioned four times (2.199, 201, 206, 207), with additional, unspecified punishments in 2.194, 207. Josephus now gathers, repeats, and amplifies those notices in 2.215-17a. The emphasis implies that strict penalties indicate a high morality, and this concurs with a traditional Roman sense of discipline (*Ant.* 13.294). Josephus' point is closely paralleled in Philo's *Hypothetica*, with a similar emphasis on the death penalty and a refusal to allow extenuation or reduction in punishment (7.1-2; cf. *Ant.* 2.276).

The Ninth Commandment (Exod. 20.13, Deut. 5.17 / Ant. 3.92)

The ninth commandment according to Josephus is 'not to bear false witness'. In this he closely follows the biblical commandment prohibiting false testimony against another person. An elaboration of this law is found in Josephus' rewriting of Deut. 19.16-19 in *Ant.* 4.219. Josephus adds that the Pharisees did not swear a loyalty oath to Herod (*Ant.* 17.42) and that the Essenes avoided swearing, 'considering it worse than the false oath; for they declare to be already degraded one who is unworthy of belief without [resorting to] God' (*War* 2.135).[62]

The Tenth Commandment

The tenth commandment (NRSV: Exod. 20.17; NJPS: Exod. 20.14) is 'You shall not covet your neighbor's house; you shall not covet your neighbor's wife, or male or female slave, or ox, or donkey, or anything that belongs to your neighbor'. The greatest difficulty in this verse is whether the law forbids 'intent rather than undertaking'.[63]

Josephus writes that the meaning of לא תחמוד is 'to desire nothing belonging to another'. The Greek verb he uses is ἐπιθυμία, which appears many times in his writings as well as in the LXX, for example the David–Bathsheba affair (*Ant.* 7.130).[64] Additionally, in his retelling of the Achan story (Josh. 7.20-21; *Ant.* 5.33-44), where the root חמד appears explicitly, Josephus does not mention it. The same is true for his retelling of the Ahab–Naboth story (1 Kgs 21; *Ant.* 8.355-62), where Josephus does not use the Greek verb either. Here the root חמד is only alluded to.

Josephus apparently did not attribute much weight to this commandment.[65] In *Ant.* 12.358, he says: 'for merely to wish a thing without actually doing it is not deserving of punishment'.

Recitation of the Decalogue

Josephus writes (*Ant.* 3.90): 'All heard a voice coming from on high to all, so that none of the ten sayings escaped them that Moses left inscribed on the two tablets. *It is not permitted for us to speak them openly verbatim*, but we shall reveal their contents.'

---

62. For Greek sources advising to avoid oath-taking, see Halevy 1967–68.
63. Sasson 2014: 5.
64. See Avioz forthcoming a.
65. This theme is prominent in the story of Adam and Eve, and Philo also elaborates further on desire and lust. See Loader 2011: 246–7; Svebakken 2012; Diaz Araujo 2017.

Josephus tells us that it is not permitted to explicitly vocalize the commandments (to the letter), but only to summarize their contents (*Ant.* 3.90). We do not know the source for this statement.

Spisbury argues that Josephus conflates the first commandment with the words of Deut. 6.4 in that he writes: 'The first saying (λόγος) teaches us that God is one (θεός ἐστιν εἷς) and that it is necessary to worship him alone' (*Ant.* 3.91).[66]

However, Josephus may be correct in his merging of the Shema with the first commandment. Indeed, this is how it appears in the Nash papyrus (c. 165–100 BCE) and in the Midrash.[67] This link between the Shema and the Decalogue also appears in the Qumran tefillin.[68]

As for the reason for Josephus' addition, we do not find any rabbinic source that prohibits stating the commandments explicitly. Abraham Schalit[69] notes that 'perhaps Josephus preserves a Zadokite early halakha'. However, there is no apparent basis for this statement. Since Philo also never cited the entire Decalogue, Josephus' comment, according to Himbaza, could mean that the rabbinic prohibition of citation was already in force in the first century CE.[70]

Moses is presented as a mediator between God and Israel, and is described as the interpreter (ἑρμηνεύς, *Ant.* 3.87; see also 4.13).[71] Nonetheless, the people were close enough to hear what was being said, 'in order that the excellence of spoken words might not be harmed by a human tongue in being transmitted to their knowledge' (*Ant.* 3.89).[72]

Slavery Laws

Slavery laws appear in the Pentateuch in many places: Exod. 21.2-6, 7-11, 20-21, 26-27, 32; Lev. 19.20-22; 25.6, 39-42, 44-45, 47-55; Deut. 12.12, 18; 16.11, 14; 21.10-14; 23.15-16.[73] A person is sold into slavery not only if he stole and was caught (Exod. 22.2), but also as a result of economic distress (Lev. 25.39). From Lev. 25.43 we learn the attitude towards a slave: 'You shall not rule over them with harshness' (NRSV), as well as the notion standing at the heart of the biblical attitude toward Hebrew slaves, namely, that all Israelites are rightfully only God's slaves (v. 42).

66. See Spilsbury 2014: 481; Waaler 2008.
67. Weinfeld 2001: 107.
68. See Nakman 2009.
69. Schalit 1944.
70. Himbaza 2004: 171.
71. Spilsbury 2014: 468.
72. Spilsbury 2014: 481.
73. See the categorization of Chirichigno 1993: 147.

From Deuteronomy it is clear that the slave should be granted the slave generous compensation once he is freed (Deut. 15.13-14) while identifying with him, since the Israelites were all slaves in Egypt (Deut. 15.15). There are repetitions of these laws as well as contradictions elsewhere in the biblical text, as we shall see presently.

In *Ant.* 4.273 Josephus rewrites Exod. 21.2:

> Let someone who has been sold to a fellow countryman be a slave (δουλεύω)[74] for six years, but in the seventh year let him be set free. If he has had children from a slave woman at the house of the one who bought him, however, and wishes to be a slave because of good will and affectionate love for his own things, let him be freed when the year of the jubilee arrives – this is the fiftieth year – and let him take along both his children and his wife who is free.

Josephus merges Deut. 15.12 with the law in Exodus 21. He understands the word לעולם as referring to the Jubilee year, in a way similar to Lev. 25.40 as well as in accordance with rabbinic interpretation.[75] Josephus harmonizes the biblical texts so that they will not contradict themselves. Urbach surmises that Josephus preserves a trace of the earlier halakha.[76]

Josephus omits the ear-piercing ceremony since it may have seemed cruel and unnecessary to him. Alternatively, the reason may have been that in ancient Greece piercing was limited to women's earrings.[77] Another omission relates to the ethnicity of the slave in question. While in the MT he is referred to as עברי, Josephus does not designate the slave as Hebrew. According to Harvey, Josephus wanted the Greek term Ἑβραῖος 'not to be linked to slavery but with the Laws, constitution and virtues of the "Hebrew nation" from the time of Moses and continuing into Josephus' own time'.[78] However, Josephus tells us about Jewish leaders who enslaved fellow-Jews.[79] He himself also had slaves (*Life* 429).

Josephus also omits the grant given to the released slave (Deut. 15). He does not mention the female slaves here, but refers to them in *Ant.* 4.244.

---

74. For terms of slavery in Josephus see B. G. Wright 2008: 232–5. See also Gibbs and Feldman 1986.
75. Mekhilta *Nez.* 2 (see Lauterbach and Stern 2004: 3:60). LXX translates here literally εἰς τὸν αἰῶνα.
76. Urbach 1960.
77. Lee 2015: 84. Dio Chrysostom (*Discourses* 32.3), a contemporary of Josephus, satirized the custom of ear-piercing.
78. Harvey 1998: 138–9.
79. Hezser 2005: 94.

Josephus disregards the laws in Exod. 21.7-11 (female slave), vv. 20-21 (striking a slave), and vv. 26-27 (the infliction of physical injury).

Josephus does not elaborate on the moral values found in these laws. He could have compared the biblical laws with Greek or Roman laws, emphasizing the superiority and virtue of the Jewish laws.[80] But he does not do so, and refers solely to the biblical text, albeit omitting several details.

Three Capital Offenses (Exod. 21.12–17)[81]

Exodus 21.12-17 elaborates on three prohibitions: murder, dishonoring parents, and kidnapping. The penalty for violating these laws is death. Of these, Josephus rewrites only the law in Exod. 21.16, prohibiting kidnapping. The reason for this omission may be that murder and dishonoring parents were already rewritten in Josephus' version of the Decalogue (*Ant.* 3.91-92) and in his other writings.

The law against kidnapping appears in Deut. 24.7 as well. Josephus refers to this law only once: 'Let death be the penalty for the stealing of a person' (*Ant.* 4.271). He discusses this law together with other theft laws. Josephus does not explain whether the kidnapped person was meant to be sold as a slave, and thus differs from the LXX to 21.17(16), which adds 'and treating him like a slave' (καὶ καταδυναστεύσας αὐτὸν).

Infliction of Bodily Injury (Exod. 21.18-27)

Exodus 21.18-19 deals with injury which occurs in the course of a quarrel. Does the attacker have to compensate the victim only for the time he has spent ill in bed, or also for the period of recovery? This was disputed by the rabbis in *b. B.Q.* 85a. Josephus (*Ant.* 4.277) rewrites this law as follows:

> In a fight where there is no iron weapon, if someone is struck and dies on the spot, let him be avenged and let the one who has struck him suffer the same. If he is carried to his home and after being ill for several days then dies, let the one who struck him be free from punishment. If, however, he has been saved but has incurred much expense, let him [the one who struck him] pay for all that he has spent during the time of his confinement to bed and all that he has given to the physicians.

---

80. In *Ant.* 18.21 he refers to the Essenes, who do not practice slavery, since they believe the ownership of slaves contributes to injustice.

81. The title is adopted from Sarna 1991: 121.

There are many differences between Josephus and biblical law. Here Josephus does not mention the punishment of an intentional murder, namely, that the killer is taken from the altar and is executed. He also does not mention the law concerning beating a slave. While biblical law refers to the use of a stone or a fist, Josephus only mentions 'no iron weapon'. According to biblical law, one who strikes is exempt from the death penalty only if the victim does not die. Josephus adds that even if the victim dies after a few days, the one who strikes will not be punished. Finally, Josephus' addition that the one who strikes has to pay the money given to the physicians is unparalleled in biblical law.

Weyl[82] and others believe that Josephus mistakenly combined two biblical laws: the killing of a freeman and the killing of a slave (Exod. 21.20-21). In contrast, Goldenberg[83] points out that both Philo (*Spec. Laws* 3.105-107) and Tannaitic halakha[84] agree with Josephus that one goes unpunished if the person whom he struck remains alive several days before dying. Goldenberg concludes that these sources divide the possible results into three cases:

> 1) Death is immediate; the penalty to the striker is death; 2) Death is delayed; the striker is not punished by death (Philo and the Tannaim demand compensation, Josephus does not); and 3) There is no death but only injuries; the striker provides compensation.[85]

As for the altar as a refuge, it is mentioned in Josephus' retelling of Joab's and Adonijah's fleeing from Solomon (1 Kgs 1.49; 2.28; *Ant.* 7.361; 8.13). Josephus understands the compensation for the victim to include only the time when he rested. The physician's fee is also mentioned in Targum Onkelos, the LXX, the Vulgate, and in rabbinic literature (*b. B.Qam.* 85a; *b. Ketub.* 52b).

Striking a Pregnant Woman (Exod. 21.22-23 // Ant. 4.278)

The law in Exod. 21.22-23 deals with a pregnant woman who was beaten in the course of a brawl between two men. Interpreters[86] have debated over the meaning of אסון and פלילים. Josephus (*Ant.* 4.278) understands the word אסון as connoting death (θνήσκω), namely the death

---

82. Weyl 1900: 54–7; Gallant 1988: 255 n. 154.
83. Goldenberg 1987: 200–203.
84. Lauterbach and Stern 2004: 3:391.
85. Goldenberg 1987: 202–3. After a detailed discussion, Nakman (2004: 135–6 n. 81) eventually tends to accept Goldenberg's explanation.
86. Sprinkle (1993) summarizes the many difficulties in this text.

of the pregnant woman. This is also the interpretation in the Mekhilta,[87] Onkelos, the Vulgate and modern commentators.[88] Josephus explains this law as follows:

> If one has kicked a pregnant woman and the woman miscarries, let him be punished by the judges with a monetary fine, since he has diminished the population through the destruction of what was in the belly, and let money also be given by him to the husband of the woman. And if she should die of the blow, let him die himself, since the law considers it just for a life to be laid down for a life.

Josephus (*Ant.* 4.278) says that if a man kicks a woman and causes her to have a miscarriage, he is to be fined by the judge and a further sum is to be given to her husband, whereas the MT (Exod. 21.22) speaks of one fine only to be determined by the judge.

Josephus explains v. 22 as referring to monetary compensation, and this interpretation is also found in the LXX, the Mekhilta (*Mishp.* 8),[89] Onkelos, and Philo.[90] Josephus explains פלילים as referring to judges, and a similar conclusion is found in the Mekhilta and in the Aramaic targums. He understands the two clauses in Exod. 21.22 concerning the money paid to the husband and ונתן בפלילים as separate issues: the latter is a fine paid to the court for a criminal act, and the former is compensatory damages to the husband.[91]

Animal Theft (Exod. 21.37–22.3 // Ant. 4.272)

In Exod. 21.37–22.3 there is a series of laws: theft of animals (Exod. 21.37); housebreaking (22.1-2a); and restitution if stolen cattle are still in the possession of the thief (Exod. 22.3).[92]

---

87. Lauterbach and Stern 2004: 3:62–6. For other rabbinic sources, see Aptowitzer 1924. It is unclear to me how Schiff (2002: 21) wrote that 'The *Antiquitates* extract is reminiscent of Exod. 21:22-25, although it does not address the loss of the woman'.

88. Cassuto 1967: 275; Phillips 1970: 88–9; Paul 1970: 72; Cohen 2009. Isser (1990: 38) divides the interpretations into two traditions: 'one represented by the Mesopotamian law codes, Josephus, Tg. Onqelos, Vg, and rabbinic literature, and the other by the Hittite Laws, LXX, Philo, and VL'.

89. Lauterbach and Stern 2004: 3:401–402.

90. *Spec. Laws* 3.108-19. Cf. Cassuto 1967 and Paul 1970. However, in *Ag. Ap.* 2.202 Josephus describes taking the life of a fetus as murder. For various explanations regarding the differences between *Antiquities* and *Against Apion*, see Schiff 2002: 22–3.

91. Isser 1990.

92. Levinson 1994: 48.

While the rabbis interpreted שור או שה as referring to ox and sheep only (*b. B.Q.* 7.1; *t. B.Q.* 7.11; Mekhilta *Nez.* 12;[93] cf. LXX), Josephus interprets שור או שה to include all cattle.[94] Philo (*Spec. Laws* 4.11-12) explains why the theft of an ox should require greater restitution (fivefold) than for a sheep (fourfold), but Josephus does not give any explanation.

Josephus omits the laws in Exod. 22.4-5 which deal with the destruction of crops by livestock or by fire. The reason for this omission is unclear.

Deposit Law (Exod. 23.4-5; Deut. 22.1-3 // Ant. 4.274)

The biblical laws demand that lost property be returned to its owner. However, the law does not state how long the lost property can be kept by the finder. Likewise, we do not know in which cases the finder may retain the lost object for himself. These details are discussed in the rabbinic sources (*m. B.M.* ch. 2; *b. B.M.* 21–33a). Although the wording in Exodus and Deuteronomy is different, the principles are similar.[95]

Josephus combines the two sources into one. He also omits the identity of the one who lost the objects ('your enemy' in Exod. 23; 'your brother' in Deut. 22). Josephus, like the rabbis, rules that the finder proclaims where he found the object, and that if he cannot locate the owner immediately, he is to keep it in his home (*Ant.* 4.274).

Josephus speaks of 'farm animals' (βόσκημα). This term may refer to an ox or a sheep, but may include other animals as well. Interestingly, the Samaritan Pentateuch adds או כל בהמתו ('or any of his beasts'). The last sentence in Josephus ('calling God to witness that he is not appropriating other people's property') is Josephus' addition, and he is quite precise in connecting the law of lost objects with theft.[96]

As in other cases, here too we find that the rabbinic discussion is much more elaborate than Josephus. Yet this does not necessarily make Josephus inferior. First, the rabbinic interpretation is not always the plain understanding of the text. Second, if Josephus' aim was to make the text clearer, he has certainly done so, albeit there remain issues to be clarified.

Exodus 22.6-14 deals with stealing of or damage to property given for safe-keeping, borrowed, or rented.[97] There are certain difficulties in this section: should we view vv. 6-7 and 9-12 as one topic dealing with two

---

93. Lauterbach and Stern 2004: 3:425.
94. Revel 1923–24: 296.
95. See Baker 2007.
96. Cf. Houtman 2000: 243.
97. Houtman 2000: 196.

variations, or perhaps we are dealing with two different issues? Mishnah *B.M.* 7.8 distinguishes four guardians: a gratuitous bailee, a borrower, one who takes a fee, and a hirer. Weyl[98] notes that Josephus does not differentiate between the various types of guardians. However, why should we expect Josephus to offer such a distinction? It seems that Josephus reflects the proper understanding of the plain meaning of the text: there is not a hint in the text of such a distinction.[99]

Another exegetical problem relates to the understanding of the word אלהים. Josephus takes this word to mean 'judges' (the defendant, 'having come before the seven judges', takes an oath, *Ant.* 4.287). Philo uses the term 'the divine court' (*Spec. Laws* 4.34).

The Prohibition of Sorcery (Exod. 21.17 // Ant. 4.279)

This law raises the question of whether it should be applied solely to a sorceress, or whether a male sorcerer is also included (cf. Onkelos over against *b. Sanh.* 67a; *y. Sanh.* 7.19, 25d). Josephus does not deal with this question. At first glance, in *Ant.* 4.279 Josephus gives a completely different interpretation to the law against sorcery (found as well in the LXX: φαρμάκους οὐ περιποιήσετε). However, modern scholars have proposed a scenario that could be in accord with Josephus' suggestion. Karel van der Toorn writes:

> Juridically, a woman could only undertake an action against her husband or in-laws in extreme cases… One may imagine the following situation: a newly married woman seems to be no longer fertile after a first pregnancy. Not satisfied with one child, her husband takes a concubine. What must the first woman do with her anger over the humiliation; does she swallow it? Possibly. But she could also try to make her rival sick by means of spells, or deprive her husband of his potency by adding magical materials to his food. In other words, she became a sorceress.[100]

Thus, Josephus may not be so far from the reality that lies behind the biblical law.

---

98. Weyl 1900: 131, 133.
99. Henshke 1991; Jackson 2006: 335. In n. 18, Jackson mentions other scholars who reject the rabbinic labels for the various guardians.
100. Van der Toorn 1994: 113. Cited by D. P. Wright 2009: 201. Sorcerers are mentioned in *Life* 149 as well.

The Altar Law (Exod. 20.23)[101]

Exodus 20.23 (ET: 26) prohibits exposing one's nakedness when ascending the altar steps. Does this law refer to the priests or to the laymen?[102] Josephus rewrites this law as follows: 'Let the access to this be not by steps but by a sloping ramp' (*Ant.* 4.201). Josephus added the 'sloping ramp' in accordance with Second Temple practices (*m. Mid.* 3.3; *Mekhilta de R. Ishmael*, Jethro, 11; Josephus, *War* 5.225).[103] Feldman's assertion that 'Josephus omits any reason for the prohibition of steps'[104] is unnecessary, since the biblical text does not tell us the reason for this prohibition either. Josephus does not explicitly state whether this law is intended for priests or laymen. If Josephus was considering priests, then covering the priests' genitals is already mentioned in *Ant.* 3.152.

Goring Ox (Exod. 21.28-36 // Ant. 4.281-82)

The laws in Exod. 21.28-36 present cases of 'injuries or damages caused by someone's property (ox or pit) to a human being or to another person's (live) property, and the question of the degree of the owner's liability'.[105]

Josephus rewrites these laws as follows:

> Let the owner slaughter an ox that strikes with its horns. If on a threshing-floor it should kill someone by striking him, let it alone die by being stoned, and let it be considered unsuitable even for food. But should the owner be proven to have known its nature beforehand and not to have guarded it, let him also die, since he would have turned out to be responsible for the slaying by the ox.
>
> If an ox should kill a slave or a maid-servant, let it be stoned, and let the owner of the ox pay thirty shekels to the master of the one who has been slain. If an ox should die after being beaten thus, let both the one that died and the one that beat him be sold, and let their owners divide between themselves the price of both. (*Ant.* 4.281-82)

---

101. There are many traditions regarding the verse division here: it is marked as vv. 22, 23 and 26. We follow the Aleppo Codex, where it is marked as v. 23.
102. See the differing views of Cassuto 1967: 257 and Sarna 1991: 117. See also Propp 2006: 185.
103. See Heger 1999: 63–70.
104. Feldman 2000: 400 n. 590.
105. Sprinkle 1994: 104.

As to the liability of the owner, Josephus argues that the owner should kill the ox that gores. This opinion also appears in Philo (*Spec. Laws* 3.145) and *m. B.Q.* 4.9: 'It (i.e. the ox) can only be guarded by the knife'.[106] Josephus follows the LXX, where v. 29, ולא ישמרנו, is translated as ולא ישמידנו (ἀφανίσῃ, 'destroy').[107]

When dealing with the non-goring ox, Josephus does not note that after the ox is stoned, the owner is exempt from paying. He also does not mention the possibility of ransom when a harmful ox killed a person and disregards the case of when a harmful ox killed another ox (vv. 30, 31, and 36). Josephus adds that a harmful ox should be killed. He also adds the threshing-floor ('If on a threshing-floor it should kill someone by striking him').[108]

Conclusion

Josephus rewrites most of the laws in Exodus. In his retelling, he follows neither the MT nor the LXX's sequence. Rather, he offers a new one where he rearranges the laws with his own creative mind.

He worked mainly as an interpreter, seeking to clarify the laws of the Torah for his readers. This is mainly shown in his retelling of the tefillin. Josephus tried to avoid contradictions and doublets. In the Pentateuch, there are repetitions either in the same book or among two or three books. He sometimes conflates laws, differentiates between them in a nuanced way, omits them altogether, or adds to them. His additions sometimes supply a rationale to the laws.

As for the relationship between Josephus and the rabbis, we saw that in some cases there is resemblance between Josephus and the rabbis and other times there is divergence. In any case, one cannot conclude that Josephus had a written copy of one of the early rabbinic sources.

---

106. See Jackson 1974: 68.
107. Wevers 1990: 336.
108. For various explanations of this component, see Feldman 2000: 451 n. 944.

2

The Laws of Leviticus in Josephus' Writings

The book of Leviticus has always presented a great challenge for readers and interpreters, both Christian and Jewish. Devoid of plot and full of technical terms, its style is repetitive. However, this did not prevent the rabbinic Sages from advising educators to use Leviticus as the first book that children should be taught.[1] The rabbis attempted to shed light upon the complicated ritual laws as well as the moral issues raised in Leviticus.[2] Other early Jewish sources in which Leviticus plays a prominent role are the Pseudepigrapha, Philo, Josephus, and some of the Qumran scrolls.[3] One must also take ancient textual witnesses of the Bible into account.[4] As Harrington points out,[5] in Second Temple literature there are attempts to clarify the ambiguities that accompany the different laws. Various parties resolved these ambiguities according to their biases, culture, and traditions.

Josephus rewrites the book of Leviticus mainly in *Ant.* 3.188-286, but a small part of Leviticus is retold throughout *Ant.* 4.196-301. The purpose of this chapter is to provide insights into Josephus' rewriting of this book: what was preserved, what was omitted, what was changed, and why.

---

1. See *Lev. Rab.* 7.3: 'R. Isi said: Why do young children commence with the Priests' manual (i.e., Leviticus) and not with Genesis? Surely, it is because young children are pure and sacrifices are pure; so let the pure come and engage in the study of the pure.' Milgrom 1991: 3.

There are differences between the numbering of Lev. 6.1-7 in the Hebrew MT and in English translations (6.1-7 ET = 5.20-26 MT). The numbering of the Hebrew text is given in brackets where it differs from the English. See Willis 2009: 49.

2. See Harrington 1996; Stemberger 2005.

3. On the reception of Leviticus in Second Temple literature, see Lange and Weigold 2011: 80–8; Metso 2014. See also Choi 2018.

4. On the Greek text of Leviticus, see Metso and Ulrich 2003; Voitila 2015.

5. Harrington 1996: 229.

The Structure of Leviticus

The following table presents a comparison between the book's structure as proposed by Wenham[6] and its reconstruction in Josephus' rewriting of Leviticus:
  I. Laws on Sacrifice (1.1–7.38).
  II. Institution of the Priesthood (8.1–10.20).
  III. Uncleanness and its Treatment (11.1–16.34).
  IV. Prescriptions for Practical Holiness (17.1–27.34).

Laws of Leviticus in Josephus' Antiquities

Josephus juxtaposes laws from Exodus, Leviticus, Numbers and Deuteronomy, beginning with the appointment of Aaron as high priest (Exod. 28; Lev. 8; *Ant.* 3.188-92).[7] He proceeds with the dedication of the tabernacle (*Ant.* 3.200-203) and the consecration ceremony for Aaron and his sons (Exod. 29 and Lev. 8–9; *Ant.* 3.204-207). Next comes the story of Nadab and Abihu (Lev. 10.1-7; *Ant.* 3.208-11).

There follows an expanded interpretation of Moses' humility (§§212-13) and an explanation of the ephod and breastplate (§§214-18; Exod. 28.30; Lev. 8.8). Next, Josephus summarizes the sacrifices of the twelve tribes according to Numbers 7 and praises the laws revealed to Moses (§§219-23).

Josephus then rewrites some of the laws concerning purifications and sacred rites (§224). He summarizes the rules for holocausts for individuals in Leviticus 1 (§§225-27); peace offerings ('thank offerings') in Leviticus 3 (§§228-29); sin offerings in Leviticus 5 (§230); sacrifices for deliberate sins in Lev. 6.1-7 and the sins of rulers in Lev. 4.22-26; public and private offerings of cereal, oil, and wine in Num. 15.4 (§§232-34); offerings of fine flour in Lev. 2.1-3; 6.14-23 (§235); and some miscellaneous rules concerning sacrifices in Lev. 22.27-30 (§236).

Next he discusses the Bread of the Presence in Lev. 24.5-9 (§§255-56) and the priestly offering in Lev. 6.12-16 (ET 6.19-23) (§257), and then moves on to the rules concerning clean and unclean animals in Leviticus 11//Deuteronomy 14 (which he promises to explain in detail in a future work) (§259). He then discusses the prohibition of the consumption of blood, that which dies of natural causes, and animal fat, found in Lev. 7.22-27, 11.39-40, and 17.10-16 respectively (§260).

---

6. Wenham 1979. For other suggestions, see Watts 2013: 12–20.
7. The following summary is based on Davila 2005: 170–2, with some corrections and changes.

He refers briefly to the laws concerning leprosy, menstruation, and contact with the dead in Leviticus 13–15 and Num. 19.1-13 (§§261-64), and ridicules those who claim that Moses was a leper (§§265-68).

Josephus then summarizes the rules for purification of women after childbirth in Leviticus 12 (§269), the laws for intimate relationships in Lev. 20.10-21 (§§274-75), the special limits on contact with the dead and marriage limitations for priests and the high priest in Lev. 21.1-15 (§§276-77), the laws concerning physical blemishes for both priests and animal sacrifices in Lev. 21.16-23, 22.17-25, and the prohibition against priests drinking wine while on duty in Lev. 10.8-11 (§§278-79). Next he rewrites the laws of the sabbatical year and the jubilee year in Leviticus 25 (§§280-85). He concludes by emphasizing that Moses received these laws from God and transmitted them in written form to the Hebrews (§286).

Other laws from Leviticus are rewritten in *Antiquities* 4.

Overall, most of the book of Leviticus is paralleled in Josephus' adaptation; the differences chiefly lie in the units' order and specific details. Sarianna Metso[8] counts twenty out of twenty-seven chapters in Josephus' rewriting of Leviticus. Josephus placed the story of Nadab and Abihu in his rewriting of the building of the Tabernacle in Exodus 25–40 (*Ant.* 3.208-11).[9] This change was probably due to logical considerations on Josephus' part: the narrative episode's placement in the MT, in a sense, interrupts the structure of Leviticus, while the story is an integral part of the consecration of the Tabernacle narrative; five priests are reduced to three when two of Aaron's sons meet their death.

In *Ant.* 4.197 Josephus states that the laws were 'in scattered condition', so he therefore reorganizes them:

> The arrangement of each topic according to its class has been innovated by us. For the writings were left by him in scattered condition, just as he ascertained each item from God. I considered it necessary to mention this beforehand, so that some blame may not be assigned to us for having erred by my fellow countrymen who encounter this text.

Josephus apologizes for making changes to the text of the Torah. This apology is intended to appeal to his Jewish readers. However, this does not serve to settle the controversial issue of Josephus' audience; in many other places, he seems to have a gentile audience in mind.[10]

---

8. Metso 2012: 77.
9. See Begg 2009.
10. See the discussion in Sterling 1992: 297–308.

The Starting Point of Leviticus

In his book *Ritual Words and Narrative Worlds in the Book of Leviticus*, Brian Bibb asks the following questions:[11]

> Can Leviticus even be considered a proper subject for literary analysis? In other words, can one distinguish Leviticus in any useful way from the material before and after it, and can one discern the internal logic and consistency expected in a work of literature? Is Leviticus, read as a book, sufficiently unified in its composition and distinct from its literary surroundings?

The opening words of the book, ויקרא, 'And [the Lord] summoned', connects Leviticus firmly to the preceding book of Exodus, in which God charges Moses with the building of the Tabernacle, or the 'Tent of Meeting'.[12] There, the glory of God is manifest, and the divine will is periodically communicated to Israel. The priesthood is appointed as a mediating body between God and the nation, and priestly duties and vestments are prescribed.

Josephus' adaptation lacks the formal opening of Leviticus, as he views the books of Exodus, Leviticus and Numbers as continuous. He begins his retelling of Leviticus in the third part of Exodus 25–40. Some modern scholars view Leviticus similarly;[13] they hold that Leviticus is not an independent narrative but is part of the priestly narrative context of the Sinai pericope, found in Exod. 19.1–Num. 10.10. In this sense, Josephus may be regarded as the first source that considers a different division of the books of Exodus–Numbers.

The Ending of Leviticus

In the MT, Leviticus 27 serves as the final chapter of the book. Milgrom suggests that this conclusion was designed to generate closure with the book's opening topic (chs. 1–9). Both deal with sanctification: of sacrifices (chs. 1–7); and of people, animals, houses, and land (ch. 27).[14]

Josephus ends Leviticus in ch. 25, with the following statement:

> Moyses ascertained carefully from God the arrangement of the laws, when he encamped the army beneath Mount Sinai, and he transmitted it in written form to the Hebrews. (*Ant.* 3.286)

---

11. Bibb 2009: 18–19.
12. Kellogg 1906: 18.
13. On the continuity between these books, see Ruwe 2003.
14. Milgrom 2000: 28.

Episodes found in the book of Numbers appear at different points during Josephus' retelling of Leviticus: Numbers 7 appears in the middle of Leviticus 10 (*Ant.* 3.220-22); Numbers 15 appears during Josephus' retelling of Leviticus 5 (*Ant.* 3.234); Numbers 28 appears after Leviticus 22 (*Ant.* 3.237-48). The opposite is true as well: Josephus transfers verses from Leviticus to Numbers. Thus, Leviticus 27 is retold in *Ant.* 4.73, in the middle of a passage that rewrites laws from various places in Numbers.

Laws Omitted by Josephus

Josephus omitted many laws from Leviticus 19: the laws from 19.16, 17-18, 26-31, 32, 33-34 are missing in his rewriting. Neither does he mention the law against child sacrifice to Molech (Lev. 18.21).

Josephus may have excluded some of these laws for apologetic reasons in order to show how highly Jews value life compared to non-Jews. Thus, we find some of these laws in *Ag. Ap.* 2.210, 257, 261, which present Judaism as compassionate with high moral values, compared to other religions.

Other laws may have been omitted for the sake of brevity. Josephus did not want to burden his readers with too much detail about Jewish law. The same seems to hold true in regard to the slave laws of Exodus. Obviously, this explanation does not explain why particular laws were omitted.

The blessings and curses in Leviticus 26 were rewritten in his discussion of Deuteronomy 28 (*Ant.* 4.305-308), thus avoiding repetition.

Sacrifices in Josephus (Ant. 3.224-57)

There are various sacrifices in Leviticus: *Olah* (burnt offering; Lev. 1.3-17; 6.1-4); *Mincha* (meal offerings; Lev. 2.1-16; 6.7-11); *Shelamim* (peace offering; 3.1-17; 7.11-34), *Hattat* (sin offering; 4.1–5.13) *Asham* (guilt offering; 5.14-26; 7.1-10); burnt offering (6.2-6); offerings at priestly inaugurations (7.35-36); and purification offerings (6.17-23). Additional sacrifices are brought for the Sabbath, New Moon celebrations, as well as for the annual festivals, namely, Tabernacles, Passover, and Pentecost (Lev. 23; Num. 28).

Josephus evidently planned the writing of a book on Judaism in four volumes, entitled 'The Customs and Causes' (περὶ ἐθῶν καὶ αἰτιων, *Ant.* 4.198), a plan he eventually abandoned. This book was to have contained certain sections devoted to sacrificial rites (περὶ θυσιῶν, *Ant.* 3.205) and Jewish laws (περὶ τῶν νόμων, *Ant.* 3.223).[15]

---

15. See Altshuler 1978–79.

Josephus deals in several places with the intention behind these sacrifices: 'it is necessary, first of all, for us to have one who will assume the duties of a priest and *to serve for the sacrifices and for the prayers* on our behalf' (*Ant.* 3.189). Their aim is 'to honor God' (*Ant.* 3.250) and thus they are gifts (δωρεά; *Ant.* 3.219). The sacrifices atone for the sins of Israel (παραίτησις; *Ant.* 3.238, 241, 246, 247).[16] Another role that Josephus attributes to sacrifices is that of purification (ἁγνεία; *Ant.* 3.224, 273) as part of the forgiveness for sins (ὑπὲρ ἁμαρτημάτων; *Ant.* 3.204, 230-32, 239-40, 249, 253).

Some scholars hold that Josephus had little knowledge of these matters. One such scholar is Louis Feldman. In his extensive commentary on Josephus, Feldman's assessment of Josephus' knowledge of sacrifices is negative: 'Despite Josephus' statement that these two types of sacrifice are performed in a similar manner, the only feature in common between thank-offerings and sin-offerings is the burning of fats upon the altar'.[17] In this context, he then lists all the differences he believes that Josephus should have noted between the two rites.

In contrast to this approach, Christoph Batsch in a recent article[18] defends Josephus, arguing that the book of Leviticus does not provide clear classification of the sacrifices. Various scholars identify four, six, eight, or nine such categories. Unlike Philo,[19] who suffices in enumerating the sacrifices, Josephus attempts to classify them.

Josephus writes in *Ant.* 3.224-25:

> Now I shall mention some few of the *regulations pertaining to the rites of purification and types* of sacrificial ceremonies. For it happens that my discussion is presently concerned with the sacrifices. There are two *types of sacrifices*, those carried out by individuals and those by the community; and they are of *two forms*. In the one case all of the sacrifice is burnt whole and for this reason it has acquired such a name. The other is for thanksgiving and is offered as a feast for those who have offered the sacrifice. I shall speak about the former.

The first axis is defined by the contrast between community, or collective, ceremonies (δῆμος), and ceremonies executed by individuals (ἴδιος). The second is defined by the opposition between two *modus*

---

16. Schalit (1944: 99) and Feldman (2000: 295) translate 'atoning for sins' in *Ant.* 3.232; yet the Greek verb does not appear there.
17. Feldman 2000: 294 n. 16.
18. Batsch 2011.
19. *Spec. Laws* 1.162-256.

operandi: sacrifices completely burned on the altar, which are entirely dedicated to God, versus sacrifices of which a part is consumed by those who offered the sacrifice. These definitions are followed by a detailed list of the various Israelite sacrifices.

With regard to Feldman's note, Josephus did not mean קרבן תודה but rather something closer to *Shelamim*, using the Greek word, χαριστηρίοι, a word unparalleled in the LXX (which translates in Lev. 7.12 αἰνέσεως). According to *Ant.* 3.229, 'After presenting the breast and the right leg to the priests they feast for two days upon what is left of the flesh, and they burn whatever remains'.

Olah *and* Shelamim *(Ant. 3.226-29)*

Leviticus 1 discusses the burnt offering. The age of the sheep[20] is not mentioned and Josephus (*Ant.* 3.226) adds that it is a year old. That is in line with the rabbis (*m. Par.* 1.3) and Milgrom adopts this addition.[21] Another parallel to the rabbis emerges when Josephus writes that 'It is permitted to sacrifice oxen that are also older'. This matches the opinion of Rabbi Yose (*m. Par.* 1.2).

Josephus does not refer here to burnt offerings of birds (Lev. 1.14-17). The reason for this omission is unclear. In fact, he does not even mention ὄρνεον ('bird') in any law in Leviticus! Is it coincidental or should we relate this to the foreboding bird omens,[22] the omission being motivated by apologetic concerns?

In *Ant.* 3.228-29 Josephus refers to the *Shelamim*[23] sacrifices. He mentions the splashing of blood on the four sides of the altar (Lev. 3.2, 8, 13; *Ant.* 3.228) and that for the lamb the kidneys and the caul and all the fat together with the lobe of the liver and the tail were reserved for God (Lev. 3.16-17; *Ant.* 3.228). The priest received the breast and right thigh; he boiled it then ate it (Lev. 7.28-34; 10.14-15; Num. 18.11; *Ant.* 3.229).

---

20. Josephus deviates again from the LXX. He translates כבש as ἀρνίον in *Ant.* 3.221, 226, 251 as well as in other dozens of places. This is contrast with the LXX who uses ἀμνάς or ἀμνός. See Johns 2004: 32–4.

21. Milgrom 1991: 163. Nakman (2004: 94) attributes Josephus' addition to a 'coincidental parallel with the rabbis'. That is part of his negative assessment of Josephus. If Josephus is not aware of the rabbinic opinion, he is to be denounced. If he knows it, it must have been coincidental! See Feldman's lengthy explanation (2000: 292 n. 593) on Josephus' sources of this addition.

22. See *Ag. Ap.* 1.200-204. On bird omens in Josephus and in Greco-Roman literature, see Bar-Kochva 1996: 57–71.

23. In *Ant.* 3.22 he uses σωτήριος in a similar way to the LXX (Norton 2011: 73). Philo follows the LXX (*Spec. Laws* 1.212, 224).

Yet as Altshuler[24] noted, Josephus does not mention the rules for goats (Lev. 3.12-16) or the exact procedure for slaughtering (vv. 2, 8).[25]

Hattat *and* Asham *(Lev. 4–5 // Ant. 3.230-32)*

Leviticus 4–5 deal with purification and guilt offerings. They are directed towards any member of the community and include a female goat (Lev. 4.27-30) or a female lamb (vv. 31-35).

In *Ant.* 3.231 Josephus writes:

> One who through ignorance has fallen into this [sin] brings a lamb and a female goat a year old; and the priest sprinkles the altar with its blood, not as at first but the protrusions of the corners. They lay upon the altar the kidneys and the other fat along with the lobe of the liver, but the priests carry off the skins and the flesh from it, intending to consume it within the day in the temple. For the law does not permit leaving it until the following day.

Josephus' addition that the lamb and the she-goat should be a year old is in accord with *Sifra* 7.10. His addition that 'the law does not permit leaving it until the following day' finds analogy in *m. Zevah.* 5.3 (cf. Philo, *Spec. Laws* 1.240, 243).

Grain Offerings and Libations (Num. 15.1-16 // Ant. 3.233-34)

Numbers 15.1-16 detail the ingredients of the grain offerings and libations that were to be offered together with the major sacrifices. Josephus (*Ant.* 3.233) points out that 'for private and public sacrifices perfectly pure wheat-flour should be offered... They present this, kneaded with oil, as a sacrifice on the altar'. In Regev's view,

> It seems that he believed that the grain offerings accompanying these sacrifices should be fully burnt on the altar, including that which is attached to the sacrificial offering. The rabbis (*Sifre* Num. 107) held a similar view. In their opinion, these verses in Numbers command that the grain offerings were to be burned on the altar together with the *Shelamim*.[26]

Numbers 15.7 does not describe the performance of libations in great detail. Was the libation poured directly on the altar?[27] Ben Sira

---

24. Altshuler 1977: 75.
25. Josephus uses σφάζω with regard to animal slaughter only six times, whereas in the MT and LXX to Leviticus–Numbers it appears 38 times.
26. Regev 1996a: 376.
27. See the discussion in Rubenstein 1994.

(50.14-15) and Josephus (§234) agree that wine is poured around the altar. According to *Jubilees* (7.5) and the Temple Scroll (11QT 34.11-14)[28] libations were sprinkled upon the sacrifices or upon the fires that burned on the altar. Rabbinic sources (*m. Suk.* 4.9; *Sifre* Num. 107) claim that the Sukkot water and wine libations went into bowls. Wine offerings were to be poured either on the base of the altar or into the bowls.

Various Laws Pertaining to Sacrifices (Ant. 3.235-36)

In *Ant.* 3.235-36 Josephus joins together various laws pertaining to sacrifices: offerings of fine flour (Lev. 2.1-3; 6.14-23); prohibition on sacrificing the mother and its offspring on the same day; prohibition on sacrificing an animal before it is eight days old; the thanksgiving offering (Lev. 22.28-29); pastries offered with sacrificial animals; the prohibition of leaving sacrifices for the following day; and the priests receiving a special portion (Lev. 7.11-16; 22.29-30). Josephus emphasizes that 'the priests took the rest as food'. A similar note appears in 11QT 9-12 and *m. Menah.* 6.1-2.[29]

Josephus omits frankincense from the grain offering (*Jub.* 21.7 also omits it). Perhaps he did not consider frankincense an integral part of the grain offering, since in Numbers 15 it is not mentioned. Yet, both Josephus and Philo do mention the frankincense on the Showbread (*Ant.* 3.256; Philo, *Spec. Laws* 1.175).

Josephus and the rabbis (*t. Zevah.* 5.3; *m. Menah.* 6.2) hold that the grain offering is not to be viewed as independent of the preceding burnt offering but as merely adjunct to it. Both are burned together on the altar.[30]

Regarding sacrificing the mother and its offspring on the same day, the law in Lev. 22.28 commands: 'But you shall not slaughter, from the herd or the flock, an animal with its young on the same day'. The biblical law remains silent as to the rationale behind it. Josephus does not add his explanation (unlike Philo, *Virt.* 125-30, 142).

Josephus adds that the sacrifice of thanksgiving is brought 'on behalf of escape from sickness'. Though not mentioned in the Bible, it is a very reasonable addition, and one finds it in modern research as well.[31]

28. Dimant and Parry 2015: 929–30.
29. Noam 2003: 251.
30. Milgrom 1991: 390.
31. Gunkel 1998: 199–221. Gunkel found this in Pss. 18, 30, 32, 34, 40, 41, 66, 92, 116, 118, and 138.

Rosh Hashanah – New Year's Day (Lev. 23.23-25; Num. 29.1-6 // Ant. 3.239)

The development of Tishri 1, the first day of the seventh month (New Years' Day), in the Bible is obscure. It is mentioned in Lev. 23.23-25 and Num. 29.1-6. The Pentateuchal laws forbid work during this festival, command a cultic assembly, and provide a list of sacrifices. Ideas of creation, remembrance, judgment, and eschatology were attached to this festival throughout the ages.[32]

Josephus (*Ant.* 3.239) says of Rosh Hashanah: 'In the seventh month, which the Macedonians called Hyperbetaeus, adding to what has been mentioned, they sacrifice a bull and a ram and seven lambs and a kid for their sins'.

As he has done with regard to Passover, here he also equates the Hebrew and the Greek months. Josephus does mention the seventh month (and adds its name in Greek). However, he does not point out the specific day of the month (the first day) or even write that it is called Rosh Hashanah. Neither does he define it as a day of judgment or mention the blowing of the shofar. He refers only to the sacrifices brought at this time (according to Num. 29).

Even when Josephus rewrites the book of Nehemiah 7–8 (*Ant.* 11.155), where it is told that all the people gathered on the first day of the seventh month and heard Ezra reading the Torah, Josephus does not tell us that it is Rosh Hashanah. How are we to understand his silence with regard to Rosh Hashanah? Some hold that Josephus was ignorant, not knowing the practices related to this festival.[33] This would explain why he did not mention them. However, we should recall that there is no hint in the Bible that the first of Tishri is Rosh Hashanah. Likewise, in the biblical account of Nehemiah the shofar is not mentioned.

With regard to the non-mention of the blowing of the shofar, Meir Bar-Ilan[34] thinks that the reason may be that in Josephus' days the halakha of 'All are under obligation to blow the shofar' (*b. R.H.* 29b) was not yet in effect, since Josephus' departure from Jerusalem near its destruction cut him off from the centers of influence where halakha was developed. According to this explanation, Josephus could not have known of this halakha.

---

32. Elgvin 2003.
33. That is the general attitude of Olitzki 1885.
34. Bar-Ilan 1982: 77.

Philo (*Spec. Laws* 2.188) also says that 'it is customary to sound the trumpet in the temple at the same time that the sacrifices are brought there, and its name is "trumpet feast"'.

Leviticus 23.23-25 prescribes the rites for the first day of the seventh month.[35] The law appears in Num. 29.1-6 as well. Josephus (*Ant.* 3.239) says of Rosh Hashanah: 'In the seventh month, which the Macedonians called Hyperbetaeus, adding to what has been mentioned, they sacrifice a bull and a ram and seven lambs and a kid for their sins'.

As for the mention of Rosh Hashanah as a day of judgment, the rabbis (*b. R.H.* 8a) discussed this idea based on Ps. 81.5. However, Josephus doesn't mention it, nor do we have Josephus' version of the Psalms. Others tried to differentiate between blowing the shofar in the temple and outside it or argued that Philo and Josephus preserve an older halakha.[36]

The Scapegoat (Lev. 16 // Ant. 3.240-43)

Leviticus 16 describes the entrance of the high priest into the holy of holies on the Day of Atonement. In the rituals he performs, his aim is to atone for the sins of himself, his family, and for the whole people of Israel. Josephus' description of Yom Kippur is an amalgamation and condensation of the ritual outlined in Leviticus 16, Lev. 23.26-32, and Num. 29.7-11.

Josephus lists the prescribed sacrifices for Yom Kippur: a bull, two rams, seven lambs, and a goat as a purification offering. This is a rewriting of Num. 29.8, 11. While Josephus specifies two rams, Num. 29.8 (and the LXX[37]) prescribes only one.

Returning to Leviticus 16, Josephus refers to the two goats mentioned in Lev. 16.7-10, 20-22) separately: one goat is sent into the wilderness while the other is conducted to the 'suburbs' (προάστειος, 'suburban'). The purpose of the scapegoat, according to Josephus, is twofold: (1) to remove evil (sin) from the inhabited area, and (2) to serve as an expiation for the sins of the people. Omitting most of Lev. 16.7-9, Josephus does not specify that one is for God and the other for Azazel. In *Ant.* 3.241 he writes that the function of the goat sent into the wilderness is 'to be an aversion and pardon for the sins of all the multitude'.

---

35. Milgrom (2000: 2013) calls this the 'Festival of Alarm Blasts'.
36. Belkin 1940; Milgrom 2000: 2018.
37. For the difference between Josephus and the LXX here, see Scullion 1990: 189 n. 204. Scullion concludes: 'Josephus was not using the LXX as his source here'.

After the description of the burning of the goat and bull, Josephus recounts the blood rite (*Ant.* 3.242-43; Lev. 16.11-19). He condenses the description by combining the blood rite of the bull (Lev. 16.11-14) and the goat (Lev. 16.15) and omitting any reference to the bringing of incense into the Holy of Holies. The high priest brings the blood of the bull and the goat into the sanctuary. He then sprinkles the blood: on (1) the ceiling; (2) the floor; (3) inside the sanctuary; and (4) around the golden altar. The high priest brings the rest of the blood into the outer court and sprinkles it around the larger altar, viz., the altar of holocaust. The order and description here are somewhat strange. The burning that Josephus is describing here is that of the hide, flesh, and offal of the bull and the goat (*Ant.* 3.241-42; Lev. 16.27). One gets the impression that since they were burned 'skin and all, without any cleansing whatsoever', there would be nothing left. Yet he will later describe another burning of these two animals on the altar of holocaust (*Ant.* 3.243; Lev. 16.25).

This description of the blood rite differs from both the MT and the LXX. According to the MT, two locations in the holy of holies are sprinkled with the blood of the bull and the goat: (1) the forepart of the mercy seat (16.14, 15); and (2) in front of the mercy seat.

The later mention of the altar of holocaust (referred to above) allows Josephus to conclude his account of the Yom Kippur liturgy with a description of the burning of the goat and the bull on this altar (*Ant.* 3.10.3 §243; Lev. 16.25).

Whereas rabbinic sources (mainly *m. Yoma*) describe the cultic rite of Leviticus 16 vividly, Josephus' depiction of sending the goat to Azazel is somewhat dry. Furthermore, Josephus does not mention the origin of Yom Kippur, the requirement to refrain from work, the bringing of incense into the holy of holies, or the confession of sins over the scapegoat. Nor does he provide a firsthand account of the high priest performing the various rites.

Josephus' vocabulary seems to deliberately recall Greek ritual language, presumably in order to suit a non-Jewish audience: in *Ant.* 3.240-41 he describes the scapegoat as 'disgusting' (ἀποτροπιασμός). The very same root was used by Julian.[38]

Josephus also does not describe the clothes of the High Priest or his immersion; the two lots associated with two sacrificial goats; the incense; the priests' placing of their hands upon the goat's head; or the confession of sins.

---

38. Stökl Ben Ezra 2002: 226.

Josephus refers to Yom Kippur in his rewriting of Num. 29.8-11: according to Josephus, three rams should be offered. This is supported by 11QT 25.14-16 and Philo (*Spec. Laws* 1.188). According to these sources, Num. 29.8-9 is a stipulation for additional offerings, distinct from those specified in Lev. 5.59 and 16.3. However, the Mishnah says it is two (*m. Yom.* 7.3).[39]

Sukkot – Festival of Booths (Lev. 23.33-43 and Parallels // Ant. 3.244-47)

The festival of Sukkot is mentioned in Exod. 23.13 (as חג האסף); Lev. 23.33-43; Num. 29.12-38, and Deut. 16.13-16. Josephus refers to Sukkot in *Ant.* 3.244-47. He assembled all the pentateuchal sources and tries to present a clear picture of this law. In *Ant.* 8.100 (cf. 15.50) he adds: 'At this same time the season of Tabernacles (σκηνοπηγία), a feast that is very sacred and important to the Hebrews'. This is supported by rabbinic sources (*m. Suk.* 4.4-5; 5.1-4).

Josephus (§244) connects Sukkot with climatic issues: 'On the fifteenth of the same month, when the season finally turns to winter, he bids them, apprehensive of the cold, in each dwelling to erect tents, for protection against the year'.[40] Rubenstein[41] explains that Josephus is motivated by apologetic concerns: 'Apparently Josephus felt uncomfortable with the fanciful notion that God actually provided booths for the Israelites, an idea that his Hellenistic audience would have ridiculed'. Yet, Josephus' explanation should not necessarily be regarded as apologetic. We may surmise that Josephus took his cue from Isa. 4.6: 'It will serve as a pavilion, a shade by day from the heat, and a refuge and a shelter from the storm and rain' (cf. Jon. 4.5). From Deuteronomy 16 Josephus took the need to bring the four species to the chosen city. That is not mentioned in the other sources.

In *Ant.* 3.245 Josephus writes that the Israelites should bear in their hands 'a bouquet made up of myrtle and willow-branch (εἰρεσιώνην μυρσίνης καὶ ἰτέας) together with a branch of palm, with the fruit of the persea'. Josephus does not specify how many myrtle and willows should be brought, since he follows the MT. This number was added by the rabbis (*m. Suk.* 3.4).

---

39. Scullion 1990: 189; Stökl Ben Ezra 2003: 22 n. 15.
40. Cf. Philo (*Spec. Laws* 2.33, 206).
41. Rubenstein 1995: 76.

Josephus (*Ant.* 3.245) identifies 'the fruit of *hadar*, goodly trees' (Lev. 23.40) as the persea (περσέα; *Ant.* 3.245). Feldman erroneously blames Josephus for failing to identify this fruit as the biblical citron. Feldman believes that Josephus identified the etrog as the avocado.[42]

Let us look at Josephus' text in its original Greek: τοῦ μήλου τοῦ τῆς περσέας. Thackeray translates 'the fruit of the persea', while Schalit translates 'the fruit of the peach'. Schalit's translation is erroneous, as the Greek for peach is μῆλον περσικόν. And while 'persea' can refer to a persea-tree[43], here *perseas* comes from 'Perseis' and 'Persea', meaning 'Persian' and should be translated: 'The Persian apple' or 'Persian fruit'.[44] Josephus clearly refers to the citron. If so, then the law of the etrog serves as another example of a case where Josephus' view concurs with the rabbinic law. Additionally, in this case, Josephus deviates again from the Septuagint, whose translation literally means καρπον ξύλου ὡραῖον – the 'ripe fruit of a tree'. Josephus actually mentions the citron in *Ant.* 13.372. In fact, Josephus' definition of the four species is identical to the rabbinic definitions (*m. Suk.* 3.4).[45]

*Omer (*Ant. *3.250-51)*

The phrase ממחרת השבת is problematic: does it designate the day after Sabbath (Sunday) or the day after Passover (the 16th of Nisan)? Josephus (*Ant.* 3.250) follows the latter view, in parallel with the Pharisees (*m. Menah.* 10.3), the LXX to Leviticus 23, Philo (*Spec. Laws* 2.1262), and the Aramaic translations.

Shavuot (Weeks, Pentecost: Lev. 23.15-21; Num. 28.26-31 // Ant. *3.252-53)*

Pentecost (or the Feast of Weeks) is mentioned in Exod. 23.16; 34.22; Lev. 23.15-21; Num. 28.26-31; and Deut. 16.9-12, 16. As in the Bible, Josephus does not add a specific date for the Feast of Weeks.[46] In Josephus' rewriting of the laws regarding Shavuot he does not refer to the Hebrew מקרא קדש. As for the abstention from work, he refers to it in *Ant.* 3.254. He adds in *Ant.* 13.252: 'for the festival of Pentecost had come round, following the Sabbath, and we are not permitted to march either on the Sabbath or on a festival'.

42. Feldman 2000: 301 n. 700.
43. See Liddell and Scott 1996: 1395.
44. Rubenstein 1995: 74.
45. Feldman 2000: 301 n. 697.
46. In *Jub.* 1.1. it is the fifteenth of the third month (i.e., Sivan). Cf. *Jub.* 14.1, 10, 20; 15.1; 16.3. See Park 2008: 99. This was adopted in the Qumran calendar, as in 4Q320, Temple Scroll, etc.

Josephus uses the term ἀσαρθά (*Ant.* 3.252), which is in line with the rabbinic term עצרת, meaning assembly.[47] Yet, he does not mention its other names (חג הקציר: Exod. 23.16; חג הביכורים: Num. 28.26). Josephus refers to it as πεντηκοστή, 'feast of fifty' (*Ant.* 3.252; 13.252; *War* 1.253; 6.299).

There are a few differences between Josephus' rewriting of the law and the MT: in Josephus' account, one loaf of two assarons (omers) of wheat flour is presented to God (*Ant.* 3.252), whereas in Lev. 23.17, it is two loaves. Second, Josephus says that the whole burnt offering consists of three calves, two rams, fourteen lambs, and two kids in atonement for sins (*Ant.* 3.253).

As to the numbers of animals, Josephus (*Ant.* 3.253) notices the contradiction between Leviticus and Numbers 29 regarding the number of bulls and rams: Leviticus speaks about the sacrifices accompanied by the two breads, while Numbers speaks about the additional offerings of the holiday, which are brought regardless of the bread. Therefore one should add the numbers of the animals in the two sources in order to reach the absolute number of offerings of Shavuot.[48] Josephus should be commended for reaching the same conclusion that Rabbi Akiva (*b. Menah.* 45b) has reached. But on the other hand, although Josephus joined the number of bulls in the two sources (2 + 1 = 3) as well as the bull numbers (7 + 7 = 14, apart from the two intact sheep, which he already mentioned with the two breads), he did not join together the ram numbers, and put in the number of two rams instead of three (2 + 1).

Bread of the Presence (Lev. 24.5-9 // Ant. 3.255-56)

The bread of the presence is also described in Exod. 25.23-30; 35.13, 39.36 and Lev. 24.5-9. Loaves of bread were placed in the sanctuary on a golden table before God. Leviticus 24.5-9 describes the bread itself. The bread of the presence consists of twelve loaves, placed in two rows of six each. Each is made with two tenths of an ephah of flour. The bread of the presence functioned like a grain offering which was sprinkled with frankincense.

Josephus has added several details.[49] According to him, the showbread was paid for by public money (§255). At first sight, this addition may seem baseless. However, we find such a claim in the scholion for the Megillat Ta'anit of Nisan,[50] and in *b. Menah.* 65b it is also noted that the

---

47. See *m. R.H.* 1.2 and *Ḥag.* 2.4. cf. Onkelos and Neofiti to Num. 28.26.
48. Nakman 2004: 76–7 n. 26.
49. Altshuler 1977: 89; Feldman 2000: 305 n. 746.
50. Noam 2003: 165–73.

Pharisees favored payment of half a shekel by each person once a year for the purpose of financing the Temple service. The Sadducees, however, objected to this regulation and apparently preferred that the service of the sacrifices be financed by individual donations, as was the case before the regulation of the half-shekel, probably during the Hasmonean period.[51] Thus, one may conclude that Josephus held the opinion of the Pharisees; yet it may reflect the practice at his time.

He further adds that it is baked on the Sabbath eve, as written in *m. Menah.* 11.2. He then writes that the frankincense is placed in two golden dishes (§256). Philo (*Spec. Laws* 1.175) views things similarly. The Temple Scroll (11QT 8.9-10) is of a similar opinion. The rabbis (*Sifra* Emor 18.19) also claim that the frankincense is not actually placed on the bread, but above it in two gold or silver containers. Milgrom[52] remarks: 'Josephus's view remains a puzzle, unless we assume that by his time, the loaves were placed inside a tiered vessel, thus permitting the frankincense containers to be placed on top of the vessel and not on the loaves'.

Josephus' mentioning the unleavened bread is paralleled by *m. Menah.* 5.1. Josephus writes that the loaves are baked by twos, a detail mentioned in *m. Menah.* 11.1.

On the other hand, Josephus does not repeat the biblical identification of the loaves as a 'token offering' (Lev. 24.7) and a 'covenant' (24.8), nor does he say that Aaron is the one charged to set the offering in order. The LXX (Lev. 24.7), Philo (*Spec. Laws* 175) and the rabbis (*b. Menah.* 20a) note that salt was also placed on the frankincense. Josephus does not mention this, perhaps because it is not explicitly stated in Scripture.

The High Priest's Daily Cereal Offering (Lev. 6.12-16 // Ant. 3.257)

Josephus writes that the (high) priest sacrifices at his own expense. That is in line with *m. Menah.* 4.5.[53] Philo, however, writes that this daily cereal offering is binding on every priest (*Spec. Laws* 1.255-56). The rabbis agree that this pericope deals with the high priest *and also* with every priest (*Sifra*, Tzav 3.3).[54]

---

51. See Nakman 2004: 74 n. 10 and the literature cited there.
52. Milgrom 2001: 2098.
53. 'If they did not appoint another priest, at whose charges was the offering made? R. Simeon says: At the charges of the congregation. R. Judah says: At the charges of the heirs; and a whole Tenth must be offered.'
54. Milgrom 1991: 395–6.

Animals Forbidden for Consumption
(Lev. 11 and Deut. 14 // Ant. 3.259)

Josephus has dealt with the issue of clean and unclean animals in general in *Ag. Ap.* 2.173-74:

> Rather, starting right from the beginning of their nurture and from the mode of life practiced by each individual in the household, he did not leave anything, even the minutest detail, free to be determined by the wishes of those who would make use of [the laws], but even in relation to food, what they should refrain from and what they should eat, the company they keep in their daily lives, as well as their intensity in work and, conversely, rest, he set the law as their boundary and rule, so that, living under this as a father and master, we might commit no sin either willfully or from ignorance.[55]

Josephus also deals with eating pork in *Ag. Ap.* 2.137, 141. He considers the Mosaic laws rational. In *Ant.* 3.259 Josephus gives a very brief description on the unclean animals. He promises to give a broader description, but he never fulfilled his promise. His decision not to develop this issue in his *Antiquities* but rather in *Apion* was probably motivated by the apologetic concerns of *Apion*, which is a better platform to enter into polemic.[56]

Prohibition on Eating Fat, an Impure Carcass, and Blood
(Lev. 7.22-27; 11.24-47; 17.10-16; Ant. 3.260)

The prohibition to eat blood is mentioned in Lev. 7.22-27; 11.24-47; 17.10-16; and Deut. 12.16, 23. It appears also in the book of *Jubilees*, Damascus Covenant, Aramaic Levi and the Temple Scroll.[57]

Josephus refers to this law only in *Ant.* 2.260 and does not rewrite Deuteronomy 12, probably wishing to avoid repetition.[58] Josephus says with regard to blood: 'He prohibited the use of all blood for food, however, considering it to be the soul and the spirit'. He refers to this prohibition also in his rewriting of 1 Sam. 14.31-35, where the people in

---

55. Cf. Arist. 128–9, 142–57.
56. For Jewish-Hellenistic sources, see Rosenblum 2006: 46–76.
57. Hanneken 2015.
58. In fact, there are several differences between Leviticus and Deuteronomy. See Hanneken 2015, with earlier literature. Eating blood is mentioned in Gen. 9.4 as well, but Josephus (*Ant.* 1.102) and the rabbis (*Sifre* Deut. 76; *b. Sanh.* 59a) understand it as referring to flesh cut from a living animal. See Werman 1995.

Saul's reign eat blood 'before they had duly washed away the blood and made the flesh clean' (*Ant.* 6.120) and that 'this was not pleasing to God' (*Ant.* 6.121). These additions basically follow the biblical explanation, without developing it further. Josephus refers here also to the eating of the flesh of an animal that has died due to natural causes and abstaining from the 'tissue covering the entrails and the fat of goats and sheep and oxen'.

Josephus understands נבלה as 'eating of the flesh of an animal that has died due to natural causes'. Here Josephus diverges from the MT's וחלב נבלה...לא תאכלהו. The verse refers to eating the fat of a dead animal, despite the fact that all parts of this animal were prohibited for consumption. Josephus correctly ignores the fat and relates to the whole flesh of the animal.[59]

As for eating fat, Josephus writes that 'we abstain from the tissue covering the entrails'. Josephus combines justifiably Lev. 7.23 with 3.3-4 to reach the conclusion that חלב refers to fat that covers the internal organs and entrails.[60]

Altshuler[61] remarks that Josephus excluded from his list the prohibition of flesh torn from living beasts (Exod. 22.30; Lev. 7.24; 17.15). That is a very strange remark, since this prohibition is clearly post-biblical and thus we cannot expect Josephus to mention it.[62] The reference to abstention from the caul of goats, sheep, and oxen is Josephus' addition, but it is a good understanding of the role of Lev. 7.25 as a clarification of v. 23.[63]

Leprosy, Menstruation, Contact with the Dead, and Seminal Emission (Lev. 13–15; Num. 19.1-13 // Ant. 3.261-64)

Josephus summarizes in *Ant.* 3.261-64 laws from Leviticus 13–15. Leviticus 13–14 deal with various cases of צרעת (leprosy) and the ways in which lepers are purified. According to Josephus (*Ant.* 3.261-62), lepers (λέπρα)[64] were banished not merely from the camp (Lev. 13.46; 14.3), but also from the city (cf. *Ag. Ap.* 1.281).[65] Josephus is supported

---

59. Cf. Levine 1989: 45.
60. Levine 1989: 45. Cf. Feldman 2000: 307 n. 775.
61. Altshuler 1977: 91.
62. See Lavee 2013. It appears in *b. Sanh.* 56b and its parallels.
63. Levine 1989: 45.
64. Milgrom (1991: 775) points out that 'it can in no way be identified with leprosy, if for no other reason than that even the LXX calls it by a distinctive term, lepra "scaly condition", not by elephantiasis "leprosy"'.
65. However, according to the rabbis, only lepers are sent out of Jerusalem altogether. Those with discharges (as well as menstrual and postpartum women) may not enter the Temple Mount. See Noam 2010: 369 n. 20.

by 4QMMT B64-72 and 11Q19 [11QT] 45.11-12.⁶⁶ Also banished were those having γονὴν ῥεομένους, probably gonorrhea.

Josephus' addition that 'if someone by imploring God successfully should be delivered from the disease and should get back a healthy skin' (3.264) is supported by 4Q274, Frg. 1 Col. i 1-4, where the leper is expected to admit his wrongdoing.⁶⁷

As for contact with the dead, we shall return to it in our analysis of Josephus' retelling of Numbers 19.⁶⁸ Josephus adds with regard to seminal emission a bath in cold water.⁶⁹

In §§265-69 Josephus refutes the anti-Jewish claim that the Jews were expelled from Egypt due to their leprosy (cf. *Ag. Ap.* 1.219-320).

As for menstruation, Josephus (*Ant.* 3.261) rewrites Lev. 15.19: 'He segregated until the seventh day women whose secretion occurs for them in accordance with nature'. As Milgrom⁷⁰ shows, the word נדה itself has a meaning of 'expelled' and quarantine is documented in many societies, including rabbinic sources (*Sifra*, Mezora 2.2). In this way, Josephus' view does not seem so strange.

Childbirth (Lev. 12.2-8 // Ant. 3.269)

Leviticus 12.2-8 deals with purification laws for women after childbirth. Josephus writes:

> He has forbidden women, when they have given birth, from entering the Temple and from touching sacrifices until after forty days if the child is a male; and it happens that twice the number of days is required for female births. Upon entering after the aforementioned fixed time, however, they offer sacrifices that the priests apportion to God. (*Ant.* 3.269)

---

66. Kazen 2010: 109–13. He mentions also Lk. 17.12-19. On p. 114, Kazen concludes: 'Such definitions are definitely interpretations of the biblical legislation, and it is reasonable to regard Josephus' statement…as reflecting a contemporary understanding of how the "leper" transferred impurity to others'.

67. Milgrom 1995: 61. See the text in Dimant and Parry 2015: 337.

68. The sacrifices of two lambs that Josephus mentions (3.262) are not mentioned in the biblical law.

69. Gallant (1988: 121) deals with the juxtaposition of all these laws by Josephus. In his view, Josephus started with the case having the least stringent purification requirement (seminal impurity) and continued with the one involving the most stringent requirement (leprosy, *Ant.* 3.264). Josephus' aim was to emphasize the severity of the latter condition in preparation for his immediately following refutation of the charge that Moses and his followers were themselves lepers (*Ant.* 3.265-68).

70. Milgrom 1990: 763–8.

Josephus does not explain why a woman who has given birth should bring a sin-offering[71] nor the extended period of impurity after the birth of a daughter. On this point Josephus may be excused, since this is a matter of debate in recent scholarship as well.[72]

We should note that Josephus does not mention any regulation with regard to bathing. He fails to mention circumcision as well. The latter omission may be related to his ambivalence towards circumcision.[73]

Lawrence Schiffman explains that Josephus' rewriting was aimed at non-Jewish readers and therefore he did not elaborate with details.[74] In my view, this assertion is problematic since a Jewish audience was also intended.[75] Had Josephus wanted to present a shorter and a friendlier version of Judaism, many of the laws of the Torah should have been omitted.

Homosexuality and Incest (Lev. 18 and 20 // Ant. 3.274-75)

The laws pertaining to incest appear in Leviticus 18 and 20. The law prohibits sexual intercourse with a mother, sister, granddaughter, aunt and proximate female in-laws (Lev. 18.6-17, 22). Josephus adds stepmother and aunt. He considers incest with one's mother the 'greatest evil' (*Ant.* 3.274).

Josephus provides the rationale behind this law: 'He completely forbade adultery, considering it is blessed for men to behave soundly with regard to marriage and advantageous for both states and households that children be legitimate'. The legitimacy of children and sex for the purpose of procreation (*Ant.* 3.275) are key factors that shape Jewish families. It is interesting to note that these explanations were adopted by modern interpreters.[76]

Josephus omits Reuben's incest with Bilhah (Gen. 35.22) as well as Judah's with Tamar (Gen. 8). In many other parts of *Antiquities* and *War*, Josephus mentions cases of incest.[77]

---

71. The LXX translates חטאת as ἁμαρτίας, and is followed by Philo (*Spec. Laws* 1.226) and Josephus (*Ant.* 3.230) ἁμαρτάς, 'sin'.
72. See La Barge 2009.
73. See Spilsbury 1996.
74. Schiffman 2018.
75. See Sterling 1992: 306–8.
76. See Gagnon 2001: 312–33.
77. See Loader 2011: 348.

As for homosexuality, Josephus speaks against the 'unnaturalness' of same-sex relations (*Ag. Ap.* 2.273: παρὰ φύσιν). A similar line of thought can be found in Philo (*Spec. Laws* 3.39; *Abr.* 133-136: παρὰ φύσιν) and in *T. Naph.* 3.3-4 (ἐνήλλαξε τάξιν φύσεως),

Josephus retells both Genesis 19 and Judges 19, where homosexual relations are mentioned. In *Ant.* 1.200 he refers to the appearance and beauty of the intended victims of the Sodomites. However, only Philo concentrates on the homosexual sin, while Josephus stresses hatred of strangers along with pride and impiety. This avoidance of stressing homosexuality as a sin seems to be a deliberate attempt to differentiate the Jews from the Greeks. In his version of the Gibeah story (Judg. 19), Josephus again emphasizes violence, rape, and abuse of hospitality while disregarding homosexuality.[78]

Various Laws for Priests (Lev. 21–22 // Ant. 3.276-79)

Leviticus 21–22 enumerates ways in which priests might be excluded, either temporarily or permanently, from service. Josephus rewrites these laws in *Ant.* 3.276-79. He begins with Lev. 21.6, 'they shall be holy to their God', rewriting it as 'From the priests he demanded twice as much purity'. Thus, he begins with a general statement backed by details, in contrast to MT where the opposite is presented.

Whereas Lev. 21.7 forbids a priest marrying a prostitute, Josephus (*Ant.* 3.276) adds that priests may not marry a slave, a prisoner of war, and 'those women who obtain their livelihood from tavern-keeping and from keeping an inn, or those who for whatever reasons have been separated from their former husbands'.

Thackeray explains that Josephus was thinking of Rahab, who was an inn-keeper (*Ant.* 5.7-8).[79] Others suggested that חללה was explained by Josephus as a slave or a prisoner of war.[80] However, it is possible that Josephus understood חללה to mean prostitute, and that is the reason why חללה is not mentioned separately. In other words, he considered the words זנה וחללה as hendiadys.

As for the prohibition of marrying a slave, Josephus mentions this restriction again in *Ag. Ap.* 1.35. There he explains that female slaves are suspected of having had frequent intercourse with foreigners.

---

78. Carden 2004: 76–8.
79. Thackeray 1926–56: 4:450 n. b. Josephus never mentions πορνεία to designate a prostitute.
80. Feldman 2000: 314 n. 836.

Leviticus 21.18-20 contains the most comprehensive list of physical impairments. It does not mention deafness, but Josephus adds it in *Ant.* 14.366 (// *War* 1.269), where Antigonus, the Persian candidate among the priestly rivals, sought to kill his uncle Hyrcanus II: 'because he was now mutilated, and the law requires that this office should belong only to those who are sound of body'.[81]

Josephus writes that the priest should be 'pure in all respects' (*Ant.* 3.279), thus abbreviating many details in his retelling of the blemishes of the priest.

Sabbatical Year (Lev. 25 // Ant. 3.280-85)

Josephus (*Ant.* 3.280-85) rewrites the laws of the sabbatical year and the Jubilee year in Leviticus 25. He deals with this law in several other places as well.[82] As a rule, Josephus (like Philo) does not mention the fact that the commandments are practiced only in the Land of Israel. Yet, as Safrai notes, 'we cannot conclude from that that he was unfamiliar with it'.[83]

According to Josephus, when the Jubilee comes, the debts of borrowers are forgiven, fields returned to their owners, and slaves released from their masters.

Schalit and Nakman[84] view this as an error on the part of Josephus. Nakman explains that Josephus in *Ant.* 3.281-86 summarized the laws of Shemittah and Jubilee in Lev. 25.1-55 and forgot or at least ignored the law of Deut. 15.12-18. The law pertaining to Shemittah in Leviticus 25 mentions only the abstaining from productive work and nothing about debt relief. On the other hand, the subsequent verses, which speak at length about the laws of the Jubilee (Lev. 25.8-22), include a number of references to the laws of interest, which serve as a kind of introduction to the issue of slaves and their release in the Jubilee. It turns out, therefore, that Josephus understood in some way, or associatively linked, the prohibition of interest with the matter of the remission of debts and included it by mistake with the laws of the Jubilee.

---

81. Milgrom (2000: 1826) notes that the Qumran sect mentions 'only the blind among the blemished persons prohibited from entering the Temple-city (11QT 45.12-14; cf. 1QM 7.4), where clearly they also included the defects of Lev 21'. MMT B 52-54 adds deafness.

82. *War* 1.39; *Ant.* 11.338, 343; 12.378; 13.343; 14.202-206, 476; 15.7. See Feldman 1984: 506–7, where he summarizes the views of several scholars on the chronology of the Sabbatical year according to Josephus' writings.

83. Safrai 2018: 89.

84. Nakman 2004: 60–1. Cf. Schalit 1944: 2:74 n. 207.

However, Gilat[85] brings evidence that according to some rabbis, the Jubilee cancels debts (*y. R.H.* 58d-59a; *y. Shev.* 39c). Josephus' view is found in 11QMelchizedek, ll. 2-3 as well.[86] Thus, Josephus' interpretation is not necessarily erroneous, and may be part of a tradition of interpretation in the Second Temple period.

Votive Gifts (Lev. 27 // Ant. 4.71-73)

The laws of votive gifts are mentioned in Leviticus 27: one can dedicate certain appropriate animals as well as other properties that will be transferred to the ownership of the temple. These gifts can be redeemed by paying their value plus 20 percent (Lev. 27.13, 19, 27).

Donations include the silver equivalent of one's value in labor (vv. 1-8), animals fit or unfit for sacrifice (vv. 9-14), houses (vv. 14-16), fields (vv. 16-25), firstborn animals (vv. 26-27), and tithed produce and animals (vv. 30-33).

From the priestly dues Josephus mentions only the valuations-of-persons payments of Lev. 27.2-8 (*Ant.* 4.73). He says nothing of field consecrations as a source of revenue. Josephus refers to 'Korban' (gifts) that were given to the priests, in continuation of the practice of the valuation of persons from Lev. 27.2-8. The priests' right to these valuation payments is also mentioned in the Damascus Document (4Q270 frag. 2 col. ii),[87] where it is referred to as כסף הערכים לפדוי נפשם, 'the valuation money for the redemption of their soul'.

In *Ant.* 4.71 Josephus does not mention the tithe of animals (Lev. 27.32). Nakman[88] surmises that there may be several reasons for this omission: (1) Josephus supported the Pharisee's view (*m. Zevah.* 5.8; *Sifre* Num. 119) that the animal tithe was not given to the priests and it should be eaten by the owners;[89] (2) Josephus had forgotten it at the time he made the list of priestly gifts; (3) Josephus didn't know the precise meaning of 'shall be holy to the Lord' (Lev. 27.32) and therefore refrained from mentioning this tithe.[90]

---

85. Gilat 1995.
86. Bartos and Levinson 2013.
87. Dimant and Parry 2015: 324.
88. Nakman 2004: 109.
89. See more sources in Schiffman 2008: 142 n. 91. According to another view this tithe did go to the priests. See 11QT 60.2-4, *Jub.* 13.25-26, and Tob. 1.6.
90. Milgrom (2000: 2399) finds in this omission an indication that the law was not observed. Milgrom says that Philo omitted this law, but this is not certain. See Schiffman 2008: 142 n. 88. Schiffman mentions *Spec. Laws* 1.141; 4.98; *Virt.* 95.

The Blasphemer (Lev. 24 // Ant. 4.202)

Josephus omitted the story of the blasphemer from his rewriting, yet he does refer to the prohibition of blasphemy later (*Ant.* 4.202). According to Feldman,[91] the omission may have had apologetic motives: Josephus 'was eager not to portray the Jews as a quarrelsome people'. However, since βλασφημέω appears 40 times in Josephus, this is unlikely. The issue is not blasphemy in itself or presenting Jews as quarrelsome people. The reason for the omission may be connected to the fact that its original placement in Leviticus 24 is awkward, and since Josephus transferred it to his rewriting of the laws in Deuteronomy, the story itself becomes an interruption. In addition, Josephus had already rewritten the laws of talion mentioned in Lev. 24.17-21 (see his rewriting of Exod. 21.14-17, 23-25).

According to Josephus, a blasphemer should be hanged after stoning. This version of the law concurs with rabbinic sources,[92] but Josephus might have reached it independently in light of the law in Deut. 21.22. The question therefore arises: did Josephus' acquaintance with the tannaitic halakha teach him that the blasphemer was hanged, or did he deduce this punishment by himself? This scholarly debate remains undecided. In any case, Josephus' description implies that he aspired to provide an accurate articulation of the law, and was not satisfied with a mere technical rewriting of the verses of the Torah. Though we cannot determine whether his description is the product of logic and analytical skills or whether it is based upon oral traditions, one thing is certain: Josephus strives for accuracy in this passage.

While Goldenberg concludes that 'the restriction of the double penalty to the crime of blasphemy by Josephus is in agreement with contemporaneous tannaitic halakha and is most probably based upon it',[93] we should not dismiss the option that he reached this conclusion through careful analysis of the laws in Leviticus.[94]

Mixture of Wool and Linen
(Lev. 19.19 and Deut. 22.11 // Ant. 4.208)

Leviticus 19.19 and Deut. 22.11 deals with the composition of fabrics, specifically prohibiting the mixture of wool and linen.[95] The biblical

---

91. Feldman 2007: 214.
92. *M. Sanh.* 6.4; Sifre Deut. 221. See Chapman 2008.
93. Goldenberg 1978: 67.
94. Nakman 2004, passim.
95. Feldman (2000: 405 n. 627) explains that Josephus avoided the LXX translation κίβδηλον for apologetic reasons, since it means 'hypocritical, unprincipled,

verses do not explain the rationale of the law. Josephus adds that only priests are allowed to wear such a blend. That explanation is followed by Tigay and is mentioned in the Mishnah (*m. Kil.* 9.1).[96]

Fruit of the Fourth Year (Lev. 19.23-25 // Ant. 4.226-27)

According to this law it is prohibited to pick fruit from new fruit-bearing trees during the first three years. In the fourth year, Israelites would dedicate the first fruits to God. There is a debate between the Qumran sect (11Q19 60.3-4)[97] and the rabbis about whether the fruits go to the owners or to the priests. According to the rabbis (*m. Maas. Shen.* 4.3-5), fruits of the fourth year are eaten or redeemed by their owners in Jerusalem. Josephus' position is in line with the Pharisees. In fact, there is a possibility that in the Bible itself this question was in debate.[98]

First Fruit of Trees (Lev. 19.23-25 // Ant. 4.227)

The fruits of the fourth year must be redeemed. The produce is to be offered to the Lord. According to the book of *Jubilees* (7.36), the Temple Scroll (60.2-4), 4QMMT (13.62-63), and Philo (*Virt.* 159),[99] these fruits should be brought to the priests. However, the rabbinic sages taught that they belong to the owners, i.e. the worshippers. Josephus (*Ant.* 4.227) follows the view of the Pharisees (*m. Maas. Shen.* 5.1-5):

> But in the fourth year let him harvest all that has grown, for then it is at the right time; and having gathered it in, let him carry it to the holy city, and let him consume it, together with the tithe of the other fruit, feasting it with his friends and with orphans and widows. In the fifth year let him be master to enjoy his plantings.

In *Ant.* 3.224-57 Josephus outlines the various sacrifices required by the law, as well as the main annual festivals instituted by Moses: Tabernacles, Passover and Pentecost. In *Ant.* 3.258-68 Josephus discusses the purity laws, including a short section on clean and unclean food. *Antiquities*

---

adulterated'. That is far-fetched. A simpler explanation would be that the LXX translators guessed the meaning, while Josephus disregarded it and used Deut. 22.11 in order to understand שעטנז.

96. Tigay 2016: 2:549.
97. Dimant and Parry 2015: 449.
98. Werman and Shemesh 2011: 216–17.
99. See Noam 2011b.

3.269 deals with childbirth, and 3.270-79 with rules concerning marriage and adultery. In *Ant.* 3.280-86 Josephus discusses the sabbatical year and the year of the Jubilee.

Conclusion

Josephus rewrote most of the book of Leviticus, albeit not following the MT in every detail. He interprets Leviticus in a way that helps the reader to better comprehend this difficult book. He was motivated by apologetic concerns, especially with regard to omissions, but these are minor in comparison to his exegetical motive.

Josephus' rewritings have a very limited contribution to the recovery of the ancient text of Leviticus. This is because Josephus' adaptation reflects neither the text of the MT nor the LXX with any consistency whatsoever; sometimes his text concurs with the MT, at other times it concurs with the LXX, and on yet other occasions it reflects neither.

A study of his modes of interpretation, however, promises to yield more interesting conclusions. They recall some methods of interpretation of the Qumran scrolls.[100] Both the Qumran scribes and Josephus seem to address an audience or audiences that may have difficulty reading Leviticus without mediation. Both, it seems, made great efforts to employ their skills as interpreters to shed light upon this intricate text.

Discrepancies between Josephus' writings and rabbinic halakha may be attributed to his being in Rome during the crystallization and development of the halakha,[101] while similarities between them may be explained by Josephus' acquaintance with the oral law that would later be codified by the rabbis. However, I have not delved into these possibilities but have instead focused on the interpretive aspect of Josephus' work.

---

100. Bernstein 2013: 2:448–75.
101. See Revel 1923–24.

3

THE LAWS OF THE BOOK OF NUMBERS IN JOSEPHUS

The book of Numbers is known for its complexity.[1] There are numerous genres in Numbers: administrative lists (1.1–4.49; 7.1-89; 10.11-28; 25.19–26.65; 34.1–35.34); cultic rules and regulations (5.1-4; 5.11–6.24; 8.1–9.14; 10.1-10; 15.1-41; 17.27–19.22; 28.1–30.1); stories (10.29–14.45; 16.1–17.26; 20.1–21.9; 21.21-31; 22.1–25.18; 27.12-23; 31.1-34; 32.1-42); laws (5.5-10; 27.1-11; 30.2-17; 35.9–36.12); and itineraries (21.10-20, 32-35; 33.1-56).[2] Likewise, there are several legal narratives in Numbers: (1) the case of the second Passover (9.6-14); (2) the case of the Sabbath wood gatherer (15.32-36); (3) the case of the daughters of Zelophehad (27.1-11). Theologically speaking, the book is focused on the question of Israel's faithfulness to their God.

From the textual point of view, the book of Numbers exists in fragments of the Dead Sea Scrolls.[3] The history of its interpretation involves ancient translations and versions,[4] sectarian Qumranic compositions, Jewish-Hellenistic writings, Pseudepigrapha and rabbinic literature.

There are no boundary markers between the books of Exodus to Deuteronomy in Josephus and they are retold continuously. Josephus treats Numbers mostly in *Antiquities* 3–4. In contrast with other chapters in my book, this one will not follow Josephus' order, due to the fact that

---

1. There are many opinions with regard to the structure of Numbers. See Olson 1985; Ska 2006: 35–8. Milgrom (1990: xiii) lists fourteen distinct genres in Numbers. Levine (1993: 48) concurs: 'Numbers is the most diverse of all Torah books'.
2. Forsling 2013: 48.
3. See Jastram 2000; Ulrich 2010: 138–74.
4. See D. B. Levine 1993: 84–7; Ashley 1993: 11–15. On the LXX, see Wevers 1998; Tov 2018.

the laws of Numbers are scattered in non-consecutive order in *Antiquities* 3–4. Thus I will follow the MT sequence. Let us compare the laws of Numbers in the MT with those of Josephus.

MT	Josephus
Num. 1–4	*Ant.* 3.287-94
Num. 3 + 8	*Ant.* 3.258
Num. 5.11-31	*Ant.* 3.270-73
Num. 6	*Ant.* 4.73
Num. 9	*Ant.* 3.294b
Num. 15.4-10	*Ant.* 3.234
Num. 18	*Ant.* 4.67-75
Num. 19	*Ant.* 4.79-81
Num. 27 + 36	*Ant.* 4.165, 174-75
Num. 28–29	*Ant.* 3.237-49
Num. 35	*Ant.* 4.172-73

This comparison reveals that Josephus retold most of the book of Numbers, but not necessarily word for word in relation to the MT. A comprehensive analysis of all rearrangements, omissions, and additions is beyond the scope of this study, and therefore I will focus mainly on the laws. Thus, though Numbers 25 and 31 contain interesting legal matters, I will not discuss Josephus' rewriting of them, since they are mostly narratives.[5]

The festival calendar in Numbers 28–29 was analyzed in our discussion of Exodus and Leviticus. Josephus (*Ant.* 3.237-49) summarized daily, Sabbath, and New Moon sacrifices and the major annual festivals.

Omissions

The range of omissions in Josephus' rewriting of Numbers is large compared to other rewritings, and it necessitates a broader discussion. At first glance, Josephus seems to omit the Nazirite law (Num. 6); the second Passover (Num. 9); the law on tassels/tzitzit (Num. 15); the story of the man gathering sticks on the Sabbath day (Num. 15.32-36); the vows in Numbers 30; and many parts of Numbers 31. Yet as we shall see, the picture is more complex.

---

5. See Begg 2007; Miller 2019.

Josephus omits the law in Num. 5.5-10, which states that one who feels remorse for making a false oath defrauding another may rectify it by confession of sin. Perhaps Josephus omitted it since he considered it a repetition of Lev. 5.20-26, a law already rewritten in *Ant.* 3.232.

Josephus omits the priestly blessing (Num. 6.22-27), as does Philo. This omission is striking due to Josephus' priestly lineage.[6] The omission may be related to Josephus' view that God may bless the people himself, without the mediation of the priests, an idea found in *Num. Rab.* 11.2.

Numbers 9.1-14 relates the law of second Passover. According to this law, people who were unable to perform the first Passover on the fourteenth of Nisan due to their impurity were given the opportunity to perform it on the fourteenth of Iyyar. Philo mentions this law in *Mos.* 2.224-33, and so do some of the Qumran scrolls (4Q320; 4Q321).[7] The rabbinic sages deal with this topic in the Mishna, Tosefta, the halakhic midrashim and in the Talmud.[8]

Josephus rewrites only Num. 9.1-5, verses dealing with the first Passover. He writes: 'Then, for the first time after the departure from Egypt, he offered the sacrifice called the Pascha in the wilderness' (*Ant.* 3.294). Though in *War* 6.425-26 he notes that only pure Israelites can celebrate Passover, he does not explicitly mention the law of the second Passover.[9] Josephus does not mention it even in his retelling of the second Passover performed by Hezekiah (2 Chron. 30; *Ant.* 10.264-67). In fact, he treats Hezekiah's second Passover as a first Passover.[10]

Josephus is not alone in omitting second Passover. This oversight is also found in the book of *Jubilees*[11] and in the Temple Scroll.[12]

Colautti[13] explains this omission as follows: 'Instead, if it was not obligatory to arrive at that city, it would not have been necessary to allow this second chance. This would explain the systematic absence of the second Passover in FJ's works.'

---

6. See Feldman 1998a: 61–2.
7. Dimant and Parry 2015: 390–6.
8. See Tabory 1995: 95–9.
9. Strangely, J. B. Segal (1963) does not mention the omission of Second Passsover in Josephus.
10. According to Feldman (1998b: 366), Josephus omitted it in order not to criticize the priests, which according to 2 Chron. 30.3 'had not sanctified themselves'. The Josiah Passover is rewritten in *Ant.* 10.70-72.
11. See Saulnier 2009; VanderKam 2012.
12. Saulnier 2012: 122.
13. Colautti 2002: 232.

It is also possible that Josephus omitted this law since in Numbers 9 Moses didn't know the halakha, an embarrassing detail for a lawgiver. In the incident of Zelophehad's daughters (Num. 27 and 36),[14] Josephus simply portrays Moses as giving the daughters a direct answer, rather than portraying Moses asking God as in the MT. In contrast, Philo's Moses follows the biblical text in having Moses refer the case to God (*Mos.* 2.43, 237).

Finally, one wonders whether the reason for the omission is related to the fact that this festival is celebrated twice, a detail hard to explain for certain readers.

The law of tzitzit is mentioned in Num. 15.38-39 and Deut. 22.12. The Greek parallel is κράσπεδα. It is mentioned also in Mk 6.20 and Mt. 9.20; 23.5, and in Pseudo-Philo (*LAB* 16.1). That this law was practiced in early times can be proved by documents from the time of Bar-Kochva and in *Aristeas* 158: God 'has given us a symbolic reminder on our clothes'.[15] While it hardly appears in the Mishnah (*m. Mo'ed Qat.* 3.4; *'Ed.* 4.10; *Menah.* 3.7), it does appear at length in other rabbinic sources (*t. Ber.* 6.10; *Sifre* Num. 115; *b. Menah.* 40b, etc.).

However, there are Second Temple sources where tzitzit is not mentioned. Josephus does not mention tzitzit in his rewriting of Numbers or Deuteronomy. Archeologists have not found evidence of tzitzit at Qumran. In their 2011 book, Werman and Shemesh end their discussion on the matter with an open question: 'Is the reason for the lack of reference for the tzitzit in the Sectarian halakha that the observance of the law was regular and obvious or perhaps vice versa: the Qumran sect did not practice the law of the Tzitzit?'.[16] In contrast, Jodi Magness writes that 'Since 4QMMT indicates that the sectarians did not mix any materials in their clothing, I believe it is likely that they fulfilled this commandment by wearing all-linen tzitzit'.[17]

Shaye Cohen argues that in contradiction to the rabbinic Sages, the Judeo-Hellenistic world did not consider tzitzit a distinctive marker of the Jews.[18] Aaron Oppenheimer[19] writes that the law of the tzitzit was not widespread even in the generations after the destruction of the Second

---

14. Feldman 1998a: 393.
15. καὶ μὴν καὶ ἐκ τῶν περιβολαίων παράσημον ἡμῖν μνείας δέδωκεν. See Wright 2015: 293–4.
16. Werman and Shemesh 2011: 423.
17. Magness 2011: 116.
18. Cohen 1999: 33. See also Vogelzang and van Bekkum 1986: 276.
19. Oppenheimer 1977: 225.

Temple. These explanations can account for Josephus' omission of the law of the tzitzit. It is not a case of sloppiness. The omission may be intentional: it simply seemed to Josephus a relatively insignificant law.

Josephus also omits the wood-gatherer tale (Num. 15.32-36). The reason for the omission may be that no new laws follow this incident,[20] thus rendering it unimportant.

Josephus omits stories where law and narrative are mixed (i.e. Num. 15.32-36, where a man is stoned for working on the Sabbath). He also omits the case of the blasphemer in Leviticus 24 for the same reason.[21] These are narratives where Moses did not know the halakha and their non-inclusion is to be expected.

Another omission pertains to vows. References to prohibitive vows appear in the Damascus Document, Philo, and the New Testament. Josephus omits the laws of vows in Numbers 30, which deals with cases in which one can or cannot annul the vows of a woman, and in his rewriting of the kidnapping of the women of Shilo in Judges 21 (*Ant.* 5.169). In contrast, in his rewriting of other biblical narratives, he does mention the vow of Jacob (Gen. 28.20-21); Israel's vow (Num. 21.2); Jephthah's vow (Judg. 11); Hannah's vow (1 Sam. 1.11); and Absalom's vow (εὔχομαι, *Ant.* 7.196; 2 Sam. 15.8). The vow of Israel in Numbers 21 is omitted, but one should note that the whole story was in fact omitted. Josephus mentions also the vows of Jon. 1.16 (*Ant.* 9.209).

In a way, Josephus' decision to omit the law in Numbers is in accordance with the rabbis' view of one minimizing the amount of vows taken (*m. Nedar.* 2.1). Indeed, this notion appears already in the Bible itself (Deut. 2.22-24; Prov. 20.25; Eccl. 5.3-5).[22]

The Census and Encamping of the Tribes
(Num. 1–2 // Ant. *3.287-94)*

The laws in Numbers 1 begin with the commandment to take a census.[23] Josephus shapes the description as if it were Moses' initiative: 'he [Moses] finally turned to the examination of the army... He ordered the

---

20. See Novick 2008.
21. On this story see Feldman 2007. Philo preserved Num. 15 in *Spec. Laws* 2.249-51 and *Mos.* 2.209-20. See also *Jub.* 2.17-33.
22. Jonquière 2007: 79.
23. Surprisingly, this was not noticed by Schalit, Altshuler, and Gallant. However, the enumerating of biblical laws cannot follow the late rabbinic enumeration (Herman 2016). It is specifically stated that God ordered that the census be taken (Num. 1.1-4).

tribal leaders, except for the tribe of Levi, to learn precisely the number of those who were able to take part in war' (§287). Josephus discerns that the aim of this census is military, a detail not stated explicitly in the MT.[24]

Josephus gives an abbreviated form of Numbers 1, providing the total sum of those counted and specifying that Levi was not counted, based on vv. 47-49. In §288 he explains that since Levi was excluded, the tribe of Joseph was split into Ephraim and Manasseh to contribute to the total number of soldiers.[25]

Numbers 2 describes the order of the twelve tribes in the camp and on the march. It is not clear from the biblical text how the tribes should be ordered in relation to the tabernacle and Josephus doesn't solve this problem. What he does is explain (§289): 'Erecting the Tent in the middle they screened it off, with three tribes pitching their tents on each side'. This is a correct understanding of the plan of encampment, albeit not a detailed one.[26] He ignores the numbers and names of the tribes. Though not stated explicitly, he infers correctly that the priests and the Levites encamped around the tent (§290).[27]

As for the number of Levites, Josephus differs from both the MT and LXX (22,000 in MT vs. 22,800 in Josephus). In *Ant.* 3.291 Josephus incorporates the law with regard to the trumpet (βυκάνης; LXX: σάλπιγγας; Num. 10.2).

Perhaps Josephus was thinking of the trumpets of his own day; however, the trumpets engraved on the Arch of Titus appear somewhat longer than the ones he describes.[28]

The Commissioning and Purification of the Levites
(Num. 3.5-10; 8.5-26 // Ant. 3.258)

The commissioning and purification of the Levites are mentioned in Num. 3.5-10 and 8.5-26. Josephus rewrites these laws in *Ant.* 3.258, right after his rewriting of Leviticus 6, where the discussion of purity laws begins. There are close links between Numbers 3 and 8 (compare Num. 8.16-19 to Num. 3.11-13, 40-51).

---

24. Indeed, Jewish medieval commentators have raised various options. Among them, Rashbam's is closest to Josephus.
25. Cf. B. A. Levine 1993: 125: 'The two sons of Joseph, Ephraim and Manasseh, take up the slack resulting from the exclusion of the tribe of Levi'.
26. See B. A. Levine 1993: 143 for a detailed description.
27. See the illustration in B. A. Levine 1993: 143.
28. The trumpets of the Temple are probably depicted on Bar-Kochba coins. See Meshorer 1982: 2:132–50.

Numbers 8.5-26 describe the process that the Levites must undergo before assuming their position: they must be sprinkled with the water of expiation; their whole bodies must be shaved; their clothes must be washed; sacrifices must be offered; Israel must lay their hands upon them; and Aaron must wave them before the Lord. This law raises many different questions, such as: Why must the Levites wash their clothes? Why must they be sprinkled with the water of expiation? Why must they shave their hair off, and not the priests?

These questions arise because it is not clear what the Levites needed to purify themselves from. Purification rituals were usually associated with impurities from seminal emission, menstruation, childbirth, discharge, leprosy, unclean creatures, or, most severe of all, contact with the dead.[29] Moreover, the 'waters of expiation' and 'sin offering' do not necessarily seem to be related to 'sin' in this context.[30] Another question concerns the Levites' requirement to shave off all their hair. Here, too, it is problematic to compare this ritual to shaving one's hair as a result of impurity (as in the Nazirite laws of Num. 6.9).[31]

The Levites are mentioned 93 times in Josephus' *Antiquities*.[32] He mentions Levi's birth story (Gen. 29.34) and his conduct during the affair of Dinah (Gen. 34). He is aware that the Levites are secondary to the Priests (*Ant.* 3.290). He notes that they are exempt from war, and entitled to gifts from the people (*Ant.* 4.67-69). He also mentions the cities of the Levites, the laws that command the people to support them, and their role as bearers of the Ark. He cites the stories of the Levites in the books of the Prophets and Chronicles nearly verbatim (according to the Masoretic version of the texts). Among the stories he omits are those that cast the figure of the Levite in a negative light (the story of the golden calf in Exod. 32 and the story of Micah's idol in Judg. 19). However, he does rewrite some stories in which a Levite plays a problematic role, such as that of Korah and his followers (Num. 16–17) and that of the concubine

---

29. Regev 1996b; Lawrence 2006.

30. Milgrom 1974. Rashi *ad loc.*, and Milgrom 1990 are convinced that this purification is similar to that which is described in Num. 19, that is, impurity caused through contact with a dead body. See also B. A. Levine 1993: 274–5. Licht (1985–95: 1:120) perceived the sprinkling of the water of expiation as part of the rites of passage through which the Levites entered their new status. In contrast to the Hebrew Bible, at Qumran, a connection is drawn between impurity and sin. See Birenboim 2003. In Baumgarten's opinion, the Essenes' concept of purity was influenced by the text in Num. 8. See Baumgarten 2006.

31. See Olyan 1998.

32. See Begg 2004.

at Gibeah (Judg. 19). He also mentions how the Levites are divided into 24 shifts (*Ant.* 7.367) and discusses their role as singers (*Ant.* 8.176; 20.216-18).

Josephus rewrites this law as follows:

> Having separated the tribe of Levi from their association with the ordinary people, Moyses purified them to become holy with ever-flowing spring-waters and with sacrifices which, as prescribed, they offer to God on such occasions. He entrusted to them the Tent and the sacred vessels and the other things such as had been made for the covering of the Tent, in order that they might serve under the direction of the priests. For they had already been consecrated to God. (*Ant.* 3.258)

A comparison between the law of purification of the Levites as it appears in Josephus and its source in the Hebrew Bible yields several differences.

In contrast with the MT, where the law features among a number of issues concerning the Levites in Numbers 8, Josephus places the law within his reworking of Numbers 3.[33] In order to understand the changes Josephus made, let us first present the general structure of Numbers 1–8. These chapters alternate between narrative and legal text: 1.1–4.49 is narrative; 5.1–6.27 is legal text; 7.1–8.26 is narrative. In addition, while the Levites are dealt with in Num. 3.5–4.49; 8.5-26, the priests are mentioned in Num. 5.1–8.4; 9.1–10.10.[34]

Josephus' placement of the law of the Levites in his rewriting of Numbers 3 rather than 8 is part of his authorial strategy, which seems to be based on an attempt to arrange the laws by category rather than the order in which they appear in the Hebrew Bible (see his words in *Ant.* 4.197). In a sense, there is certain repetition in the description of Num. 8.5-26 and the description in 3.5-13. In order to prevent such duplication, Josephus placed the different references to the appointment of the Levites in his rewriting of Numbers 3.

While the Hebrew Bible devotes 22 verses to the purification process, Josephus summarizes it in three sentences. He omits the divine command to Moses to purify the Levites, presenting only its execution.[35] He omits the commandments to shave their bodies and wash their clothes. He does

---

33. In Gallant's opinion (1988: 113–14), *Ant.* 3.258 links the laws of sacrifice (224-57) and the laws of ritual purity (259-73). Josephus also does not mention the redemption of the first-born among the Levites.

34. See Douglas 1993: 118; Lee 2008.

35. The opposite (i.e., his expansion of a brief passage) also occurs in Josephus' writings. See, for example, his rewriting of 1 Sam. 9.3-4 in *Ant.* 6.46.

not clarify the meaning of the waving described in v. 13, nor the reason for the Levites' selection in place of the firstborn.

Josephus mentions that the Levites are holy (ἱερός), unlike their biblical description, which does not present them as holy.[36] A comparison between the Levites and the priests is also evident in §205: 'With the blood of the sacrificed animals he sprinkled the vestment of Aaron and him himself together with his children, purifying them with spring-water and with sap of the myrrh, in order that they might become God's'.[37] Josephus adds that the Levites purified themselves in water from a perennial spring.[38]

Do these changes result from the fact that Josephus had a different *Vorlage* at his disposal? While in general this could explain some of Josephus' deviations from the MT, in this particular case this explanation is not feasible, as neither the LXX[39] nor other ancient translations differ significantly from the MT, and it is therefore impossible to assume that Josephus relied on the LXX translation of the passage when he rewrote the law of Levite purification for his readers.

What is the meaning of the commandment to 'sprinkle them with the water of expiation', and why should the Levites be sprinkled with water? The Sages connect this commandment with the Levites' state of impurity of the dead after they slaughtered those who had sinned during the episode of the golden calf: '"Sprinkle them with the water of expiation"…they were all impure with impurity of the dead, for they had killed those who served the calf' (*Bam. R.* 12.15). In contrast, Josephus understood that the purpose of this purification was to enable them to serve in the Sanctuary. According to his view, this purification is not related to sin or impurity.[40]

---

36. Concerning this point, see Feldman 2000: 319 n. 869. Regarding the non-sacred stance of the Levites in the Bible, see Milgrom 1991: 519.

37. The Greek verb here is γίγνομαι, which is concerned with belonging to God. The sanctity of the Levites is also mentioned in *Ant.* 3.287.

38. We find no testimony of the use of *mikvaot* (ritual baths) in Josephus' writings. See Nakman 2004: 246–7. It should be noted that it is also rare to find mention of *mikvaot* in the Qumran Scrolls, despite the fact that archaeological excavations uncovered several such baths in the area. See Broshi 2009; Lawrence 2006: 157 n. 5. Shaye Cohen (2007: 132) notes that in all literature written since during the days of the Second Temple, including the New Testament, there is, in fact, no mention of the word *mikveh*.

39. Josephus' words do not reveal any connection to the Peshitta or the Vulgate. 4Q23 (or 4QLev-Num[a]) contains excerpts from Num. 5.7-12. However, it is fairly similar to the Masoretic version. See Ulrich 2010: 142.

40. The same is argued by Ashley 1993: 169.

In the law of the Levites' purification in the Masoretic text, there is no mention of a spring. Where did Josephus take this idea from? While the Tabernacle basin may be one possibility (see Exod. 30.17-21), Jacob Milgrom is convinced that this is not the case:

> The water could not have been taken from the basin in the Tabernacle, for the basin is a vessel reserved for the exclusive use of the priests (Exod. 30.17-21) and its waters are referred to as 'holy water' (5.17) – a fitting name, given that only those who are holy (that is, the priests) are permitted to use them.[41]

It is evident that Josephus had the words of Lev. 11.36 in mind – 'A spring, however, or a cistern for collecting water remains pure, but anyone who touches one of these carcasses becomes impure' – as well as the law of the red heifer (Num. 19), where Josephus also explains the water in question as spring water (*Ant.* 4.81). In both places, Josephus' words are paralleled in rabbinic literature: in *m. Mikv.* 1.7-8, the words מים חיים – 'living waters' – are interpreted as spring water; the same is true in the Midrash *Sifre* Bamidbar 128 regarding the law of the red heifer. Modern scholars and exegetes also follow this interpretation.[42] Josephus' explanation of 'water of expiation' as spring-water can therefore be considered a reasonable interpretation of the text.

In the MT of Num. 8.8 and onward, the Levites are required to bring two bulls as part of their inauguration. Josephus does not specify the details of these sacrifices, using general language instead: 'with such sacrifices as were usually offered to God on such occasion' (*Ant.* 3.258). Josephus is similarly vague about sacrifices in other places in his writings (*Ant.* 9.263, regarding Hezekiah's Passover: 'customary sacrifices'; 10.43; 15.147). Likewise, in his rewriting of the description of the incense mixture (Exod. 30.34-38), he adds: 'I omit to describe their nature in detail, lest it become burdensome to my readers' (*Ant.* 3.198). This abridging is inherent to his role as historian, and seems to follow in the footsteps of Herodotus, who also used the expression τὰ νομιζόμενα ποιήσα (*Hist.* 9.107).

---

41. Milgrom 1997: 59.
42. See Milgrom 1991: 923–4. In the second chapter of the *Aramaic Levi Document*, after the third verse, there is a lacuna of four lines. Scholars have reconstructed them by comparing them to the Greek *Testament of Levi* Apocrypha. See Greenfield, Stone and Eshel 2004: 58. There, Levi testifies that he washed at ὕδατι ζῶντι. In Kugler's opinion, the text was influenced by Num. 5.2. See Kugler 2000: 110. Its Aramaic source may have read מיים חיין, 'living water'. See Drawnel 2004: 102.

Different biblical sources describe the Levites as chosen by God (Num. 3.13; 8.17; 1 Chron. 15.2), but no reason is cited for this choice. The book of *Jubilees* (30.17-20) and the *Testament of Levi* explain that Levi was chosen for a reward for his behavior in the affair of Dinah's rape (Gen. 34).[43] Philo (*Spec. Laws* 1.29; 2.170-73) and the Midrash (*Bam. R.* 12.15) explain that the Levites were chosen to serve God in reward for their refusal to participate in the sin of the golden calf (Exod. 32–34). Even if we assume that Josephus knew of this exegetical tradition, he would obviously not be able to use it, as he omitted this episode from his retelling of the book of Exodus.[44] This episode was probably excluded by Josephus in accordance with his tendency to remove references to priestly zeal and violence. He chooses to postpone his mention of God's selection of the Levites until his retelling of the story of Korah and his followers (Num. 16–17; *Ant.* 4.14-66).

Why does Josephus leave out the shaving and clothes-washing mentioned in Num. 8.7: 'Pass a razor over all their flesh, and wash their clothes'? Some have attributed this omission to Josephus' wish to abridge the biblical sources,[45] but this explanation does not seem likely.

It should be noted that a parallel can be drawn between the law of purification of the Levites and the law of purification of lepers, which appears in Lev. 14.9.[46] Similarly, soon after his mention of the Levites' purification, Josephus retells the laws concerning lepers, which appear in Leviticus 13–14 (*Ant.* 3.261-64), and then immediately refutes the claim that the nation of Israel was expelled from Egypt because they suffered from leprosy (*Ant.* 3.265-68).

It seems, therefore, that this detail is omitted for apologetic reasons. Since the issue of leprosy lay at the heart of the anti-Jewish polemics in Greek and Roman writings at that time, Josephus deliberately omits the instruction for Levites to shave their bodies in order to preclude associations between the Levites and lepers.[47] Similarly, he also leaves

---

43. See Kugel 1993.

44. Concerning this passage being omitted from Josephus' writings for apologetic reasons, see Feldman 1998a: 61–2. The omission may have stemmed from his desire to protect Aaron's honor, and/or to prevent Greek and Roman authors from using this passage to claim that the Jews are also pagan.

45. Nakman 2004: 248.

46. This parallel is also drawn by the Midrash (*Mid. Agg.* on Num. 8.9) and Rashi; Licht 1985–95: 1:120; Milgrom 1991: 45. The spring is also mentioned in *Ag. Ap.* 1.282 in relation to lepers. There, it also states that the leper must shave his head.

47. For the possibility that Josephus alters biblical law and early Jewish law for apologetic reasons, see Olitzki 1885; Goldenberg 1978.

out the miracle of Moses' leprosy-smitten hand (Exod. 4.6), as well as the description of Miriam being punished with leprosy (Num. 12.10). These omissions are most likely related to the anti-Jewish polemics that sought to present the Children of Israel as a nation of lepers who were not saved from Egypt by God, but rather banished in disgust and disgrace.

Law of the Sotah (Num. 5.11-30 // Ant. 3.270-73)

Numbers 5.11-30 presents the law of the *sotah*, namely the married woman who has 'gone astray and broken faith' (5.12) and is suspected of adultery. The text explains that the crime was both consensual and clandestine, although not necessarily premeditated: 'in that a man has had carnal relations with her unbeknown to her husband, and she keeps secret the fact that she has defiled herself, without being forced, and there is no witness against her' (5.13). Undetected by her husband, she has freely engaged in sexual relations with another man. Overcome with jealousy, her husband takes her (together with the appropriate offerings) to a priest to determine her guilt. Through a ceremony involving holy water, dust of the tabernacle, and a grain offering, the priest utters a curse on which the woman takes an oath. The curse is then written on parchment, and mixed with bitter waters, for the woman to ingest. If guilty, the curse enters her body, causing intense pain: 'Her womb shall discharge, her uterus drop, and the woman shall become an execration among her people' (5.27). If innocent, the wife (and her unborn child) survive unharmed.

This striking account raises many awkward questions: What purpose does each element of this ritual serve? On what basis is the husband's jealously elicited, or justified? It is also not clear whether the guilty wife (unlike her unborn child) survives the punishment, nor is the relationship between this law and the laws that precede or follow it obvious.[48]

According to Num. 5.13, the ritual is only necessary when there are no actual witnesses who testify that the wife freely consented to sexual relations with another man. Philo (*Spec. Laws* 3.53-55) does not discuss the provision of witness testimony but adds that there is a preliminary hearing before the judges, where the husband makes his accusation, and where the wife is able to defend herself.[49] Numbers 5 is not attested in the Qumran scrolls (namely 4QLev-Num; 4Q23 and 4Q27),[50] although the

48. This is aside from the highly obscure elements: המים המרים למאררים, translated as 'spell-inducing water[s]', in the NJPS 5.27, 31.
49. Halbertal 1997: 112; Rosen-Zvi 2012: 23 n. 7. On Philo's reading of the *sotah* ritual, see Towers 2014.
50. Ulrich 2010.

Damascus Document (4Q270 col. 4 line 3) does contain a requirement for a wife's testimony in which she is able to declare her innocence by claiming that she was forcibly raped (אנוסה הייתי).[51] This recalls the provision for a wife's testimony in rabbinic law.[52]

In his adaptation, Josephus refers neither to witness testimony nor to the process of a preliminary trial. Two possible reasons may be suggested for this: first, that since the biblical scribes did not focus on either the witness' or the wife's testimony, Josephus follows their lead and omits these likewise.[53] Also, by viewing the matter as a ritual procedure, rather than a judicial one, Josephus may be deliberately keeping closer to the plain meaning of the Hebrew text.[54] Secondly, the presence of a single witness in these proceedings would contradict the law in Deut. 19.15, which prohibits any conviction based on the testimony of one person – a law that Josephus is clearly familiar with in *Ant.* 4.219. The omission of witness testimony here thus prevents any potential contradiction between the laws in Numbers and Deuteronomy, and this inner-biblical consistency may have been significant to Josephus.

The biblical account also includes the requirement for the priest to uncover the woman's hair (Num. 5.18), which many scholars interpret as 'loosening', i.e. effectively untying, or spreading out her hair, for all to see. Josephus, however, proposes that this indicates the removal of the woman's ἱμάτιον (veil) from her head.[55] He appears to read the verse in light of the Greek custom that women, and even men, covered their heads with a veil as a symbol of modesty, or else was familiar with the widespread ancient Near Eastern requirement for married women to cover their hair. Either way, the removal of the *sotah*'s veil would effectively reinforce the woman's wayward status, if not her immediate disgrace. Here Josephus, like the Septuagint,[56] Philo, and the rabbinic Sages, interpreted the verb פרע as a reference to unveiling the head rather than spreading out the hair. In this way, they were able to extend this convention to address a different halachic context, thereby claiming that covering the head of a married woman was a divinely mandated law rather than a social custom.

---

51. Wassen 2005: 64–5; Grushcow 2006: 279–81. See also Qimron 2010: 1:35 and Petersen 2009.

52. *M. Sotah* 1.1-2; *Sifre* Num. 7.12. See Halbertal 1997: 97–8.

53. B. A. Levine 1993: 193.

54. Cf. Friedman 2012.

55. Milgrom 1990: 40. NJPS translated 'to bare'; NIV: 'loosen'; NRSV: 'dishevel'.

56. For פרע in Symmachus, as well as in other ancient versions, see Salvesen 1991: 110.

Numbers 5.23 continues with the instruction that 'then the priest shall put these curses in writing and wash them off into the water of bitterness'. Josephus does not mention these curses; he only observes that the name of God must be written on parchment.[57] In view of this omission, Lisa Grushcow maintains that Josephus 'is drawing on the post-biblical emphasis on the name being the key factor',[58] a suggestion more fully developed by Sean McDonough:

> We see here that the name of God is closely associated with oaths and curses, just as it was in much of the Jewish literature already surveyed. The terrifying consequences of swearing a false oath by the name are vividly seen in the physical distress of the convicted adulteress. One can easily see how traditions such as these would have led a Jew to think twice about invoking the name of God in this way, and indeed to abstain from such swearing altogether.[59]

Josephus may have taken his cue from the MT's מים קדשים, 'sacral water[s]' (v. 17), the presence of which is unexplained,[60] and would enable Josephus to suggest that the water attained its inherent sanctity by having come into direct contact with the name of God.[61] In addition, it seems that Josephus exacerbates the *sotah*'s betrayal of God in order to reinforce the severity of her sin: 'But if she has deceived her husband in her marriage and God in her oaths' (*Ant.* 3.273).

The biblical text further specifies a spirit of jealousy that overcomes the husband – an element which Josephus entirely ignores in his rewriting.[62] In this context Lisa Grushcow claims that Josephus, like Philo,[63] refrains from using the expression 'jealousy' (ζήλωσις, the preferred term of the

---

57. See Feldman 2000: 312 n. 811. Here Josephus is not consistent with the rabbinic Sages, who hold that the written verses of the *sotah* law should be inscribed on parchment (*Sifre Sotah* 17b; *m. Sot.* 2.4).

58. Grushcow 2006: 128.

59. McDonough 1999: 85.

60. For various explanations, see the Aramaic Targums. Onkelos מֵי כִיוֹר (was basin water); Pseudo-Jonathan מיין קדישין; Neofiti: מיין דכין ('pure water'). Cf. Milgrom 1990: 29. The LXX omitted any reference to the holiness of the water (ὕδωρ καθαρὸν ζῶν). See Wevers 1998: 86.

61. Brichto (1975: 64–5) also does not view this law as an ordeal, but as a divine sign.

62. Where his 'fit of jealousy' (i.e. רוח־קנאה in 5.14) was could potentially be absolved by the 'meal offering of jealousy' (מנחת קנאת in 5.15).

63. *Spec. Laws* 3.55.

LXX) because of its potential contemporaneous political connotations: Josephus considers the Zealots a group of violent anti-Roman political revolutionaries. He alternatively uses the word ζηλοτυπία ('jealousy') in §271,[64] which suggests that exegetical, rather than political considerations, were his main concern.[65] This is aside from the obvious question: How does the husband suspect that his wife has betrayed him, since there are no available witnesses to corroborate her crime?[66] Helena Zlotnick suggests that this was based on 'a supernatural resource that inspired the husband with suspicion',[67] whereas Josephus, wishing to avoid the supernatural when possible, provides a more rational basis for the husband's suspicion:[68] 'If someone suspects that his wife has committed adultery' (§270).

According to Num. 5.21, if the woman is guilty, she will be cursed with 'a sagging thigh'.[69] According to Josephus, her punishment is dropsy, i.e. the swelling of soft tissues due to the accumulation of excess water. Elsewhere, Josephus claims that this physical condition was also manifest in Herod's punishment:

> From this time onwards Herod's malady began to spread to his whole body and his sufferings took illness in a variety of forms. He had fever, though not a raging fever, an intolerable itching of the whole skin, continuous pains in the intestines, tumours in the feet as in dropsy (ὑδρωπιάω), inflammation of the abdomen and gangrene of the privy parts, engendering worms, in addition to asthma, with great difficulty in breathing, and convulsions in all his limbs. (*War* 1.656)[70]

Here Herod appears to be consumed by a slow and painful death, which also caused reproductive sterility. Josephus (*Ant.* 3.271), and similarly Philo (*Spec. Laws* 3.54), understood the *sotah* to likewise be punished by a gruesome death, where the emphasis was laid heavily on the transgression of ancestral laws. Although Josephus is clearly aware of the

---

64. Grushcow 2006: 39–40.
65. Ortlund 2012: 108–10, with earlier literature.
66. Cf. Rosen-Zvi 2012: 23 n. 7.
67. Zlotnick 2002: 113.
68. For use of 'suspicion', see also Milgrom 1990: 38; Ashley 1993: 126; Briggs 2009: 312.
69. The rabbis interpreted this 'thigh' as a euphemism for her sexual organs. See Milgrom 1993: 42.
70. Thackeray 1927: 311. See further Kottek 1993: 61; Allen 1997.

rabbinic principle of 'measure for measure', as evident from his rewriting of several biblical sources,[71] it is clearly less relevant to the death of the *sotah* and the loss of her unborn child in his context.

Numbers 5.22 states that 'the woman shall say, "Amen Amen"', which the LXX translates as γένοιτο γένοιτο, 'so be it'.[72] Although the expression is found in the Qumran scrolls, in apocryphal literature (Tob. 8.8; *3 Macc.* 7.23; *4 Macc.* 18.24), and frequently in the New Testament, Josephus omits the word 'Amen', as he does in numerous instances elsewhere.[73] This was particularly noteworthy in his account of 1 Kgs 1.36, where he substituted the word 'Amen' with a statement that Benaiah prayed for Solomon's success (*Ant.* 7.357); this could reflect an awareness of the earlier traditions associated with the rabbinic prohibition of answering 'Amen' in the Temple.[74]

Is the brevity of Josephus' adaptation of the law of the *sotah* due to his discomfort with its magical nature ('waters of bitterness that induce the spell', 5.19), as Lisa Grushcow argues?[75] There may be other reasons for this reticence, including his lack of knowledge of individual elements, but his brevity could additionally reflect an attempt at moderating the harsh and humiliating nature of this ritual for his Roman audience.

The ceremonial elements of the *sotah* ritual emphasize the belief that the woman's guilt or innocence is determined by God and not by human authority (vv. 16, 18, 21, 25, 30). Even though Josephus does not explicitly clarify this connection, it is circumstantially recalled in his account: 'and they throw one handful of it for God', 'inscribes the name of God upon a skin', and 'if she has deceived her husband in her marriage and God in her oaths', and so on.[76] This highlights a further ambiguity in Josephus' writings where authority for the law is not always attributed to God.

---

71. See Avioz 2009, *contra* Grushcow 2006: 163–4.

72. Instances where the LXX transliterates αμην are found in 1 Chron. 16.36, and Neh. 5.13. In addition, Salvesen (1991: 120) notes that Symmachus 'consistently transliterates this Hebrew word wherever his rendering is preserved'.

73. E.g. Deut. 27.15-26; 1 Kgs 1.36; Isa. 65.16; Jer. 11.5; 28.6; Pss. 41.14; 72.19; 89.53; Neh. 5.13; 8.6; 1 Chron. 16.36.

74. See Lachs 1988 and also Schiffman 1983: 133–54.

75. Grushcow 2006: 84. In particular, Milgrom (1990: 347–8) rejects any connection of this text with magic. Cf. Ashley 1993: 124; Gane 2016. Surely the point here is that Josephus was not averse to providing his readers with accounts of ancient Hebrew magic when it suited him. See especially Duling 1985. See also Jewell 2009.

76. Entreaties for the blessing of children in Josephus' writings are noted in Jonquière 2007: 130–1.

As *Ant.* 3.273 asserts: 'Moyses ordered these provisions for his fellow countrymen with regard to the sacrifices and the purification relating to them, and he drew up the preceding laws for them', *contra* their divine attribution in Num. 5.11.

What if the wife is innocent? Numbers 5.28 states: 'But if the woman has not defiled herself and is clean, then she shall be immune and be able to conceive children', found in similar terms in the LXX.[77] Both Philo (*Spec. Laws* 3.63) and Josephus here regard the woman's pregnancy as compensation for the false charges made against her, and Josephus further claims (*Ant.* 3.273) that the woman will then bear a *male* child: καὶ ἐκσπερματιεῖ σπέρμα. Such preferences (in the promise that παιδίον ἄρρεν, 'she will have a male child') are a hallmark of the inherent misogyny of ancient Greco-Roman society.[78] Likewise, subsequent rabbinic traditions assert 'that the bearer of female children will now bear male children' (*Sifre* 19.23).[79]

Josephus adds that if the suspected woman is found innocent, she will bear a child in the tenth month (*Ant.* 3.271), but it is not clear on what basis his calculation was made. Was this no more than a pragmatic observation, which allowed a safety buffer of up to one month, in addition to the usual nine months of pregnancy?[80] If so, could it then reinforce the former *sotah*'s innocence and sexual fidelity? Or was it simply a reflection of the fact that the birth of a child 'in the tenth month' is a well-established motif? Indeed, it is found not only in Greco-Roman traditions,[81] but is also prevalent in earlier Old Babylonian tradition such as in Atra-hasis[82] as well as in Hittite sources.[83] This determination is also apparent in the Aramaic Levi Document from Qumran, which claims 'and he was born

---

77. Literally: 'shall seed seed', meaning produce offspring. See Pietersma and Wright 2007: 115.

78. See *T. Jos.* 3.7: 'In the night she would come in to me, pretending a mere visit. Because she had no male child, she pretended to consider me as a son' (Kee 1983–85: 1:820). See also Sir. 22.3; Philo, *Spec. Laws* 1.200. See Archer 1990: 19, and similarly the rabbinic view that: 'If she formerly bore children in pain she will now bear with ease; if formerly girls she will now give birth to boys' (*b. Soṭ.* 26a).

79. Rosen-Zvi 2012: 124 n. 84. See also Peshitta, Neofiti, and Pseudo-Jonathan.

80. As in 2 Macc. 7.27, where a ninth-month period of gestation in the womb appears, and which corresponds to estimates in rabbinic literature (*y. Nid.* 1.3, 49b).

81. See the sources in Solevag 2013: 73. This idea has its roots in the ancient Near East, as Stol (2000: 23–5) shows.

82. See Stol 2009.

83. As in the myth of Appu: 'After Appu follows the Sun God's instructions, his wife conceives and ten months later gives birth to a son'. See also Ashmon 2012: 143.

in the tenth month at sunset',[84] as well as in the *Wisdom of Solomon:* 'and in my mother's womb I was sculptured into flesh during a ten-month's space' (Wis. 7.2). It could thus reflect a popular literary convention.

The Nazirite Law (Num. 6.1-21 // Ant. *4.72)*

Philo mentions the Nazirite law (Num. 6.1-21) in his *Spec. Laws* 1.247-54. This law is mentioned also in Acts 21.15-27 and in rabbinic literature.[85] Nakman argues that Josephus disregarded the Nazirite law.[86] However, a more nuanced description would be that Josephus mentioned this law but with some details missing. Josephus writes:

> Those who make a vow and consecrate themselves—these are called Nazirites ναζιραῖοι—letting their hair grow long and not drinking wine, these, whenever they dedicate their hair and offer it in sacrifice, allot the shorn hair to the priests. (*Ant.* 4.72)

Josephus does not rewrite this law in his retelling of Numbers 6, but rather of Num. 15.20-21, probably because of the vow language mentioned in vv. 3 and 8. Josephus' retelling is in accordance with the biblical law in Numbers 6, namely that the Nazirites' hair should be brought to the priests (see also v. 18).

The prohibition on drinking wine is also mentioned in *War* 2.313 with regard to Bernice. Josephus refers to this prohibition in his retelling of the Samson narrative as well: 'He likewise urged her [= Samson's mother] not to cut his hair. He was to abstain from all other drink, since God had ordered this, and be familiar only with water' (*Ant.* 5.278).

Josephus avoids referring to Samson as a Nazirite and calls him a prophet. Ulrich concluded that Josephus did not consider Samson a Nazirite:

> Josephus (*Ant.* 5.347) narrates this feature exactly where 4QSam^a does. For 'Nazir' Josephus substitutes the word 'prophet', since the term would be unfamiliar to his Greek audience; understandably, he never uses the singular form of that term for an individual. The strongest proof here is that he also designates Samson, the most dramatic single example of a Nazirite (cf. Judg. 13.5), not a Nazirite but a prophet. (*Ant.* 5.285)[87]

---

84. Drawnel 2004: 145.
85. See Chepey 2005: 72–137.
86. Nakman 2004: 79.
87. Ulrich 2002: 96.

Contrary to Ulrich, Josephus' retelling of the Samson narrative reveals that Josephus did consider him a Nazirite, despite the fact that Josephus did not use this term explicitly. Samson disregarded the prohibition to drink wine (*Ant.* 5.278). In this, Josephus emphasizes the Nazirite laws with regard to Samson even more than in the MT version, since after all, in the Bible, only Samson's mother was prevented from drinking wine.

Josephus refers to this law in *Ant.* 5.347 in his rewriting of Samuel's birth: 'He [= Eli] let his hair grow freely and water was his drink'. Thus, it can be concluded that Josephus knows most of the details of the Nazirite law; however, he chooses to discuss them throughout his rewriting of the biblical narratives of the Former Prophets.

Feldman[88] notes that Josephus does not say that the standard length of time for a Nazir is 30 days (*m. Nazir* 1.3; *Sifre* Num. 25; *Sifre* Deut. 357). However, Josephus does mention this period in *War* 2.313 with regard to Bernice:

> For it is a custom for those who are being worn out by disease or by some other stresses to make a vow: before the [day] on which they were going to offer sacrifices, after thirty days, to abstain from wine and also to shave their hair.

Josephus may thus have been relying on *War* when he omitted this detail in his *Antiquities*.

According to biblical law, the Nazirite should bring three sacrifices: one male lamb a year old without blemish as a burnt offering, one ewe lamb a year old without blemish as a sin offering, and one ram without blemish as an offering of well-being. Together with the ram, the Nazirite brings a basket of unleavened bread cakes of choice flour mixed with oil and unleavened wafers spread with oil, with their grain offering and their drink offerings. None of these are mentioned in Josephus. However, he does mention the sacrifice in *War*: 'to offer sacrifices'.

Josephus omits the prohibition that the Nazirite may not contaminate himself with the dead. Philo (*Spec. Laws* 3.251) does mention it. We may suppose that Josephus omitted this detail so that it would accord with Samuel the Nazirite, who let others kill Agag rather than perform it himself (1 Sam. 15.33; *Ant.* 5.347).

We may propose that the reason for dealing with the details of the Nazirite law only in his retelling of later stories is that in the narratives, the reader is exposed to the implementation of the law in practice, thus showing its vitality and relevance.

---

88. 2000: 352 n. 174.

Grain Offering Accompanying Sacrifices
(Num. 15.4-10 // Ant. 3.234)

According to Num. 15.4-10 each animal sacrifice should be accompanied by semolina flour, oil, and wine. While the biblical law does not mention wine libation, Josephus adds it. A similar tradition is found in *b. Zeb.* 91b, according to which wine can be offered on the altar fire.

According to the biblical law, a grain offering should be brought only with the whole burnt offering, festal, and voluntary offerings. Josephus broadens this law to include all communal and individual sacrifices. The tannaitic halacha (*Sifre* Num. 106-107) exempts the sacrifices not included in these categories (such as *hattat* and *asham*) from libations. Josephus did not see it necessary to detail which sacrifices demand a grain offering since in any case he provides only a short summary.[89]

The Red Heifer (Num. 19 // Ant. 3.262; 4.79-81)

Numbers 19 deals with impurity resulting from contact with or proximity to a human corpse, a grave, or bones from a corpse. This type of impurity was regarded as the most severe of all.[90] The chapter describes the rites connected with the red heifer, namely that it is burned to ash after slaughter and its blood sprinkled by Eleazar the priest.

Josephus rewrites this rite in *Ant.* 4.78-81 and in *Ant.* 3.262. He translates as μόσχος (calf), whereas the LXX translate δάμαλις. According to Josephus, the High Priest deals with the fire while in the MT Eleazar the priest is named. Various sources indicate that while the Second Temple existed, the high priests, rather than laymen, were involved in burning the red heifer. The Mishnah (*Par.* 3.5) discusses the high priests who burnt red cows (see also *Sifre* Num. 123). This is also mentioned by Philo (*Spec. Laws* 1.268).[91]

Numbers 19.11-12 leaves a gap: what happens after the seventh day if one has failed to purify oneself? Is one impure forever, or is there some way out?[92] According to Josephus (*Ant.* 3.262), 'one who is afflicted in a state of defilement beyond the number of these days [= seven] is to sacrifice two lambs, of which it is necessary to offer one as a sacrifice; the priests take the other'. This may reflect actual practice with which Josephus would presumably have been familiar, or exegesis.

---

89. Nakman 2004: 74 n. 5; Regev (1996b) connects the citation from Josephus to a broader dispute between the Sadducees and Pharisees.

90. B. A. Levine 1993: 457.

91. See additional sources in Feldman 2000: 357 n. 212.

92. Schwartz 1990: 89.

Zelophehad's Daughters (Num. 27 and 36 // Ant. 4.174-75)

Numbers 27 and 36 narrate the story of Zelophehad's daughters and their dialogue with Moses concerning inheritance rights for daughters. Zelophehad died without a son, so his daughters brought their case to Moses, arguing that their father's inheritance ought to come to them, despite standing law. Their argument was declared correct by God. Josephus (*Ant.* 4.174-75) rewrites the law on the inheritance rights of daughters as follows:

> The principal men of the tribe of Manassitis approached him [Moyses] and revealed that a certain eminent tribesman, Solophantes by name, had died and had left no male children but only daughters, and they inquired whether the inheritance should be theirs [= the daughters'].
>
> He said that if they [= such women] were going to establish a house with one of their tribesmen, they should depart with the inheritance to them, but if they should marry some men from another tribe, they should leave the inheritance in the father's tribe. At that time he decreed that the inheritance of each one should remain in the tribe.

Josephus condensed this narrative and gave only a snapshot. First, it was not Zelophehad's daughters who came to Moses but rather the principal men of the tribe of Manasseh. It seems that since Josephus faced a clear case of a doublet (this story appears in both Num. 27 and 36), he preferred one of the versions – the one in ch. 36.

Belkin[93] notes that Josephus' remark may be regarded as a literal repetition of the biblical text, applicable only with the implementation of the Jubilee ordinances. For in Josephus' day and in tannaitic times this ordinance did not apply. Contrary to Josephus, the rabbis (*Sifre* Num. 134) held that even if the woman did marry into another tribe, the property belonged only to the son or husband and did not 'remain in the tribe'. However, it may be that Josephus omitted it since the law of Jubilee seems to have nothing to do with inheritance.

Feldman[94] suggests that Josephus omits this scene altogether because it would demean Moses' ability as a judge. However, whereas in Num. 36.1-4 the chiefs of the families of the sons of Joseph come to Moses to complain about his decision – pointing out that when the Jubilee occurs, their inheritance will be added to the tribe into which they have married – here in Josephus there is an inquiry but no reference to a previous decision by Moses and no complaint.

---

93. Belkin 1970: 305.
94. Feldman 2000: 391 n. 524.

Regulation to Redeem a Firstborn Donkey (Num. 18.15 // Ant. 4.71)

This law appears in Exod. 13.13, 34.20, and Lev. 27.27. However, there are differences between the sources.[95] There is a contradiction between Exod. 13.2 and Num. 18.15: are all unclean animals to be redeemed, or only donkeys? Philo (*Spec. Laws* 1.127, 135) and Josephus (*Ant.* 4.71) maintain that all first-born had to be redeemed. The rabbis, however, ruled that only a donkey can be redeemed (*Mekh. Pisha* 18; cf. *m. Bekhor.* 1).

Olitzki[96] attributes this omission of the donkey to Josephus' apologetic desire to avoid any allusion of esteem for the donkey in Judaism, and discusses the ass libel found in *Ag. Ap.* 2.80-81. Ritter and Teeter,[97] however, view it as a halakhic difference reflected also in the Peshitta and in the *Mekh. Pisha* 18, where the option that the law is to be applied to all domestic animals is rejected. The fact that in Lev. 27.27 and Num. 18.15 there is another inner-biblical tradition may have led Josephus to omit Exod. 13.13 in order to avoid contradiction.

Laws of the Cities of Refuge
(Exod. 21.12-14; Num. 35; Deut. 4; 19 // Ant. 4.172-73)

Laws of the cities of refuge appear in Exodus, Numbers, Deuteronomy and Joshua (Exod. 21.12-14; Num. 35; Deut. 4.4-41; 19.1-12; Josh. 20). This topic involves the designation of the number of cities of refuge and their location, laws regarding who can flee to these cities, and laws regarding the avenger of blood.

Josephus rewrites these laws in *Ant.* 4.172-73, which contain a very brief summary of the long chapter of Numbers 35. The reader gets the impression that it is Moses who built these cities at his own initiative. He seems to present Moses as the lawgiver.[98] In other places, however, Josephus argues for the divine origin of the law: *Ant.* 3.88-101, 222-23, 286; 4.197, 295, 318-19.

Josephus adds an explanation for the reason the murderer remains at the city of refuge until the death of the high priest. The length of time in the city 'should be the same as the lifetime of the high priest during whose tenure he went into exile for having committed the manslaughter'.

---

95. See Brin 1994: 196–208.
96. See Olitzki 1885: 29; Feldman 2000: 351 n. 174.
97. Ritter 1879: 121; Teeter 2014: 156.
98. Lierman 2004: 136–9; Barclay 2007: 259 n. 620.

Josephus does not mention specifically the term גאל הדם, 'Avenger of Blood', but rather gives the essence of the law concerning him: 'The relatives of the one who had been slain, if they should seize the one who committed the manslaughter outside the boundaries of the city to which he fled, had the right to kill him'. The law of the avenger seems to be operating without any judicial authority and that is why the rabbis marginalize it and constrain the avenger within the rules of their justice system.[99]

Josephus records many examples of people fleeing into the temple for protection during times of danger and distress:[100] *Life* 17–21; *Ant.* 14.4-5, 19-20, 334-35, 339, 477, 480; *War* 1.149; 4.151, 203-204; 6.248. In *Ant.* 4.172 he views the function of the cities of refuge as exile (φυγή) for the unintentional murderer, in a similar way to Philo (*Spec. Laws* 3.123) and the rabbis (*m. Mak.* 2.1).

Josephus speaks of ten cities of refuge, while the Bible records nine. He may have been referring to the four cities in the territory of Reuben, another four in Gad, and two more in the half tribe of Manasseh.

Conclusion

Uncovering Josephus' rewriting techniques of the laws in Numbers is a challenging task since Josephus does not follow the MT order and various laws are scattered throughout his rewriting of laws in Leviticus and Deuteronomy. Once we adjust our expectations of Josephus and do not assume him to be a 'Shulchan Aruch', the classic Jewish legal code, we can view Josephus' writings correctly.

Despite his declaration that he will neither add nor omit anything, Josephus never intended to discuss all the biblical laws in his book. He was selective, perhaps emphasizing the laws which were mandatory according to his understanding. It should be acknowledged that we cannot always grasp the logic of his omissions.

The laws are incorporated into Josephus' *Antiquities* narrative of the history of the people of Israel as he saw it. Therefore, one cannot expect full compliance with the halakha. The reasons for the discrepancy between Josephus and the Bible and/or the halakha are varied: he may have relied on the fact that he had already referred to part of the laws in *War*; he had not been aware of the complicated halakhic discussion; and at other times he may had apologetic reasons for omissions.

---

99. Berkowitz 2006: 97–107.
100. Stevenson 2001: 164.

On the one hand, I do not accept David Goldenberg's view which eliminates almost every apologetic reason for the omissions in Josephus. On the other hand, David Nakman's view that Josephus was sloppy or ignorant in most cases acceptable. Josephus' rewriting of the biblical laws examined here neither represent a straightforward transmission of the biblical text nor are they exclusively Josephus' own interpretation.

One cannot deduce from the omission of the laws mentioned here what Josephus' self-identification may have been, namely: Was he a Pharisee or not? Even the non-mention of the tassels is so complicated that it cannot lead to the conclusion that he was an Essene.

Time and again we saw that Josephus chose to refer to the details of the laws in later narratives of the so-called Former Prophets. Indeed, it is easier to tell a story using narratives where the details of the laws can then be incorporated more seamlessly.

4

The Laws of Deuteronomy in Josephus

The book of Deuteronomy was of great importance to the authors of the Second Temple period.[1] It contains almost a third of the biblical laws, it concludes the career of Moses, and it paves the way for the entrance of Israel into the Promised Land.[2] The book also had great impact on the development of Jewish theology and thought. It is reflected in ancient translations, and parts of the MT of Deuteronomy were preserved at Qumran.[3] It is also alluded to in the Temple Scroll.[4] Philo refers to Deuteronomy on several occasions, and it is mentioned numerous times throughout rabbinic literature.[5] However, among all Second Temple period writers, Josephus' adaptation of Deuteronomy is the most comprehensive.

In the following chapter I will analyze Josephus' rewriting of the laws found in the book of Deuteronomy. Deuteronomy consists of a prologue (chs. 1–11), laws (chs. 12–26), blessings and curses (chs. 27–28), and an epilogue that includes Joshua's installation (ch. 31) and the death of Moses (ch. 34). Before Moses' death, there is a poem (ch. 32) and a blessing for the tribes of Israel (ch. 33). However, various laws are found in chs. 1–11 as well as in other chapters before and after chs. 12–26: cities of refuge (ch. 4); the Ten Commandments (ch. 5); the Shema, mezuza, and

---

1. See Crawford 2005: 127.
2. For Israelites Josephus uses Παλαιστίνη in *Ant.* 1.136, 14 and 20.259. He uses Ἰσραηλίτης for designating the ethnos. This term appears 196 times in the *Antiquities* but is not mentioned even once in *War*, where *ioudaioi* is used. Josephus uses *ioudaioi* for the post–biblical descriptions in *Ant.* 11–20. See the discussion and scholarly literature in Tomson 2019: 202–3; Ben-Eliyahu 2019.
3. Ulrich 2010: 175–246.
4. Schiffman 2008.
5. Lim 2007; Lincicum 2010. Lincicum has written on the reception of Deuteronomy in Paul.

phylacteries (chs. 6; 11); destroying the Canaanites (7.1-2); the command to build an altar on Mount Gerizim (ch. 27); and summoning Israel to hear a public reading of specific portions of the Torah (31.10-13).

Josephus paraphrases Deuteronomy in *Ant.* 4.176-331, with a retelling of the laws in §§200-300. In an effort to make the whole more coherent and logical, Josephus systematizes the discussion of subjects and gathers passages from various places of the Pentateuch. The justification for the reordering of the laws is that Moses 'left what he wrote in a scattered condition' (*Ant.* 4.197)

I shall now present Josephus' retelling of the Deuteronomic laws in comparison with the biblical laws.[6]

Josephus, *Ant.* 4	Bible
The Holy City and the Temple (200-201)	Deut. 12; Exod. 20
Pilgrimage (203-204)	Deut. 16
Tithing (205)	Deut. 14
Harlot's fee and dog's Price (206)	Deut. 23
Summoning the people (*Hakhēl*) and studying Torah (209-11)	Deut. 31
The Shema, tefillin (phylacteries) and mezuza (212-13)	Deut. 6, 11[7]
The administration of justice (214-18)	Deut. 16
Witnesses (219)	Deut. 19
Undetected murder (220-22)	Deut. 21
The law of the king (223-24)	Deut. 17
Prohibition of moving boundary markers (225)	Deut. 19.14
Various laws of charity and tithes (231-43)	Deut. 14, 24, 26; Lev. 19
Marital laws (244-59)	Deut. 21–22, 24–25; Lev. 21
Rebellious children (260-65)	Deut. 21
Monetary (civil) matters (267-70)	Deut. 23–24
Lost and found objects, assisting a fallen animal (274-75)	Deut. 22
Torts (277-84)	Exod. 21; Lev. 24.19-20; Deut. 19.21
Deposits (285–88)	Exod. 22; Deut. 24

6. I disagree with Lim's explanation (2007: 25) for the structure of the laws in Josephus. The same holds true for Nakman 2004. Laws taken from Exodus, Leviticus, and Numbers were dealt with in the preceding chapters.

7. These laws will be dealt with in the chapter on reasons for the commandments.

Josephus, *Ant.* 4	Bible
Fathers' guilt on account of children (289)	Deut. 24
Castration (290-91)	Deut. 23
Laws of warfare (292-301)	Deut. 20, 22[8]
Blessings and curses, covenant renewal, Song of Moses (302-33)	Deut. 27–34[9]
Eradicating Amalek (304)	Exod. 17.8-16; Deut. 25.17
Idolatrous city (310)	Deut. 13

Omissions

A notable omission in Josephus' rewriting of the laws of Deuteronomy is related to idolatry. The relevant passages in Deuteronomy containing commands against idolatry are Deut. 4.15-35; 5.6-10; 7.2-5, 16, 25-26; 11.16, 28; 12.2-3, 30-31; 13.1-15; 16.21-22; 17.2-3; 18.9-14; 20.17-18; 27.15; 28.36; 29.17-18, 25; 30.17; 31.16-20. Josephus downgrades this issue by either omitting or minimizing its significance.[10]

Moreover, Josephus does not rewrite the biblical laws pertaining to true and false prophets (Deut. 13 and 18). The reader will find later allusions to these laws in *War* and in other parts of *Antiquities* (*War* 4.626; *Ant.* 10.35-36, 61, 104). In contrast, Josephus places a heavy emphasis on the fulfillment of prophetic predictions.[11]

The law of asylum (Deut. 19.1-13) is also omitted from Josephus' retelling, probably since he has already dealt with this law in his rewriting of Numbers 35 (*Ant.* 4.172).

Another omission is that of the festivals mentioned in Deut. 16.1-17. Josephus has already dealt with the festivals (*Ant.* 3.240-54) and avoids mentioning them in his retelling of Deuteronomy.

According to Feldman, Josephus' omission of the prohibition of the Ammonites and Moabites converting to Judaism until the tenth generation (Deut. 23.4) and of the Edomites and the Egyptians until the third generation (Deut. 23.9) seems to be motivated by his eagerness to answer the charge that the Jews are exclusivist and haters of mankind.[12]

---

8. It is unclear why Altshuler (1982–83) added Deut. 24 in this rubric.

9. See Waters 2006: 65–6.

10. See Vermes 1982: 300 on *Ag. Ap.* 2.215-17.

11. Cook 2011: 125–8. I do not accept Feldman's explanation (2000: 469 n. 1081) that Josephus omits this law because of the famous prophecy (*War* 6.312) that someone from Judea would become ruler of the world.

12. Feldman 1997: 53.

However, Josephus does mention this law in *Ant.* 8.191-93, where he refers to Solomon as transgressing the law of Moses, 'who prohibited cohabitating with non–compatriots' (§191). Thus, Josephus has again referenced, in a later part of *Antiquities*, a law omitted in his rewriting of the Torah. Similarly, the pentateuchal law prohibiting the capture of a mother bird together with her young (Deut. 22.6-7) is omitted in *Antiquities*, yet it is mentioned in *Ag. Ap.* 2.213.[13]

The Holy City and the Temple (Deut. 12 // Ant. 4.200-201)

Deuteronomy 12 focuses on the chosen city in which the Temple will be built, yet it does not explicitly mention Jerusalem. Theoretically, it may refer to a place in the north.[14]

Josephus restates this law as follows:

> Let there be, in the fairest part of the land of the Chananaians, one holy city that is renowned for its excellence, whichever God selects for Himself through prophecy; and let there be one Temple in it and one altar of stones that are not hewn but chosen and joined together, which, smeared with whitewash, will be appealing and clean to view. Let the access to this be not by steps but by a sloping ramp. In another city let there be neither an altar nor a temple, for God is one and the stock of the Hebrews one.

This idea also appears in *Ag. Ap.* 2.193 as well as in Philo (*Spec. Laws* 1.67). Josephus follows the MT and does not explicitly identify the chosen city as Jerusalem.[15] This is in contrast to 4Q96 (4QMMTᵉ), which identifies the central cultic place in Deuteronomy 12 as Jerusalem (col. II, ll. 11; col. III, l. 1).[16] Josephus' addition that the location will be selected by God and through a prophet is quite reasonable. Prophets serve as mediators between God and men. How else would this message be conveyed to the people?

While in Deuteronomy the phrase במקום אשר יבחר appears eleven times, in Josephus this is the only occurrence. The repetitive style of Deuteronomy may have made it seem redundant to him.

The biblical altar may be made of earth (Exod. 20.20; 2 Kgs 5.17) or stones (Deut. 27.4-6; Josh. 4.2; 1 Kgs 18.31-32). Josephus interprets the altar in Deuteronomy 12 as being constructed of stones, which is possible.

---

13. See Barclay 2007: 294 n. 865.
14. Thelle 2012: 29.
15. Josephus does mention Jerusalem in his rewriting of Gen. 14 (*Ant.* 1.180) and 22 (*Ant.* 1.224).
16. Dimant and Parry 2015: 510.

As for the unhewn stones, Josephus seems to read Deuteronomy 27 into Deuteronomy 12. Since the whitewash appears already in the Mishnah (*Mid.* 3.4), one may relate Josephus' understanding to his knowledge of the oral tradition.

Pilgrimage (Deut. 16.16 // Ant. 4.203-204)

Deuteronomy 16.16 commands, 'Three times a year all your males shall appear before the Lord your God'. Josephus omits the instruction that only male adults[17] make pilgrimages to the holy place, perhaps because it seemed obvious to him. In any case, regarding Passover, Josephus writes that 'all the people streamed from their villages to the city and celebrated the festival in a state of purity *with their wives and children,* according to the law of their fathers' (*Ant.* 11.109 [emphasis added]).

In *War* 6.425, Josephus describes the large-scale journey to Jerusalem, and he may have thought of the biblical law in terms of his Second Temple milieu. Josephus also adds that the pilgrims come 'from the ends of the land that the Hebrews conquer', thus exempting many countries in the Diaspora from pilgrimage. Josephus also says that pilgrimage builds friendship, a point mentioned by Philo as well (*Spec. Laws* 1.70).

Second Tithe (Deut. 14.22-27 // Ant. 4.205)

Josephus deals with tithes both here and in §§231-43, which I shall return to later. Here the second tithe (δεκάτη) is discussed. Josephus adds details not mentioned in the Bible, and in his additions he resembles the rabbis (*Sifre* Deut. 107;[18] *m. Pesah.* 7.3) in that the second tithe can be redeemed everywhere and not exclusively in Jerusalem.[19] In both sources the tithes may be sold and the proceeds used for meals and sacrifices.

Harlot's Fee or a Dog's Price (Deut. 23.19 // Ant. 4.206)

Deuteronomy 23.19 reads, 'You shall not offer a harlot's fee or a dog's price as any kind of votive offering in the house of the Lord, your God'. The meaning of מחיר כלב is debated: does the law refer to 'dog' in a literal sense, or does it denote a cultic prostitute? Jeffrey Tigay notes, 'there is no fully convincing explanation of this phrase [in Deut. 23.19]'.

---

17. See Exod. 23.17; 34.23-24; Deut. 16.16; *Mekhilta Kaspa* 4 to Exod. 23.17 (see Lauterbach and Stern 2004: 3:482); *m. Hag.* 1.1; *Sifre* Deut. 143.

18. Feldman (2000: 403 n. 615) refers erroneously to ch. 96a.

19. In Josephus: ἐν τῇ ἱερᾷ πόλει, 'in the holy city'.

Josephus' literal interpretation of 'dog' is possible. He adds different varieties of dogs ('hunting-dog or a protector of flocks'); types found in the ancient Near East. Yet there is no certainty that Jews in the Second Temple period were practicing hunters.[20] His use of ὕβρις is interesting since תועבה stands in contrast to the LXX's βδέλυγμα. In rewriting the laws of Deuteronomy, Josephus uses this term in 2.237-39, 251, 260 and 319. Throughout his writings it is used 232 times.[21] In *Ant.* 4.206 it connotes sexual impropriety.

*Summoning the People (*Hakhēl*) and Studying Torah (Deut. 31.9-13 // Ant. 4.209-11)*

In Deut. 31.9-13, Moses requires that all the people of Israel gather every seven years during Sukkot to hear the words of the Torah. The biblical law does not specify who is to read the Torah. The Mishnah assigns the role to the king, namely Agrippa (*m. Sot.* 7.8).[22] According to Josephus, the high priest is the reader. Fine[23] thinks that Josephus reflects 'the practice in his days under Roman procuratorial rule'.[24] Fraade assigns this to 'Josephus's own priestly lineage and advocacy of priestly theocracy (or aristocracy)'.[25] Yet doubt still remains regarding whether Josephus was influenced by Neh. 8.1-12, despite the difference between the two sources.[26]

Which part of the Torah is to be read? Josephus writes generally τοὺς νόμους ('the laws'), without indicating whether it refers to the whole book of Deuteronomy or only portions.

Israel's Judicial System (Deut. 16.18–17.13 // Ant. 4.214-18)

Deuteronomy 16.18–17.13 can be subdivided as follows: instruction to appoint local judges (16.18-20); prohibitions of idolatry in contrast to proper worship (16.21–17.1); the legal process to be followed in cases of forbidden forms of worship (17.2-7); and judicial procedures in the higher court (17.8-13).

---

20. Schwartz 2004: 257.
21. See D. B. Levine 1993.
22. Whether it is Agrippa I or II see Schwartz 1990: 159–71.
23. Fine 1999: 42.
24. Fraade (2011: 217 n. 24) mentions other supporters of Josephus' view: Philo, *Hypoth.* (in Eusebius, *Praep. Ev.* 8.7.12-13); Hecataeus of Abdera; *Let. Aris.* 310. Priests as readers of Torah appear also in 4Q266 5 ii 1-3.
25. Fraade 2011: 217.
26. On Deut. 31 and Neh. 8 see Pakkala 2004: 157.

Josephus' addition of seven men ruling in each city is debated. While some accept it as a reliable testimony of Josephus' time, others think that it is merely a literary phenomenon that 'functioned not only to harmonize the deuteronomic law for judges with pentateuchal traditions about the Mosaic appointment of deputies, but also to appeal to a popular non-Jewish tradition for apologetic purposes'.[27] In *War* 2.570-71 Josephus tells the reader that he himself had appointed seven judges in each city. These are most likely not to be identified with the טובי העיר שבעה mentioned in *b. Meg.* 26a.

As in other instances, Josephus omits any reference to idolatry. This omission contributes to the thematic unity of the passage, yet it results from apologetic reasons. Josephus adds the role of ὑπηρέτης ('assistants'), which may be his substitute for שטרים. The Levites had policing duties,[28] as is already stated in 2 Chron. 19.11. The rabbis also mention this (*Sifre Deut.* 15).

Josephus' (and the LXX's) understanding of biblical שער as a city is supported by Deut. 5.13 and 12.12, 28.52, 55, where it connotes cities.

Witnesses (Deut. 19.15-21 // Ant. 4.219)

Josephus rewrites the law of testimony as follows:

> Let not one witness be trusted, but let there be three or, at the very least, two, whose credibility their previous way of life shall attest. Let the testimony of women not be accepted because of the levity and boldness of their gender. Nor let slaves give testimony because of their ignobility of soul, since it is likely that they do not bear witness to the truth, whether because of gain or because of fear. And if someone bears false witness and is believed, let him, when convicted, suffer whatever the one against whom he bore false witness was going to suffer.

Josephus includes some additional requirements for witnesses not found in the Bible. He excludes women and slaves and demands good character from witnesses. The Mishnah also excludes women and slaves (*m. R.H.* 1.8; *Sanh.* 3.3) and likewise demands that the witnesses be people of integrity. By contrast, elsewhere in the Bible we find the story of Solomon's trial in 1 Kgs 3.16-28, where two women testified; this constitutes evidence from the ancient Near East that women and slaves were not excluded from testifying.[29]

---

27. Pearce 1995: 489.
28. See Pearce 1995; Schwartz 1992: 96–7.
29. Wells 2004: 50–3.

According to Josephus, a false witness must suffer what he might have plotted, even if the convict was not punished; this is as the Pharisees argued (*m. Mak.* 1.6). The agreement between the rabbis and Josephus cannot be coincidental. Since this issue was part of a polemic between the Pharisees and the Sadducees, one had to know the law clearly or otherwise interpret it according to the plain meaning of the text, as did the Sadducees.[30]

In regard to Josephus' addition that women are not allowed to testify, this is part of his general view of women as being inferior to men (*Ag. Ap.* 2.201; cf. *Ant.* 18.255).[31] Daube thinks that Josephus' addition accords with the Roman concept of 'levitas animi' (weak judgement).[32] Pearce notes, 'there is no certainty that he follows actual Jewish practice and that he may be influenced by his Roman context'.[33] Baumgarten points out that in 'Athenian and Roman law…women were, with few exceptions, excluded from the witness box'.[34]

Nevertheless, Josephus mentions women's testimony in the days of Herod (*Ant.* 17.64-65, 93; *War* 1.584-90).[35] In general, I concur with Tal Ilan that scholars pushed the case too far in arguing for Josephus' misogyny, since in many cases the opposite is true.[36]

Unsolved Murder (Deut. 21.10 // Ant. 4.220-22)

Deuteronomy 21.1-10 deals with an unsolved murder. The details of the ritual require explanation: (1) What is the purpose of the ritual? (2) Why is the presence of judges necessary? (3) What is the significance of the unworked heifer? (4) Why must the ritual take place by a נחל איתן? (5) Why is the animal's neck broken? (6) What role do the priests play in the ritual? (7) What is the function of the handwashing ceremony and the

---

30. Nakman 2004: 156.
31. Philo, *Hypoth.* 11.14-17. See Tilford 2013.
32. Daube 1986: 14.
33. Pearce 2000.
34. On the Testimony of Women in 1QS28a (1QSa), see Baumgarten 1957: 268; Dimant and Parry 2015: 53.
35. Wassen 2005: 87–8. Sanctions against false witnesses are mentioned in the targums: because of it there is no rain and drought comes upon the world, people are robbed of their children by wild animals, and powerful empires overrun the world sending people into exile. Pseudo-Philo (11.12) cites as consequence a talionic reprisal: against the false witness guardian angels will give a false witness. See Houtman 2000: 66.
36. Ilan 2017.

confession? (8) Why must the watercourse where the ritual takes place not be cultivated?³⁷

Josephus does not answer all these questions, but only some of them. As to the breaking of the neck, he interprets correctly the verb ערף as 'cut the cervical sinews of the cow'.³⁸ Among his additions Josephus mentions washing in *pure* water, the search for the murderer ('seek him with much diligence') and offering rewards for information. Josephus understood נחל איתן as φάραγγα ('ravine'), and a similar interpretation is found in Onkelos and the Vulgate.

It is interesting to note that a similar explanation for the rationale of this law is found in Maimonides (*Guide* III, 40):

> As a rule the investigation, the procession of the elders, the measuring, and the taking of the heifer, make people talk about it, and by making the event public, the murderer may be found out, and he who knows of him, or has heard of him, or has discovered him by any clue, will now name the person that is the murderer.

The similarity is striking. No doubt Maimonides had no access to Josephus' writings, reaching the same explanation independently. Josephus' interpretation is thus possibly a plausible reading of the law.

According to Josephus' interpretation, the biblical זקנים are γερουσία. This term appears in the book of Maccabees (2 Macc. 1.10; 4.44; 11.27), in addition to the LXX and Philo, and it may be regarded as an anachronism.³⁹ Josephus adds that the elders should wash over the head of the animal. This detail is also found in the Temple Scroll (11QT 63.5).

The subject of rewards for information (μήνυτρον) appear also in *Ant.* 15.265. It may have been inserted under the influence of Dio (*Roman History* 55.27.3). The statement that no one is suspected of having committed the slaying because of hatred is Josephus' addition, which he seems to have derived from Deut. 19.11-13.⁴⁰

As for the role of priests in this ritual, Josephus gives them the duty of reciting the prayer in v. 8 (cf. *m. Sota* 9.6).

---

37. Zevit 1976.
38. See Wright 1987: 394 n. 22.
39. For priests, Levites, and counsel of elders, see also *Ant.* 4.214-18 (in *Ant.* 4.324 they appear with the high priest). See also Philo, *Flacc.* 10, 74; *Ant.* 12.138. See also LXX to Exod. 3.16; Num. 22.4; Josh. 23.2 et al. See Sharon 2012, with earlier literature. Goodblatt (1994: 94–7), however, sees in Josephus' usage of this term merely a translation of 'elders', and not necessarily a formalized council.
40. Feldman 2000: 683.

The Law of the King (Deut. 17.14-20 // Ant. 4.223-24)

Deuteronomy 17.14-20 focus on the king. Several questions arise: Is the appointing of a king mandatory or optional? What are the reasons for the various prohibitions imposed on the king? What are his rights?

Josephus seems to follow the opinion that appointing a king is optional: 'If, however, you should have a passion (ἔρως) to have a king'. Josephus adds that the high priest and the elders will guide him.

Josephus' reasons for all the prohibitions imposed on the king include horses, women, and money. He warns that if he obtains them he will be full of contempt for the laws. On the other hand, concerning polygyny he states that it is 'an ancestral custom of ours to have several wives at the same time' (*Ant.* 17.14; cf. *War* 1.477). Josephus' words are supported by rabbinic sources, where there is no prohibition of polygyny.[41] This is to be contrasted with several sources from Qumran forbidding polygyny (CD 4.20-21; 11QT 56.17-18).

Many scholars hold that Josephus' view of monarchy was negative. This assessment is based on his rewriting of Deuteronomy 17 and 1 Samuel 8.

Flatto[42] concludes that 'Josephus expresses a general ambivalence about the very institution of the monarchy that goes well beyond any equivocation that may be detected in Deuteronomy 17'. Kingship is not the preferred form of rule but rather aristocracy. When a king is eventually chosen, he must consult with the high priest and the elders.

Likewise, in his adaptation of the people's demand from Samuel to appoint a king (1 Sam. 8), Josephus adds, 'Their words greatly grieved Samuel on account of his innate justice and hatred of kings. For he delighted intensely in aristocracy as something divine that renders blessed those who use it as their constitution.' This addition is regarded as apologetic, commenting on the current situation in Josephus' own day by appealing to the Romans' disdain for monarchy. Turning to modern interpretations of these biblical sources, one finds that most scholars view them as restrictions of the king's power in Israel. Deuteronomy 17 provides no rights for the king – only obligations. He is neither a military commander nor a judge. Likewise, Samuel's speech does not contain even one positive evaluation of the king.

However important as these passages may be, one cannot base an assessment of Josephus' view of monarchy solely on them.[43]

---

41. See Satlow 2001: 190; Schremer 2003: 218.
42. Flatto 2010: 49–50.
43. See Avioz 2015.

Prohibition on Moving Boundary Markers
(Deut. 19.14 // Ant. 4.225)

Deuteronomy 19.14 forbids moving boundary markers. Josephus expands on this law and explains why it is forbidden. First, it is 'God's pebble', which helps avoid wars and seditions.[44] Among commentators, it is debated whether this law refers to disputes between neighbors or to disagreements among the tribes or between Israel and its neighbors.[45] In Josephus, the addition 'through the wish of those who are *greedy* to go further than the boundaries' seems to refer to a domestic rather than an international boundary. In Josephus' writings, the word στάσις refers to inner quarrels (*War* 1.10, 25, 31; 4.131) between Jewish groups. In some other occurrences (e.g. *War* 2.487; *Ant.* 19.278) it refers to quarrels between Jews and Greeks. There is no compelling reason to assume, as Nakman[46] does, that in retelling this law Josephus refers to peaceful nations.

The mention of God is not of Josephus' arbitrary addition, but it rather emerges from biblical law: 'The land was allocated to the people of God when their ancestors first entered the promised land, and their descendants do not have the right to change these divinely ordained allocations'.[47]

In Roman law, as mentioned by Dionysius of Halicarnassus (*Roman Antiquities* 2.74),[48] the punishment for moving boundary markers is death. In contrast, Josephus does not mention any punishment regarding this law.

Various Laws of Charity and Tithes
(Deut. 14, 24, 26 and Lev. 19 // Ant. 4.231-43)

The laws of tithes appears in Lev. 19.9-10; 27.30-33; Num. 18.21-32; Deut. 14.22-27; 15.19-23; 24.19-22; and 26.12-15.[49] According to the tanaitic halakha (*Sifre* Deut. 63; *m. Terum*; *t. Demai*; cf. *y. Sheb.* 5b), some of the gifts are given to the priests and Levites (Num. 18.12, 25-32 and Deut. 18.4).[50] Josephus has dealt with these gifts in his retelling of Num. 18 (*Ant.* 4.67-75).

---

44. Cf. Ibn Ezra ad loc., who mentions this linkage as well.
45. See *Encyclopedia Talmudit*, vol. 9, s.v. 'hassagat gevul' ('boundary moving').
46. Nakman 2004: 160.
47. Baker 2009: 100. Pace Feldman 2000: 416 n. 714.
48. See Castelli 2001: 157.
49. Baker 2009: 241. In Josephus tithes appear in *Ag. Ap.* 188; *Life* 12, 15; *Ant.* 11.182; 14.245; 20.181, 206-207.
50. The rabbis found three types of tithes in pentateuchal law: the first tithe is for the Levites (Num. 18.20-32); the second tithe is eaten by the Israelite layperson from whom it originates (Deut. 14.22-27; Lev. 27.30-31); the third tithe is designated for the poor (Deut. 14.28-29; 26.12). See the literature in Stackert 2007: 167 n. 6.

Other gifts were given to the poor, the orphan, and the widow (Lev. 10.9-10; 23.22; Deut. 14.28-29; 24.19-22; 26.1-12). Gifts to the poor are called עוללות, פרט, פאה, שכחה, לקט.

As in other cases of repetition, Josephus had to decide how to refer to a law appearing several times in the Torah. Likewise, the repetition may not be in identical terms, and it may include variances and contradictions. How should one interpret the tithe law in Deut. 14.22-29 in relation to the one described in Num. 18.21-32? What is the relation between Deut. 24.19-22 and Lev. 19.9-10?

Josephus adds the gratitude that the poor will feel for those who leave behind sheaves and grapes. While the MT mentions only the divine reward, Josephus also includes the motivation for the farmers to help the poor. At first glance, Josephus seems to be influenced by Cicero and Seneca. Seneca expects the poor to express gratitude and calls such giving a social act ('socialis res', *De Beneficiis* 3.8.3; 4.10.5, 11.1; 5.11.5). However, the 'needy' in the works of Cicero and Seneca 'are respectable citizens, and not the most desperate members of their society'.[51]

Josephus understands that the law commanded to leave for the poor a small amount of the crop in the field, vines, and olive trees. According to Shemesh, it represents a tradition that did not differentiate between different types of gifts. The two laws in the Torah are interpreted as one law, namely, to leave for the poor different species of crops of each kind in its own way. He argues that a similar tradition is to be found in 4Q270 3 ii 12-19.[52] A different tradition is reflected in Philo (*Virt.* 90–94) and the rabbis (*t. Peah* 2.13), according to which there are two types of gifts, a custom extended to include olives. In contrast, the tradition reflected at Qumran and in Josephus did not distinguish between the various laws in Leviticus 19 and Deuteronomy 24 and interpreted all the verbs in one sense: everything must be collected at the end of the harvest, and the form of gift-giving varies from one growth to another according to its nature.

According to the rabbinic Sages (*b. R.H.* 12b; *y. Shev.* 2.7; 34a), the tithes of the poor are brought in the third and in the sixth year of the seven-year sabbatical cycle in place of the second tithe. Thus, each year only two tithes are served: the first and second tithes, or alternatively, the first tithe and the tithe of the poor. But Josephus says, 'a second tithe must be brought every year', and in the third and sixth years a third tithe is added to it for the poor.

---

51. Parkin 2006.
52. See Dimant and Parry 2015: 325.

Josephus is not alone. The LXX to Deut. 26.12, the book of *Jubilees* (32.11), the book of Tobit (1.7-8), and the Targum *Pseudo-Jonathan* on Deut. 26.1-13 all held that all three tithes had to be paid in the third and sixth years, including the poor man's tithe.

Feldman concludes that Josephus agrees with the Mishnah in *Ma'aser Sheni* 5.6, where it states that 'in every fourth and seventh year not only the Levite and poor tithes but also the second tithe had to be separated'.[53] Werman and Shemesh[54] conclude that 'there is no way to determine whether according to the sectarian law, the poor tithe was given in the third year instead of the second tithe, according to the Sages, or perhaps apart from the second tithe, according to the tradition of Josephus'.

The law regarding the muzzling of an ox (Deut. 25.4 // *Ant.* 4.233) may seem unrelated, but Josephus ties it in via the discussion of fruits in §§231-34. Who is violating the law? One who puts a muzzle on an ox before threshing, one who threshes with a muzzled animal, or one who does both? Josephus dwells on the reasoning of this law: 'for it is not right to bar from the fruit those who joined in the work and who have exerted themselves with regard to its production'.[55] This is a very reasonable explanation which is retained until today by oriental societies.

In §§234-37, Josephus rewrites the law in Deut. 23.25-26,[56] stating that those 'walking on the road' should not be prevented from picking and eating the ripe fruits to fulfill all their needs. The addition, 'walking on the road', is reasonable and is to be preferred over the rabbinic suggestion (*b. B.M.* 87b) that it relates to workers only. Josephus adds that the law also applies to non-Israelite foreigners. This addition is recorded in *b. B.M.* 92b as well and thus is not necessarily apologetic.

---

53. Feldman (2000: 421 n. 759). Some hold that that the older halakha provided also for a 'third tithe' Against this, see Finkelstein 1930. Olitzki (1885: 16–17) denies that there was a third tithe. He maintains that Josephus, ignorant of the traditional law, was misled into supposing that three tithes were given in the third year when he noticed that some of the second tithe of the second year was used in Jerusalem in the third year.

54. Werman and Shemesh 2011: 198.

55. Dr. Michael Graham noted to me that Paul cites this text in 1 Cor. 9.9 and 1 Tim. 5.18 and he makes a very similar argument.

56. There are verse numbering differences between the Hebrew text and English translations. While in the English translations the numbering is Deut. 23.1-25, in the Hebrew it is Deut. 23.2-26.

Josephus also adds a long passage regarding God who 'grants an abundance of good things not for the enjoyment of us alone' (§237). A very similar assessment is found in a thirteenth-century guide to Jewish law called *Sefer Hachinuch* (precept #576): 'the root of this commandment is to teach the Children of Israel to have a nice soul and goodwill; and through this the blessing of God will descend upon them'.

Liturgical Declarations Recited When Bringing the First Fruits (Deut. 26 // Ant. 4.242-43)

Deuteronomy 26 contains liturgical declarations that the farmer is to recite when he brings the first fruits (ביכורים) to the Temple (vv. 1-11) and after he gives the poor-tithe every third year (vv. 12-15).

There are many differences between Josephus, the Bible, and the rabbis. Josephus omits any reference to the difficult phrase ארמי אובד אבי. He does not mention that the poor-tithe is aimed at the Levite and the alien as well. He adds that the third year tithe is brought in addition to the other tithes[57] and that sacrifices are brought together with the first fruits. Josephus' view appears already in *Jubilees* (32.11) and Tobit (1.7). The contrasting view is found in the LXX to Deut. 26.12 and in rabbinic literature (*Sifre* Deut. 302). Perhaps there were differing traditions in this regard.

It also seems that Josephus combines the two liturgical recitations declared by the farmer into one text. Another deviation from the rabbis is that in Josephus' view, the fruits are not necessarily brought only from the seven species that Israel was blessed with (see *m. Bik.* 3.9; *b. Ber.* 44a), but rather any fruit. In this he again deviates from the rabbinic view. The explanation may be that he was interpreting biblical law where there is no hint that the fruits should be from the seven species.

Finally, in §242 Josephus adds that the one bringing the tithe stands 'right opposite the Temple precincts'. This addition is supported by *m. Meg.* 2.5-6.[58]

Marital Laws (Deut. 22–25 // Ant. 4.244-59)

In Deuteronomy 22–25 we find scattered laws regarding marital issues and improper sexual behaviors: marriage, adultery, divorce, rape, and virginity.

---

57. On *Jubilees*, see Baumgarten 1977: 140–2. Philo mentions bikkurim in *Virt.* 95; *Spec. Laws* 2.215-22.

58. Henshke 2007: 152–3.

Concerning Deut. 22.22, Josephus deals with this law prior to his rewriting of Deut. 22.13-21 (§244).[59] He adds a non-biblical reference to 'those who have arrived at the age of marriage'. But what is this age? Josephus was married at the age of 30,[60] while Philo (*Quest. Gen.* 4.154) recommends marrying at the age of 40. The rabbis debate whether it should be 18 or 20.[61]

He also writes that Moses demanded that young men should marry freeborn virgins of good parents. Virginity preserves the woman's purity and the purity of the seed, and it also denotes her modesty and loyalty to her husband. This is possibly why Josephus emphasizes this issue.[62] Josephus' understanding accurately reflects the values in the biblical world as found in the Pentateuch: a daughter was expected to remain a virgin before her marriage.[63] It is not unique to the Greco-Roman world.

He goes on to declare, 'Let not free men marry female slaves'. This reflects Josephus' hierarchical assumptions.[64] The passion Josephus alludes to may refer to Pheroras' 'mad passion' for a slave girl (*Ant.* 16.194-95).

Josephus adds (§245) that no Israelite should marry a prostitute, a prohibition found in the Bible with regard to the High Priest (Lev. 21.7). This point was not shared by Philo ('Nor let anyone else be prevented from taking her in marriage', *Spec. Laws* 1.101-102). It seems that Josephus was inspired by both Lev. 19.29, 21.5, and Deut. 22.22. In both books there is a negative attitude toward prostitution.[65]

The law of the slandered bride (Deut. 22.13-21) raises several problems: What is the meaning of עלילות דברים? What is the role of the parents in the procedure? Why is the bride punished by death?

---

59. Josephus deals with marriage also in *Ag. Ap.* 2.199-203.
60. *Life* 414 – on 67 CE. However, we do not know whether he was married before this point. See Mason's comment on *Life* (2001: 164).
61. See Schremer 2003.
62. For earlier literature dealing with virginity in the ancient world, see Avioz 2011: 4 n. 15.
63. See Frymer-Kensky 1998.
64. Hezser 2005: 94, 196. Hezser points out that Josephus is not interested in their ethnicity but rather in the boundaries between slaves and free persons. Prohibitions on marrying slaves appear also in 4Q270 4, 12-21; 4Q266 12, 4-9. See Wassen 2005: 68–71.
65. See Goodfriend 1992. A negative view of prostitution is found in 1 Kgs 22.38 and Amos 7.17. A similar prohibition is found in 4Q271. See Dimant and Parry 2015: 331–4; Shemesh 1998; Wassen 2005: 80–8. Shemesh does not mention Josephus in his paper.

Josephus (§§246-48) understands אשה as a betrothed woman (μνηστευσάμενος); he is supported in this by modern scholars who claim that Deut. 22.13-29 should be contrasted with Deut. 22.28-29.⁶⁶

Josephus omits that the accusation is to be brought before the elders of the city in the gate (Deut. 22.15). He may have relied on other mentions of this found both earlier and later (*Ant.* 4.218, 220-22, 224, 255-56). There is no need to explore why Josephus omitted the שמלה garment and why he did not specify which evidence is to be brought.⁶⁷ Tigay, in his commentary on Deuteronomy,⁶⁸ points out that we need not interpret the שמלה literally⁶⁹ and that any kind of evidence can be brought – just like Josephus commented.

If the accusation turns out to be false, the husband should be יסר. Josephus understands the root יסר correctly as flogging, or whipping, as he did in his rewriting of the law of the wayward son. He deviates from the LXX which translates it as αιδεύουσιν ('educate, chastise'). The law does not specify the number of lashes, but Josephus adds that it is '40 minus 1', in line with the Mishnah (*Makk.* 3.10).

In §§249-50 Josephus rewrites the law found in Deut. 21.15-17 regarding a man marrying two wives and the law of primogeniture. His changes are minor.

In §251 Josephus rewrites Deut. 22.23-24, which involves adultery with a betrothed woman. Josephus does not mention stoning, despite the fact that he is aware of such a punishment (*Ant.* 4.202; 20.200; *Ag. Ap.* 2.206):

> If the one who violates a young woman, who is betrothed to another, persuaded her and received her consent to the violation, let him die together with her, for both are similarly guilty, he for having persuaded the young woman to undergo the greatest disgrace willingly, and to value this more highly than honorable marriage, she for having been persuaded to offer herself for the outrage because of pleasure or because of gain.

The law concerning the violation of an unbetrothed virgin is recorded in Deut. 22.28-29. Josephus deals with it in *Ant.* 4.252, where he conflates it with Exod. 22.15-16 (cf. Philo, *Spec. Laws* 3.65-71 and 11Q19 66

---

66. Wells 2005.
67. Nakman 2016: 285.
68. Tigay 2016: 2:560.
69. Cf. *Sifre* Deut. 237. Cf. 4Q159 as following the non-literal understanding of שמלה. See Schiffman 2008: 532.

ll. 8-11).⁷⁰ Scholars debate as to whether the sex in Deut. 22.28-29 is consensual or non-consensual. Josephus uses ὕβρις to connote violence.

Josephus omits the prohibition imposed on the rapist to divorce his victim and adds, 'But if it does not seem best to the father of the young woman to give her in marriage to him, let him pay fifty shekels as compensation'. The omission follows the law in Exodus 22, where no prohibition on divorce is mentioned. The addition also follows Exodus 22. There is a striking resemblance between Josephus and the halakha (Mek. de R. Ishmael, *Nez*. 17), according to which in both Exodus 22 and Deuteronomy 22 the father has the right to resist these marriages. Tigay summarizes by stating, 'Since the father does not have to consent to his daughter's marriage with the seducer who was lying with her consensually (and against the father's will), it is inconceivable that the father would have to agree for his daughter's marriage to the one who raped her'.⁷¹

According to Deut. 24.1 a man can divorce his wife if he found in her עֶרְוַת דָּבָר ('something obnoxious about her', NJPS; 'something objectionable about her', NRSV). The cause for the divorce is not clear: does the law refer to chastisement or to another reason? When Josephus came to rewrite this law, he states, 'One who wishes for whatever reason – and many such arise among human beings – to be divorced...' (*Ant*. 4.253). According to Josephus, it could be for any cause. This is in line with Philo (*Spec. Laws* 3.30), Ben Sira (25.26), and Hillel (*m. Giṭ*. 9.10). In *Life* 426–27 Josephus tells us that he has 'sent away' his woman, 'being displeased with her habits'.⁷²

Levirate Marriage (Deut. 25.5-10 // Ant. 4.254-56)

The law in Deut. 25.1-5⁷³ deals with a woman whose husband died childless. She was then required to marry one of her husband's brothers in order to perpetuate the name of the deceased. Josephus omits the detail that the brothers should be living together, probably not understanding its significance here.

---

70. Hiebert 1994. For the text of 4Q19, see Dimant and Parry 2015: 948.
71. Tigay 2016: 2:559.
72. See Instone-Brewer 2002: 115.
73. Related to this law are the following biblical sources: Gen. 38; Ruth 4; Lev. 18.16; 20.21; Num. 27.1-11; 36.1-13. Of these, Josephus omits Gen. 38.

In case of a refusal of the brother to marry his widowed sister-in-law, she should bring him to the elders, pull his sandal off, spit in his face and speak words of disdain (Deut. 25.7-10). Josephus adds that this procedure is performed whether the brother-in-law mentions a slight or a more significant reason. This addition probably stems from the fact the biblical law contains no exceptions.

Another addition is that the widow says her brother-in-law has insulted the memory of the deceased brother by not marrying her; the woman is then free to marry again. Josephus intensifies the shaming of this person. In contrast,[74] in the Mishnah (*m. Yebam.* 12.3), spitting is not mandatory.

Josephus also adds:

> This will be of advantage to the community, if houses do not disappear and the possessions remain with the kinsmen; and it will bring to the women, as they live with those nearest to their former husbands, an alleviation of their suffering.

This is in line with modern commentators who believe that one of the primary purposes of the law of levirate marriage is to maintain the property of the deceased brother within the family.[75]

As for calling the child born of levirate marriage by the name of the deceased, it is unclear whether Josephus means the giving of a personal name or making him an heir.[76] A reading of Tigay's commentary leads to both possibilities.[77] In any case, Josephus is not in line with the rabbinic Sages who declared (*m. Yebam.* 4.7) that the levir is the heir. Josephus is not to be treated as a testimony for the development of the halakha but as a commentator.

Josephus replaces the MT's בן with ἄτεκνος, which means 'childless'. In this way, the child's gender is insignificant. The LXX translates בן as σπέρμα, pointing to the same direction. The rabbis (*Sifre* Deut. 289) also follow this line.

The Law of a Captive Beautiful Woman
(Deut. 21.10-14 // Ant. 4.257-59)

Among the laws concerning warfare, the law of a captive beautiful woman (Deut. 21.10-14) raises several difficulties: Why does the woman 'do' her

---

74. In the MT to Ruth 4, spitting is not mentioned and Josephus (*Ant.* 5.335) adds it.
75. Pressler 1993: 69. Pace Altshuler 1977: 133.
76. Weisberg 2009: 37-8.
77. Tigay 2016: 2:616.

nails and trim her hair? What is the meaning of removing 'her captive's garb?' Is it the garment that she was wearing when taken prisoner, or something she is required to wear when in captivity? Why must the captor wait a month before marrying her?

Josephus adds that the woman is 'a virgin or a woman who has been married', a point not specifically addressed by the biblical law. Josephus is in accord with the rabbis (*Sifre* Deut. 211; *b. Kid.* 21b), who point out that a Jewish soldier may marry a married captive woman as well.

Josephus omits reference to the nails,[78] either because he considered it an unimportant detail or because he did not see the nails' relation to the mourning rites mentioned in vv. 12-13. According to Josephus, the Jewish soldier is not permitted to have marital relations with the captive woman 'before she has her hair cut and puts on a mourner's appearance and laments her relatives and friends who have perished in the battle'. In this Josephus expands on the biblical law, which mentions only her parents. There is debate among the medieval commentators whether she laments the killing of her parents in battle (Ibn Ezra) or because she will never see them again (Nachmanides). Josephus adopted the first option.

Josephus adds that the purpose of taking this woman is for procreation, a point mentioned in various places throughout his writings.[79] One notes the emphasis of Josephus on the morality of the Israelite army even in taking captives.

Josephus interprets the thirty days to refer to the time passed in mourning. This is supported by Tigay,[80] who referenced Num. 20.29 and Deut. 34.8 as evidence. The command לא תתעמר בה is unclear, and Josephus understands it as making her a slave, a possible interpretation.

The Law of the Rebellious Son (Deut. 21.18-21 // Ant. 4.260-64)

The law of the rebellious son (Deut. 21.18-21) is retold in *Ant.* 4.260-64. The main difficulties and questions arising from the biblical text include: Is the context of the law and its position within the series of laws

---

78. Stern (1998: 102) errs when he says that Josephus understand ועשתה את צפרניה as pairing her nails. Josephus does not mention any nails. That interpretation is found only in Philo (*Virt.* 111). Despite some resemblance between Philo (*Virt.* 110–15) and Josephus, there are differences between them as well. For instance, while Josephus speaks of a virgin or married woman, Philo speaks of a virgin or widow. While Philo mentions the option of selling the captive woman as a prostitute, Josephus remains silent in regard to selling her. Philo speaks of cutting off the hair, but Josephus retains the MT shaving.

79. See below for my discussion on the rebellious son.

80. Tigay 2016: 2:533.

significant? (The law of the rebellious son follows the law of the hated wife's son, and it precedes that of the proper treatment of the corpses of executed criminals.) Does the law apply to daughters as well as sons? (The Hebrew word בן could refer to either.) What is meant by 'disciplining' (ויסרו) him? What does סורר ומורה mean? What, exactly, is the sin of the son? Does זולל וסובא denote something different than סורר ומורה, or are they synonymous? What is the elders' place within the legal procedure described in these verses? Is the punishment proportionate to the crime?

While reworking the deuteronomical law of the wayward son, Josephus' adaptation deviates considerably from the biblical law and legal procedure in both its additions and omissions.

Josephus adds a characteristically Greco-Roman twist. He states that marriage is purely for procreation's sake, a principle which has its origin in the Greco-Roman world.[81] Thus, in this case, Josephus' description of parenting may be understood as a fusion of Greco-Roman culture and homiletic technique.

An interesting addition of Josephus is that the law refers to a rebellious daughter as well. According to the rabbinic sources, the law of the wayward son applies only to male children: 'If a man has a son – a son and not a daughter, a son and not an adult' (*Sifre* Deut. 218); 'If a man has a son – not a daughter' (*m. Sanh.* 8.1). Josephus understands בן generically, explicitly applying the law to daughters in §263 'in seeing neither son nor daughter punished'. This interpretation is logical, as a daughter may also rebel against her parents.

Josephus is likely connecting this law to the commandment in the Decalogue about honoring parents (Exod. 20.12), since he emphasizes lack of 'honor' as opposed to disobedience. Thus, he assumes that this law applies to son and daughter alike, as in the Decalogue. This is supported by his phrasing of this law in his *Ag. Ap.* 2.206, which combines elements of the Decalogue and the law in Deuteronomy (Deut. 5.16): The law ranks honoring one's parents second only to honoring God, and if a son does not acknowledge the benefits received from them – for the slightest failure in his duty towards them – it hands him over to be stoned.

Do the words ויסרו אותו mean lashes or a warning? The NJPS translates this as 'they discipline him'. The root יסר has various meanings in the Hebrew Bible. In some places it refers to physical punishment, whereas in others it means verbal rebuke (Prov. 1.8; 8.33; 19.27). The rabbis understood this verb to mean 'lashes/flogging' (*b. Sanh.* 71a), and some

---

81. See Dixon 2015: 84–6. This principle appears also in *Ag. Ap.* 2.199, 202 (Barclay 2007: 283 n. 797); Philo, *Spec. Laws* 3.32-36. For more Hellenistic sources, see Wassen 2005: 179–81.

modern commentators also understand יסר this way.[82] Josephus, however, interprets it as a verbal warning,[83] an explanation advocated by other ancient commentators (LXX; Onkelos; Pseudo-Jonathan). He therefore invents a dialogue between the son and his parents, in which they explain to him all they have done for him and attempt to convince him to repent. Josephus' embellishment fills in details that help the reader grasp the spirit of the biblical law.

What is the meaning of סורר ומורה? This phrase is usually understood as a hendiadys, and this appears to be how Josephus understands it as well. He describes the sin of the wayward son by essentially saying the same thing twice, 'young men disdain their parents and do not grant them their honor'. Moreover, Josephus' understanding seems to be in line with modern interpretations as connoting the violation of duties toward one's parents.[84] Contrary to the rabbinic approach, Josephus does not feel the need to mention specific violations committed by the son, such as stealing from his parents (*m. Sanh.* 8.3; *b. Sanh.* 71a).

The phrase זולל וסובא, which describes the son's actions, is enigmatic. It is most commonly understood as a related pair of terms, 'glutton and drunkard'. The LXX translates it as συμβολοκοπῶν οἰνοφλυγεῖ, 'being disposed to feasting, he is a drunkard'. The word זולל is not translated in the LXX, presumably because it was not understood. Josephus omits this pair of words from his rewriting, possibly due to his inability to decipher their meaning. Alternatively, he may have considered them synonymous with סורר ומורה. Another possibility is that Josephus may have been aware of the phrase's meaning but chose to focus on what he considered the main offense: a child disrespecting his or her parents.

The rabbis take a completely different approach. They offer very specific interpretations for each term. A glutton is considered one who consumes semi-cooked meat, while a drunkard drinks partially mixed wine, among other voracious tendencies (*m. Sanh.* 8.2). Moreover, for the rabbis, these details are crucial; if the boy does not fit the exact definitions of glutton and drunkard, he cannot be executed! These different approaches relate to a broader legal issue. The rabbinic Sages took great pains to render this law inapplicable and absurd so that it could never be applied in practice. Josephus, however, treats this law like any other, and he gives the reader no reason to think that such cases never resulted in execution.

---

82. See Bellefontaine 1979.
83. The LXX translates similarly παιδεύσωσιν, 'educate'. Targum Onkelos and Pseudo-Jonathan also translate the verb as verbal reproach.
84. See Bellefontaine 1979.

The biblical account of the elders' role in the case of the wayward son lacks significant details; they do not hold a trial or render a verdict. Rather, immediately after the parents testify, the child is stoned to death by the community. Perhaps because of the vague role extended to the elders in the Bible, Josephus cuts them out altogether, instead describing how the parents bring the child directly before 'the masses' for punishment. This is not in line with the rabbinic view that held the court responsible for carrying out the sentence (*m. Sanh.* 8.4).

Some scholars suggest that Josephus wished to point out the similarities between Jewish law and Roman law, where the rule concerning the *patria potestas* (the supreme judicial authority granted to the father of the family) was prevalent.[85] Feldman objects to such an idea:

> As to Josephus' indebtedness to Roman law, Josephus nowhere indicates that he had studied or admired Roman law – modesty is not one of his virtues and, moreover, he did seek to ingratiate himself with the Roman imperial family, at least – and, on the contrary, he insists on the unique excellence of Jewish law (*Ant.* 1.22-23; *Ag. Ap.* 2.163).[86]

In addition, in biblical law, both parents decide whether to bring their son to trial, whereas Roman law awards unilateral authority to the father. An alternative explanation may be that Josephus provides his own interpretation of the law due to his ignorance of rabbinic halakah in this regard. However, Goldenberg argues that Josephus' adaptation reflects prevalent contemporary custom and that severe punishment of rebellious sons is documented in other Second Temple sources.[87] This suggestion is plausible, but I find Goldenberg's theory that Josephus had a written record of the rabbinic sources doubtful.

In regard to the proportion between crime and punishment, Josephus underscores the gravity of the offence by emphasizing that it was not only against the parents but also against God – the 'parent of humanity' – thus justifying the wayward son's harsh sentence.[88] The rabbis make a similar point through a midrashic comparison of verses commanding the honor and fear of parents and those commanding the honor and fear of God (*b. Kid.* 30b). Josephus does not reveal the source of this claim, but

---

85. Weyl 1900; Halbertal 1997: 63–7.
86. Feldman 1989: 417.
87. Goldenberg 1987: 47–8.
88. Cf. the tannaitic sources brought by Goldenberg 1978: 46. See also Burnside 2002: 51 for a similar assertion (without reference to Josephus).

his phrasing of the law in *Against Apion* ('the Law ranks second only to honor to our God') implies that he derives it from the fact that the law of honoring parents follows the laws of worshipping God and keeping God's Sabbath in the Decalogue. Additionally, it is worth noting that this biblical law is less harsh than the Roman equivalent, the *patria potestas*. This rule seems to inform Philo's version of this law (*Spec. Laws* 2.232):

> Fathers have the right to upbraid their children and admonish them severely, and, if they do not submit to threats conveyed in words, to beat and degrade them and put them in bonds. And further, if in the face of this they continue to rebel, and carried away by their incorrigible depravity refuse the yoke, the law permits the parents to extend the punishment to death.

Whereas Philo essentially turns the biblical law into the Roman law, Josephus follows the biblical (and not Roman) description of the offended party, reading 'parents' and not just 'father', implying that both parents have a say in the matter. Moreover, in biblical law, parents are not given a free hand in the execution of their wayward child; they are required to bring him (or her) before the entire town for punishment. This would presumably give the parents an opportunity to consider their actions rather than act in the heat of anger. This implies that a child is an independent human being, whose death should not be taken lightly and who should be given over to public scrutiny. These differences, found in Josephus but not Philo, would have made the biblical law seem more lenient than Roman law in the eyes of Josephus and his contemporaries.

Prohibition on Exposing Corpse after Hanging (Deut. 21.22-23 // Ant. 4.265)

Deuteronomy 21.22-23 instructs that after execution, the body of a sinner should not be exposed beyond sunset and must be buried the same day. These verses raise various difficulties: is hanging intended as a means of punishment or should he be hanged after his death? In addition, the ambiguous phrase קללת אלהים, 'a curse of God', can be understood as 'a curse towards God' or as 'a curse from God'.[89]

---

89. Bernstein 2013: 594 (published originally in 1983). Scholars discuss these verses as reflected in ancient translations, Philo, Josephus, Qumran, rabbinic and Christian literature.

Josephus (*Ant.* 4.265) omits reference to God in his retelling. Instead, he explains the reason for the law as double punishment for a single sin. Chapman[90] thinks that Josephus understands קללת אלהים as blaspheming God, yet it is not clear that Josephus is trying to interpret this difficult phrase.[91]

Chapman[92] notes that whereas Philo associates Deut. 21.22-23 with crucifixion, Josephus was much more reluctant to do so. Josephus refrains from speaking of the Jews as 'hanging' anyone – they merely expose people's bodies for common view before burial. The suspension is clearly post-mortem, given that the person is 'stoned to death'.[93]

Taking and Holding Distrained Property
(Deut. 24.10-13 // Ant. 4.267-70)

The law in Deut. 24.10-13 restricts the lender's freedom to foreclose and hold the borrower's assets.

Josephus (*Ant.* 4.268) rewrites this law as follows:

> If, however, they are shameless with regard to the restoration, one should not walk around the house to take a security deposit before judgment has been rendered concerning this. One should ask for the security deposit outside and the debtor should bring it of himself without contradicting the one who has come to him with the support of the law.

Josephus is in accord with the Mishnah (*B.M.* 9.13: 'and he may not enter his house to take his pledge') in understanding that the law forbids entering into the creditor's house. This is also how Tigay understands it.[94] However, Feldman[95] maintains

---

90. Chapman 2008: 136–7.
91. It seems that Chapman understood Bernstein incorrectly. Bernstein (2013: 597–8) writes 'we have no reason to relate these words in Deuteronomy to the specific crime of blasphemy without the midrashic reading'. Chapman (2008: 137) refers in n. 147 to Bernstein as supporting the view that 'the 'curse of God' construct phrase in Deut. 21.23 had been interpreted by Josephus as 'one who curses God', i.e., as a 'blasphemer'.
92. Chapman 2008: 37.
93. Chapman 2008: 136.
94. Tigay 2016: 603.
95. Feldman 2000: 438 n. 883.

Josephus has understood the biblical statement about pledges (Deut. 24.10) as rendered by the LXX, i.e., 'If your neighbor [already] owes you a debt... you shall not go into his house to take his pledge', whereas the Hebrew says, 'When you make your neighbor a loan...you shall not [at the time when you make the loan] go into his house to fetch his pledge'.

However, Feldman's explanation has no textual basis. The biblical text narrates a situation *after* collecting the debt. It is part of the concern of the law that the creditor has to safeguard the dignity of the debtor.[96] Therefore, in this case Josephus has interpreted the law correctly.

Another issue connected with this law is its similarities with Exod. 22.24-26. These similarities may explain Josephus' omission of Exodus 22 in his rewriting as it may be deemed redundant.

Caring for the Blind (Deut. 27.14; Lev. 19.14 // Ant. 4.276)

Josephus combines the law in Lev. 19.14 with the curse in Deut. 27.18. In both there is a reference to עיור, 'blind'. Commentators through the ages have debated whether this word relates to a person physically disabled or to 'metonyms for all the helpless'.[97] In joining these two references to the blind, Josephus has paved the way toward a multiple understanding of עיור. We should note that a similar technique can be found in Josephus' retelling of the *talio* laws.

Torts (Exod. 24.2; Lev. 24.19; Deut. 19.21 // Ant. 4.277-84)

The law of 'an eye for an eye' (*Lex Talionis* or *talio*) appears three times in the Pentateuch: Exod. 24.2; Lev. 24.19; and Deut. 19.21. Does 'eye for an eye' mean physical punishment, or is the law intended to compensate the victim or his relatives with monetary restitution? Was the injury caused intentionally or accidentally? In order to answer these questions, scholars have compared the biblical laws to parallel laws from the ancient Near East and have also discussed sources from the Apocrypha, Hellenistic-Jewish literature, the New Testament, and rabbinic literature.

In general, the idea underlying the demand for an eye for an eye is to create a symmetry between the injury to the victim and the desire to punish the offender. Josephus rewrites this law in *Ant.* 4.280:

---

96. Tsai 2014: 157.
97. Milgrom 2000: 1401.

> Let one who mutilates someone suffer similarly, being deprived of that which he deprived another, unless the one who had been mutilated should be willing to accept money, since the law gives the one who has suffered the power to assess the suffering that has occurred to him and grants this, unless he chooses to be more embittered.

According to Josephus, the basic meaning of 'an eye for an eye' is bodily punishment: punishing the same organ that caused the offense committed against the human body. This means mutilation in the offender's eye. However, it is also possible to convert the bodily punishment into monetary compensation. The decision whether to receive a monetary fine and the amount of this fine will not be heard by the court but will be part of negotiations between the offender and the victim.

Although Josephus is generally aware of issues of social justice,[98] in this case there is a striking inequality: only the wealthy can buy their lives with money, but the poor do not. In Josephus' writing, there is no distinction between intentional bodily harm and accidental injury, nor does he mention a difference between harming a slave and harming a free person.

Josephus' interpretation of this law deviates from what is stated in the Mishnah (*B.Q.* 8.1). The underlying assumption of the Mishnah is that 'eye for an eye' means financial compensation for the damage. The Bavli (*B.Q.* 83a) asks what is the source of this Mishnah, since money itself is not mentioned in the text. Rabbi Dosthai asks, 'What then will you say where the eye of one was big and the eye of the other little, for how can I in this case apply the principle of eye for an eye?' Thus, it is necessary to understand the punishment as monetary.

Similarly, R. Simeon b. Yohai maintains that 'eye for an eye' means pecuniary compensation:

> You say pecuniary compensation, but perhaps it is not so, but actual retaliation [by putting out an eye] is meant? What then will you say where a blind man put out the eye of another man, or where a cripple cut off the hand of another, or where a lame person broke the leg of another? How can I carry out in this case [the principle of retaliation of] 'eye for an eye', seeing that the Torah says, Ye shall have one manner of law, implying that the manner of law should be the same in all cases?[99]

---

98. Feldman 1993: Chapter 7; Kasher 1996: 553.
99. Translation adopted from Neusner 1975: 65–6.

A number of explanations have been suggested for Josephus' literal interpretation of 'eye for an eye'.[100] A study of the meaning of the biblical verses shows that there is a reasonable likelihood of interpreting the law of *talio* literally, and this possibility also arises according to some of the opinions in rabbinic literature.[101] Having dealt with this in detail, Yael Shemesh presents evidence that the law in the Torah was originally intended for corporal punishment: (1) in the Torah it is not explicitly stated that a person shall pay monetary compensation for the imposition of an injury on his friend; (2) it is difficult to understand Lev. 24.19-20 ('Anyone who maims another shall suffer the same injury in return… the injury inflicted is the injury to be suffered') as a proof of monetary compensation. All of this suggests that Josephus interpreted the law of *talio* not necessarily for apologetic reasons or to please the Romans but in a way that did not contradict the philological analysis of the law.

This interpretive tradition already exists in Philo (*Spec. Laws* 3.181-83, 195). Such a tradition is also found in the Pseudepigrapha, the Apocrypha, the New Testament, and in the Scholion on Megillat *Ta'anit*:

1. *Jub.* 4.31: 'At the conclusion of this jubilee Cain was killed after him in the same year. His house fell on him, and he died inside his house. He was killed by its stones for with a stone he had killed Abele and, by a just punishment, he was killed with a stone.'[102]
2. Wis. 11.16: '…that they might know that by those things through which a man sins, through them he is punished'.[103]
3. Mt. 5.38-42, from the Sermon on the Mount: 'You have heard that it was said, "An eye for an eye and a tooth for a tooth". But I say to you, do not resist an evildoer. But if anyone strikes you on the right cheek, turn the other also; and if anyone wants to sue you and take your coat, give your cloak as well; and if anyone forces you to go one mile, go also the second mile. Give to everyone who begs from you, and do not refuse anyone who wants to borrow from you.'
4. According to the Scholion for Megillat *Ta'anit* (in the Oxford manuscript), the Boethusians interpreted the rule of 'eye for an eye' literally.[104]

---

100. See Avioz 2009.
101. Amram 1911–12; Regev 2005: 118–19.
102. VanderKam 2018.
103. Winston 1979: 230.
104. Noam 2003: 78–9.

Building a Parapet on the Roof (Deut. 22.8 // Ant. 4.284)

Deuteronomy 22.8 provides instruction for the building of parapets on the roofs of houses. Josephus, like Philo (*Spec. Laws* 3.27.148-49) and the rabbis (*b. B. Qam.* 15b), combines the two laws concerning wells and battlements that appear separately in the Bible (Exod. 21.33; Deut. 22.8). This is a reasonable interpretation, since there is some resemblance between these laws. They both emphasize the responsibility (and culpability) of the owners for the fate of other people who might be injured.[105]

Timely Payment of Wages (Deut. 24.14-15 // Ant. 4.288)

Deuteronomy 24.14-15 contains the law of the hireling, prohibiting the oppression of a day laborer and requiring compensation of a laborer on the day of work. Josephus omits reference to והיה בך חטא, which connotes punishment. In his retelling, Josephus emphasizes that God is not satisfied with such behavior ('we know that God has given this to him in place of land and the other possessions'; 'God does not wish that the one who has worked should lack the enjoyment of the things for which he labored') and that the sinner should be hated.

Josephus omits the word גר ('alien') from his rewriting here and elsewhere in *Antiquities* 1–4. Nor does he use the word προσήλυτος in his writings,[106] but refers to foreigners using other terms throughout his corpus.

Preventing Transgenerational Punishment
(Deut. 24.16 // Ant. 4.289)

Deuteronomy 24.16 forbids transgenerational punishment. The sinner is punished according to his or her own sin, regardless of the wrongdoings of his or her ancestors. A fulfillment of this law is found in 2 Kgs 14.6 (//2 Chron. 25.4). However, this law contradicts other biblical sources

---

105. §§277-83, 286-87 were already discussed in the chapter on Exodus.
106. Barclay 2007: 232 n. 447. Josephus refers to *gerim* in various ways, such as 'those who wish to come and live under the same laws' (θέλουσιν ὑπὸ τοὺς αὐτοὺς ἡμῖν νόμους ζῆν; *Ag. Ap.* 2.210); *Ant.* 3.318 (οὐ νομιζομένων); 13.257-58, 318-19; 15.254-55; 18.82; 20.17 (εἰς τὰ Ἰουδαίων ἔθη); *Life* 149 (θέλοντας εἰς τὰ παρ' αὐτοῖς ἔθη). In the MT of Deuteronomy, *ger* appears in 1.16; 5.13; 10.18-19; 14.21, 29; 16.11, 14; 23.8; 24.14, 17, 19-21; 26.11-13; 27.19; 28.43; 29.10; 31.12.
Philo mentions the gerim in *Spec. Laws* 1.9.52; *Virt.* 20.102-103.

where collective punishment is implemented: Exod. 20.5-6 (// Deut. 5.9); Josh. 7.24-25; and 2 Sam. 21.8-9. Josephus omits Exod. 20.5, retelling the other biblical narratives in Joshua (*Ant.* 5.33-44), Samuel, and Kings.[107] It appears that Josephus was aware of the distinction between civil law, in which each person shall be judged according to his or her deeds, and divine law, in which a collective punishment can be inflicted upon the people. Indeed, he understands the narratives in Joshua and Samuel as sins against God, while Deuteronomy and Kings are interpreted as referring to civil law.

As for the second part of the law, Josephus believes parents should not be punished for their children's deeds, since 'young people, in their contempt for being taught, permit themselves many things contrary to our instruction'.[108]

Finally, Josephus softens the death penalty and speaks generally on punishment.

Castration (Deut. 23.2 // Ant. *4.290-91)*

It is unclear whether the prohibition in Deut. 23.2 applies to all those who have these defects, or only to those who voluntarily carry them out. Voluntary castration was practiced in the ancient Near East for various purposes; at least some royal officials were indeed eunuchs in the full sense of the word. We know nothing about the frequency of castration in Israel where officials were also sometimes called eunuchs (e.g., in 1 Sam. 15.15), but there is no certainty that it was always referring to true eunuchs. Why was it prohibited? Josephus connects it to the inability of the eunuch (γάλλος) to bear children (*Ant.* 4.290). Since castration disqualifies priests from the work of the Temple (Lev. 21.21) and forbids such animals from going up to the altar as a sacrifice (vv. 22-24), this practice was considered to be unfitting for the sanctity required of Israel.

While biblical law goes into graphic details of crushed genitals, Josephus refers to eunuchs instead. Josephus linked the taboo on eunuchs with a ban on castrating men or animals, and a similar double ban is articulated in *Hypoth.* 7.7 (cf. *b. Sabb.* 110b). In *Ant.* 10.186, he reports that Nebuchadnezzar castrated Daniel. The harsh language of Josephus in viewing eunuchs as monsters, nonhumans, or a third type of human being

---

107. On Joshua, see Begg 2004; on Samuel, see Avioz 2015: 148–51; on 2 Kgs 14 in Josephus, see Begg 2000: 227. Cf. Philo, *Spec. Laws* 3.164-68.

108. On children in Josephus' writings, see Reinhartz and Shier 2012; Bons 2012–2013. In *Against Apion* the obedience of children figured prominently.

was shared by others as well.[109] Leviticus 22.24 could be read as banning not only the sacrifice of animals with crushed or missing testicles, but also the infliction of such damage upon them.

Laws of Warfare (Deut. 20–21; 23.10-15; 24.5 // Ant. 4.296-300)

Laws of warfare appear in Deut. 20–21, 23.10-15, and 24.5. In ch. 20 there are three laws concerning war: preparing the army for battle (vv. 1-9), treatment of the conquered enemy (10-18), and the treatment of trees in the vicinity of besieged cities (19-20).

As for preparing the army for battle (Deut. 20.1-9), Josephus summarizes the laws of those exempt from military service and inserts slight changes (*Ant.* 4.298).[110] He adds that the reason for the exemption of those who 'are betrothed and those who have recently married' is because 'through longing for these things they do not spare their lives and, preserving themselves so as to enjoy these, play the coward deliberately on account of their wives'.

Josephus (*Ant.* 4.296) then rewrites the law in Deut. 20.10 as follows:

> When you are about to go to war, send an embassy and heralds to those going to war against you deliberately. For before taking up arms it is right to carry on discussions with them, revealing that though you have a large army and horses and weapons and, above all, have God who is benevolent and an ally; nevertheless, you do not think it right to be forced to go to war with them, and by removing what is theirs to obtain in addition undesired gain for yourselves.

While the rabbis (*m. Sanh.* 1.1; *Sifre* Deut. 190) classify wars as either mandatory or voluntary, Josephus does not do so. In his retelling, there is no option for voluntary war. In fact, there is no certainty that this classification was known to the biblical authors.

Feldman explains that Josephus' addition, 'send an embassy and heralds', is based on Josephus' acquaintance with Roman ideals and their methods of warfare.[111] However, that assessment is unnecessary, since a declaration of war sent by messengers is attested in the first millennium BCE in Assyrian and Babylonian sources.[112]

---

109. See, e.g., Herodotus, *Hist.* 8.105-106; Philo, *Spec. Leg.* 1.325; 2.344; *Somn.* 2.184. See Wilson 2015: 120 n. 22.
110. See Feldman 2000: 462 nn. 1020–5.
111. Feldman 1998a: 415; Lincicum 2010: 176.
112. Altman 2012: 168–71.

Deuteronomy 20.19 forbids the cutting down of trees in war. Josephus ascribes a voice to a tree by the comparison in Deut. 20.19 of trees to men. Josephus dramatically supplies the reason why the besiegers cut down the trees, the reason why they should not be cut down, and what the trees would say (cf. Philo, *Spec. Laws* 4.41.226-29). He omits the statement that the rule only applies when the Israelites have been besieging a city for a long time, that the trees are not to be likened to men, and that only non-fruit-bearing trees may be destroyed.

Josephus extends the biblical prohibition to include the burning of the enemy's land and the slaughter of their livestock. The looting of an enemy country without a direct military advantage should be denounced as wanton destruction. In *War* (4.264; 5.523) there is a detailed description of a massive felling of trees.

Cross-Dressing (Deut. 22.5 // Ant. 4.301)

According to Deut. 22.5, a man is not permitted to wear women's clothes and vice versa. What is the rationale behind this law? What does כלי mean? Josephus understands כלי as weapons of war (Cf. Onkelos; *Sifre* Deut. 226). Josephus writes, 'Be especially careful in battles that a woman not wear a man's clothing nor a man wear a woman's garment'. Here, the case is specifically referring to battles (μάχη).

Josephus does not explain the reason for this law, but he refers to it when he describes the zealots who 'unscrupulously indulged in effeminate practices, plaiting their hair and attiring themselves in women's apparel, drenching themselves with perfumes, and painting their eyelids to enhance their beauty' (*War* 4.561). This is part of excess and luxury.[113] Gender boundaries should be kept according to Josephus. In addition, cross-dressing is expanded to prohibit other behaviors associated with women.[114]

Eradicating Amalek (Exod. 17.8-16; Deut. 25.17 // Ant. 4.304)

Exodus 17.8-16 and Deut. 25.17-19 refer to the encounter between Israel and the Amalekites. Exodus 17 is a blend of law and narrative, while Deuteronomy 25 contains legal details only. Josephus relocates the law of eradicating Amalek in Deuteronomy 25 to just before Deuteronomy 31:

---

113. See Wilson 2015: 46.
114. See the review of Jewish sources in Liebman 2002.

And he exhorted the people, after conquering the land and settling there, not to forget the insolence of the Amalekites, but to undertake a military expedition against them and to avenge themselves for the wrong they did to them when they happened to be in the desert.

This short reference to the Amalekites builds on an earlier longer reference of Josephus (*Ant.* 3.39-61).[115] Johann Maier understood Josephus' retelling as an attempt 'to avoid the impression of an existing linkage between Esau's grandson Amalek and Rome', and to identify the Amalekites with an actual enemy of the latter, thus transferring 'the emotional aspects of the hostility between Israel and Amalek to the relationship between Romans and Arabs'. Amalek, according to Maier, was thus presented by Josephus primarily for political reasons – as 'an enemy common to Rome and Israel'.

Apostasy (Deut. 13 // Ant. 4.310)

In Deuteronomy 13 there are three laws dealing with apostasy. The first two refer to incitement to worship other gods that originates with a false prophet (Deut. 13.2-6) or via a family member, spouse, or close friend (13.7-12). The third deals with the apostasy of an entire city. This third law requires that the entire population of the city, together with its cattle and property, be destroyed (13.13-18).

While in the biblical law, idolatry is the sin, Josephus omits any sign of idolatry and only speaks generally of τῶν νόμων – the laws. This law was relocated from Deuteronomy 13 and embedded here as a conclusion to Deuteronomy, where Moses puts great emphasis on keeping the laws. Its transposition seems to reflect a Josephan apologetic, downplaying idolatry and emphasizing the significance of keeping the laws.

Conclusion

The book of Deuteronomy occupies an important place in Josephus' rewriting of the laws. Being the last speech of Moses, it foreshadows the history of Israel in the post-Moses era. Josephus reflects on many central issues of Deuteronomy, such as monotheism, devotion to God, and humanitarian values. Idolatry was left aside due to apologetic reasons.

---

115. Other references to Amalek in Josephus are found in *Ant.* 1.174; 2.5-6; 5.210; 6.129, 131-55, 323, 336, 356-67, 371-72; 7.1-6; 9.188-98; 11.209, 211, 277. See Feldman 2008.

As was the case with the laws in Exodus, Leviticus, and Numbers, in this chapter we saw that Josephus adheres to the MT and rewrites most of its laws; his understanding of many biblical laws is quite reasonable. There are cases in which he accords with the later halakha and cases where he deviates from it, but that was not my focus. I attempted to point to Josephus' careful reading of the laws, and how he takes great effort to make them more uniform and comprehensible.

5

JUXTAPOSITION IN JOSEPHUS' REWRITING OF THE LAWS

One of the most vexing problems related to biblical laws is the sequence and arrangement of each law.[1] The biblical texts do not always clarify the connection between the laws and initially they may seem unrelated. Moreover, narrative and laws appear sometimes side by side and the difficulty of understanding the logic of their sequence is even greater. The biblical authors and redactors employ various devices to connect certain scenes or compositions, such as association, key words, and others. Cassuto[2] focused on association as a motivation for juxtaposition, noting that laws were grouped together by associated words or expressions (and sometimes ideas).

Scholars usually refer to the rabbis as the first to discern various connections between laws and narratives. It is commonly called *semukhin* or *smikhut parshiot*. They assume that there exists a meaningful relation between the close units.[3]

However, prior to the rabbis, Josephus, though not using terms of juxtaposition directly, utilized several techniques throughout his works to juxtapose laws and narratives that may seem unrelated. Thorough research on this topic was undertaken by Gallant.[4]

Gallant shows how Josephus transferred material from one biblical law to another and treated one law as analogous to another to which it is juxtaposed, either in Scripture or in Josephus' arrangement of the laws. Josephus used wordplay to draw out implicit linguistic connections

---

1. See Shinan and Zakovitch 2015; Gottlieb 2009; Gilmour 2015.
2. Cassuto 1973.
3. Gilmour 2015: 13.
4. Gallant 1988.

between different laws. Gallant's explanations are not always persuasive.[5] Likewise, Gallant does not delve into the principles behind the biblical laws themselves to examine whether Josephus was innovative or correct in his juxtaposing of various laws.

Below I will present my understanding of Josephus' use of juxtaposition as an exegetical tool.

The so-called Covenant Code in Exodus 21–23 starts with: 'These are the ordinances that you shall set before them' (Exod. 21.1). There are no connecting words between the Ten Commandments, mentioned earlier, and the subsequent laws. Josephus clarifies the connection with his own addition:

> The multitude, having heard from God Himself concerning the things Moyses had discussed, rejoicing in what had been said previously, separated themselves from the assembly. On the following days, however, resorting frequently to his Tent, they asked him also to bring them laws from God. (*Ant.* 3.93)

Josephus transferred most of the laws in Exodus 21–23 to his writing of the laws of Deuteronomy (esp. *Ant.* 4.271-87). The reason may be that the Exodus laws seemed more fitting in the πολιτεία ('constitution') present in Deuteronomy (*Ant.* 4.184, 194, 302-304; *Ag. Ap.* 2.145-296). Josephus created a smoother transition from the Sinai revelation to the tabernacle laws (*Ant.* 3.100-218).[6]

One of the chronological problems in the book of Numbers is the displacement between Num. 1.1 and 9.1. While Num. 1.1 begins 'on the first day of the second month, in the second year after they had come out of the land of Egypt', Num. 9.1 dates to the 'first month of the second year after they had come out of the land of Egypt'. This discrepancy was already noticed by the rabbis (*Sifre* Num. 64). In order to avoid this displacement, Josephus does not mention the dates in these narratives.

Josephus places the law of *sotah* (Num. 5.11-31) within a series of provisions relating to women,[7] where it appears immediately after instruc-

---

5. Feldman (2000; 2006: 361–411) follows Gallant in many of his comments on Josephus' placement of the laws.

6. The word πολιτεία has several meanings: Jewish people's form of government (*Ant.* 4.223; 6.35, 44, 83, 268); the whole order of life that God gave to Moses (*Ant.* 3.84, 322; 4.191, 195, 196, 310); laws that relate to communal affairs and relations between people (*Ant.* 4.198; cf. *Ant.* 4.230, 292, 302). See Cowan 2019: 81.

7. For a different opinion, see Gallant 1988: 13: 'the meal offering and rituals to which the woman is subjected are presented in succession, without any intermingling.

tions for a mother who has just given birth (Lev. 12), after which he describes the punishment for adultery (from Lev. 20.10). This thematic arrangement contrasts with that of the rabbinic sages, who connect the *sotah* law with that of the Nazirite, by means of word association: both laws contain the root פרע, and therefore 'anyone who sees a *sotah* in her [state of disgrace] should separate himself from wine [by vowing to become a Nazirite]' (*b. Sot.* 2a).

Josephus transferred the law of the red heifer from Numbers 19 to his rewriting of the purity laws (Lev. 12–15; *Ant.* 3.261-69). The reason for this transposition may be that in its original location it interrupts the wilderness narrative, and therefore joining it with other impurity laws may be more fitting.[8] The second time he mentions the red heifer (*Ant.* 4.79-81) he connects this story with the death of Miriam related in Numbers 20 (cf. *b. Mo'ed Qat.* 28a).

The laws of the cities of refuge in Numbers 35 are also disconnected from the rest of the book. By placing these laws within his retelling of Deuteronomy 4, Josephus gives them a more appropriate context, since Deuteronomy 4 deals with the distribution of asylum cities in the Transjordan.

How are the laws in Deuteronomy 21 connected? Rashi, following the Midrash *Tanchuma*, explains the connection between the three main laws found in Deut. 21.10-23 (the captive woman, the son of the hated wife, and the wayward son) as follows (21.11):

> 'You may take her [= a beautiful woman from the enemy camp] for yourself as a wife'. – The Torah is speaking only against the evil inclination... But if he marries her, he will ultimately come to despise her, as it says after this, 'If a man has [two wives-one beloved and the other despised]' (v. 15); [moreover] he will ultimately father through her a wayward and rebellious son (see v. 18). For this reason, these passages are juxtaposed.

Josephus was likely influenced by the law of the eldest son born to the man's hated wife that immediately follows the law of the wayward son;

To highlight the topical transition from one category to the next, Josephus begins his discussion of the second category with an accusative-first sentence, "as for the woman"...(3.270).'

8. There are indeed some similarities between theses chapters. Cf. Num. 19.6 and Lev. 14.4, 6, where cedar, hyssop and scarlet thread appear. Likewise, compare the sprinkling in Lev. 14.7, 16, 27, 51, and Num. 19.4, 18, 19, 21. Feldman (2006: 397–8) refers only to the connection with Miriam but disregards the connection between Lev. 13–14 and Num. 19.

this may explain part of the parents' speech which Josephus writes. The claim of the parents that 'they did not come together for pleasure' may reflect the knowledge that this may be the child of a 'despised' wife and not a 'loved' wife.

Juxtaposition also explains the final difference between Josephus and the biblical text. The legal section following that of the wayward son concerns the proper disposal of bodies (21.22-23): 'If a man is guilty of a capital offense and is put to death, and you impale him on a stake, you must not let his corpse remain on the stake overnight, but must bury him the same day. For an impaled body is an affront to God: you shall not defile the land that YHWH your God is giving you to possess.' The Torah has the law of the corpse as an independent law; ostensibly, it would apply to the wayward son and any other executed criminal. Josephus, however, incorporates it into the passage about the wayward son, telling readers that despite the child's sinful behavior, no bodies may be left overnight according to Jewish practice. Apparently, Josephus believed that the juxtaposition of the two laws was meant to tell the reader to apply the law specifically to the case of the wayward son as a paradigm for all others.

In conclusion, Josephus does not use rabbinic terminology to connect different laws, but he is aware of the phenomenon and makes various attempts to solve it. Though we cannot always understand why he transposed laws or juxtaposed them, in several cases we can detect exegetical awareness that can be logically justified.

6

Reasons for the Commandments in Josephus' Writings

The subject of Ta'amei ha-Mitzvot (the reasons for the commandments) was mainly dealt with by the medieval Jewish philosophers, as one can see in Isaac Heinemann's important book on this topic.[1] Some of the explanations for the rationale behind the commandments are explicitly stated in the Torah, while most of them are not explained at all.

Heinemann mentions two motivations for focusing on this topic: (1) the belief in the authority of the legislator, and (2) the belief in the value of the commandments. We may add another one: 'to know how to respond to a heretic' (*m. Abot* 2.14), a strategy of silencing objections and criticisms against Judaism. It may also simply derive from independent, self-evident study.

In this chapter I will reexamine Heinemann's conclusions with regard to Josephus' discussion of the reasons for the commandments. I will try to show Josephus' indebtedness to the plain meaning of the text as part of his exegetical motivation *vis-à-vis* his assumed apologetic motivation.[2]

Josephus informs his readers that he intended to write a book about the reasons for the commandments, but he did not succeed (*Ant.* 1.29):[3]

---

1. See Heinemann 2008. See also Hayes 2015. Josephus is mentioned once in her book, and only in passing.
2. Schiffman (2018: 70) mentions the following options for Josephus' rationale: 'While some of the rationales do indeed fit with the polemical purposes of Josephus, it appears that most are simply drawn from the common Judaism of the time or represent rationales fitting with Josephus's notion of Moses as a kind of philosopher king whose legislation was totally wise and just'. He does not consider the possibility that Josephus' rationales are based on a good grasp of Scripture.
3. Cf. 1.25, 214; 3.94, 143, 205, 218, 230, 257, 259; 4.198, 302; 15.371; 20.268; *Ag. Ap.* 1.92. See Altshuler 1978–79.

And this would be the first day, but Moyses called it one day. I am capable of giving the reason even now, but since I have promised to give an account of the reasons for everything in a separate work, I am postponing to that time also the explanation concerning this.

Despite the fact that such a treatise was not eventually written, one can find such explanations throughout his works. Josephus does not supply a rationale for each law, and we do not know why he did it for specific laws and not for others.

A preliminary study of the subject is found in Heinemann's famous book on the reasons for the commandments. He brings Philo and Josephus to stress the autonomous-based reasons for observing the mitzvot, in contrast to the heteronomous reasons given by the rabbis.

Heinemann distinguishes between three types of explanations of the commandments:

1. The apologetic motive – the need to defend Judaism against charges by non-Jews.
2. The rational motive – the religious-theoretical need to understand the commandments and to demonstrate that God's commandments are just and useful.
3. The practical-religious motive – 'The educational value of the mitzvot will be diminished if we fulfill them only to discharge our obligation and earn our future reward; it will be enhanced to the extent that the intentions of the Torah, both explicit and hidden, will find an echo in our souls'.[4]

In the fourth chapter of Heinemann's book, the framework for the discussion of 'Hellenistic Jews' is set out and Philo and Josephus are placed in the first category, i.e., apologetic explanations. He does not regard Josephus as an interpreter; this claim is explicitly made in his article on Josephus: 'Josephus did not come to interpret the Bible before the public, but rather to present a substitute for it to people who do not need it at all'.[5]

It is evident that his attitude towards the 'Hellenistic Jews' is quite negative. In general, Heinemann's discussion of Josephus' explanations is hard to accept due to several reasons.

---

4. Heinemann 2008: 4.
5. Heinemann 1940.

First, Heinemann binds together Philo, Josephus and other contemporary compositions. He does not pay any attention to the generic differences between these sources and the aims of each. Thus, for example, the very extensive rewriting of the Ten Commandments by Philo, the philosopher, contrasts sharply with Josephus' meager rewriting of these commands; Josephus dedicates to the Ten Commandments one sentence in total.

Second, Heinemann does not distinguish between the various works of Josephus. While *Against Apion* is defined by many as an apologetic composition,[6] the same does not necessarily hold for *Antiquities*. *Antiquities* is defined by some scholars as 'rewritten Bible'. The main disadvantage of this approach is that it does not let the sources speak for themselves but rather imposes models on them.

One should not be prejudiced with regard to Josephus. The rationale he gives for certain commandments may well accord with the plain sense of the Bible. Scholars should compare what Josephus designates as the rationale of the commandments with what modern scholars write. Heinemann, however, assumes that Josephus should conform to the model of Hellenistic thought, and as a result his own interpretation becomes secondary. This is because in Heinemann's view medieval thought has the best answers, whereas Hellenistic thinking is seen as inferior.

Josephus – Between Interpretation and Apologetics

In analyzing the motives for the changes introduced by Josephus to the biblical text, we should distinguish between interpretive motives and apologetic motives. The distinction is not always easy to make, but it is possible in many cases. Gallant[7] offers the following approach. Before accepting a Josephan passage as a testimony to the history of his time, it is asked whether the passage is intended to justify Josephus' military conduct; to cast the Jewish people and their religion in a favorable light in the eyes of a Hellenistic audience; to refute detractors of Josephus and his people; or to please his Roman patrons. When we do not identify an attempt by Josephus to defend himself or his people, it is clear that the motive is interpretive.

On the one hand, the omission of the story of the golden calf (Exod. 32–34) and the omission of stories that relate to leprosy (i.e. Moses, Exod. 4.6; Miriam, Num. 12) may be influenced by apologetic motives. On the other hand, when we compare Josephus' explanations for the reasons of

---

6. See, e.g., *Ag. Ap.* 2.171-74.
7. Gallant 1988: 3. For a summary of Gallant's view, see Pearce 2013: 39.

the commandments to those of commentators and scholars through the ages that have not been defined as apologetics, then this may point to interpretive motives.

The Sabbath Law

In *Ag. Ap.* 2.20-27 Josephus rejects the absurd explanation given by Apion for the Sabbath. Josephus' own explanation (2.27) is: 'According to the language of Judeans, *sabbaton* means rest from all work'. However, in *Ant.* 1.33 he writes:

> Moyses says that the universe and all the things in it came into being in six days in all and that on the seventh day He ceased and took a rest from his activities, whence we also on this day take leisure from our activities, calling it the Sabbath. This word means 'rest' in the language of the Hebrews.

There is not a hint of apologetic in this explanation and it is quite reasonable. Scholars call it *imitatio dei*.[8] There is no dispute that the law in Deuteronomy has a social reason. Deuteronomy 5.14 says: 'your male and female slave may rest as well as you'.

The Law of Shemittah

The law of the sabbatical year appears in Exodus, Leviticus, and Deuteronomy. The rationale is not given in every source. Heinemann writes in this regard: 'Even more than Josephus, Philo emphasizes the ethical and social character of the Torah's commandments'.[9] Let us see what Josephus says of the Shemittah. Josephus (*Ant.* 3.281) writes:

> In the seventh year he grants respite to the land from the plough and from planting, just as he commanded them a cessation on the seventh day from labors. The enjoyment of those [products] brought forth of their own accord from the soil is to be for those who wish it, both compatriots and foreigners, nothing being withheld from them. And he also ordained that this be done after the seventh week of years.

Josephus points out the need for the land to rest or for a 'periodic fallowness of agricultural land'.[10] Tsevat[11] also claims that implied in this

---

8. See Davies 1999.
9. Heinemann 2008: 43.
10. Milgrom 2001: 2153.
11. Tsevat 1970.

law is the assertion that all the inhabitants of the land are equal before God.

At first glance it may appear that Josephus is being apologetic by focusing on the social aspect of the sabbatical year laws. Yet, a similar explanation is also found in Maimonides:

> As to the precepts enumerated in the laws concerning the year of release and the jubilee some of them imply sympathy with our fellow-men, and promote the well-being of mankind; for in reference to these Precepts it is stated in the Law, 'That the poor of thy people may eat' (Exod. 23.11); and besides, the land will also increase its produce and improve when it remains fallow for some time. Other precepts of this class prescribe kindness to servants and to the poor, by renouncing any claims to debts [in the year of release] and relieving the slaves of their bondage [in the seventh year].[12]

As in Josephus' first part, Maimonides offers an agricultural rationale: the sabbatical year is essential for the land to renew its strength. This shows that Heinemann's placing of Josephus in 'the Hellenistic Jews' group and Maimonides' placement among the medieval thinkers is artificial; they have similar points of view with regard to the Sabbatical year.

Keun[13] notes independently that the sabbatical year is closely related to the idea of the Sabbath. The ideas of freedom and equality of human beings before God are among the basic motifs of the Sabbath, for on the Sabbath every human being is called to rest from the burden of work. Finally, the concept of social equity is echoed by Kochman.[14] He writes that the sabbatical year is meant to place God's creatures in an equal starting position.

The Law for Interest on Loans

The law of loans on interest is mentioned in Exod. 22.24, Lev. 25.1, and Deut. 23.20-21. In these biblical sources, there is no explanation for the prohibition of charging interest. Josephus explains its rationale as follows:

> Let it not be permitted to lend either meat or drink to any one of the Hebrews at interest, for it is not just to profit from the misfortunes of one's compatriot; but in helping his needs you should consider as a gain the gratitude of those men and the reward that will come from God for this generosity. (*Ant.* 4.266)

---

12. Maimonides, *Guide*, part III, ch. 39, 340.
13. Keun 1993: 168–9.
14. Kochman 1987: 182.

What is the origin of this explanation? In Gallant's opinion,[15] meat and drink were mentioned here under the influence of the law of the rebellious son in Deut. 21.20. Goldenberg[16] claims that Josephus substituted money for food and drink because these are the things that were customary to offer a person in distress rather than money. Goldenberg's opinion is more convincing then Gallant's, since the connection to the law of the rebellious son is very weak. Nevertheless, Josephus' explanation that the giver profited socially by expressions of thanks directed to him and also by reward from God accords well with Ezek. 18.8, 17; Pss. 15.5, 37.26, and 112.5.[17]

*Tefillin (*Ant. *4.213)*

The law of tefillin (phylacteries) appears in Exod. 13.9, 16, Deut. 6.8, and 11.18. Josephus explains the rationale behind this law:

> And as many things as we are able to show forth the power of God and His goodwill toward them let them display on the head and the arm, so that the favor of God with regard to them may be readily visible from all sides.

The meaning Josephus ascribes to tefillin seems quite reasonable. As Tigay explains: 'This means that you have to remember well the great deeds of the Lord'.[18] Though Josephus did not elaborate the halakhic details of tefillin, he has offered a rationale that was followed by modern scholars.

Pledge (Deut. 24.10-13 // Ant. *4.267-70)*

The biblical law in Deut. 24.10-13 states: 'When you make your neighbor a loan of any kind, you shall not go into the house to take the pledge. You shall wait outside, while the person to whom you are making the loan brings the pledge out to you. If the person is poor, you shall not sleep in the garment given you as the pledge. You shall give the pledge back by sunset, so that your neighbor may sleep in the cloak and bless you; and it will be to your credit before the Lord your God'.

Josephus rewrites this law as follows (*Ant.* 4.267-70):

---

15. Gallant 1988: 243.
16. Goldenberg 1978: 83–4.
17. See Tigay 2016: 2:586, who accepts Josephus' explanation for this law.
18. Tigay 2016: 2:279.

> Let those who have received some things, whether of silver or of fruits, moist or dry, if matters have gone according to their plan through God's blessing, bring them with pleasure and give them back to those who have given them, as restoring them to their own place; they might have them again if they needed them. If, however, they are shameless with regard to the restoration, one should not walk around the house to take a security deposit before judgment has been rendered concerning this. One should ask for the security deposit outside and the debtor should bring it of himself without contradicting the one who has come to him with the support of the law. If the one from whom a deposit has been taken is wealthy, let the creditor hold on to it [the deposit] until the repayment; but if he is poor, let him return it before the setting of the sun, especially if the deposit is a coat, in order that he may have it for his sleep, since God by nature dispenses pity to those who are poor. *But it is not permitted to take as a deposit a hand-mill and the utensils connected with it,* in order that they may not be deprived of the implements for preparing food nor be subjected to some worse sufferings through lack of food.

Josephus' explanation that 'it is not permitted to take as a deposit a hand-mill and the utensils connected with it' (*Ant.* 4.270) appears also in the Aramaic targums, in Philo, and in tannaitic literature.[19] Josephus' addition of 'subjected to some worse sufferings through lack of food' is mentioned also by modern interpreters, who point out that this creates pressure on the borrower, which causes him distress.[20]

Kilayim (Mixed Species)

The laws of Kilayim appear in Lev. 19.19 and Deut. 22.9-11. Forbidden combinations are: agricultural hybrids, plowing with an ox and donkey simultaneously, and shaatnez, a mixing of wool and linen. The rationale behind these laws is unclear. Josephus (*Ant.* 4.228) writes that:

> Do not sow the land that is planted with vines, for it is sufficient for it to raise this plant and to be freed from the toils of a plough. Plough the land with oxen, and lead no other animal with them under the yoke, but do the ploughing even with them according to their own kinds. The seeds should be pure and unmixed; and do not sow two or three kinds together, for nature does not rejoice in association of dissimilar things.[21]

---

19. See *m. B. Mes.* 9.13.
20. Tigay 2016: 2:600.
21. On nature in Josephus, see Attridge 1976: 140–3.

In a similar way, the biblical scholar Jacob Licht[22] writes: 'It appears that the combination of both sexes found in nature separately is considered an unnatural act'. Sforno, Rashbam, and Bekhor Shor pursue this explanation in a similar vein.

It is interesting to note that a modern scholar concludes his essay on hybrids in a language very reminiscent of Josephus, even though he does not refer to Josephus: 'Blurring separation and variety may induce a reversal of cosmos to chaos and must be before being invented'.[23] Thus, if contemporary scholars, none of whom are suspected of apologetics, reach the same conclusion as Josephus, Josephus' interpretation of the text may be regarded as legitimate.

Levirate Marriages (Ant. 4.254)

Regarding the law of Levirate marriage in Deut. 25.5-6, Josephus adds a utilitarian rationale:[24] 'This will be of advantage to the community if houses do not disappear and the possessions remain with the kinsmen; and it will bring to the women, as they live with those nearest to their former husbands, an alleviation of their suffering'.

Josephus here introduces two rationales for this law. First, it provides for orderly transmission of property and maintenance of 'houses', that is, clans within the tribe. Second, it provides the unfortunate widow both with material support and with a husband who would in many ways resemble her first husband.[25] Altshuler[26] labels Josephus' explanation as apology, but this is unnecessary, since 'societal benefits' are not a real criteria for deciding whether an interpreter is apologetic or not.

Josephus articulated this aim of the law as many modern commentators do, namely, that one of the primary purposes of the law of levirate marriage is to maintain the property of the deceased brother within the family.[27]

---

22. Licht 1971.
23. Houtman 1984.
24. Schiffman 2018.
25. Satlow (2001: 186) argues that Josephus' explanation translates 'the biblical levirate marriage into the Greek *epiklerate*. In this Greek institution, if a man dies without sons, his nearest male relative "inherits" both his widow and his property.' However, if my intrinsic explanation is acceptable, Satlow's explanation is unnecessary.
26. Altshuler 1982–83: 4.
27. Pressler 1993: 69.

Conclusion

Scholars assume that Josephus is apologetic and therefore forego his testimony in halakhic and interpretive discussions. This study has shown that such an assumption is unnecessary. Although there is no denying the existence of apologetic elements in the writings of Josephus, one should not eschew an individual analysis of each and every case. The aforementioned generalization, which is a shortcoming of these scholars' works, must be abandoned. If there is no particular distinctiveness in the interpretations of Josephus, and other writers, contemporary or later, have also reached similar conclusions, this would greatly weaken the apologetic explanation.

Josephus described the reasons for the commandments in a way that is not allegorical as in Philo, and this applies to his approach to all the commandments. And yet, in those places where he explained the reasons for the mitzvot, he was followed by later generations, albeit he is not always credited for his original interpretations.

7

Josephus' Perspective on Defining Moses as a Lawgiver or Mediator

Moses plays two distinct roles in the Pentateuch. He is, on the one hand, presented as a mediator,[1] relaying messages from God to Israel (Deut. 5.5) and vice-versa. His intervention involved transmitting laws, covenant making, and interceding with God on behalf of Israel. Moses is unique in the frequency of his contact with God and in the multiplicity of messages he delivered. His communion is defined as 'face to face' (Exod. 33.11; cf. Num. 12.8), i.e., in direct revelation. His absence during the golden calf narrative (Exod. 32–34) was so acute that it led the people into sin. Israel turned to Moses for divine instruction in Exod. 18.13-27, Leviticus 24, and Numbers 9, 14, and 27.

However, there is another Pentateuchal outlook that tries to minimize Moses' stance as a mediator. In Exod. 19.19 there is a distinction drawn between the words of God and the words of Moses. In addition, during the Sinai theophany Aaron joins Moses (Exod. 19.24) and in the climax of the scene God gives the Ten Commandments directly to Israel; Moses stays at the bottom of the mountain with the people. In this view, Moses is not giving the people the commandments, but rather is presented as part of the Israelites.[2]

In this chapter, I will present Josephus' view on the role of Moses as mediator or lawgiver, based on his presentation of Moses in *Antiquities* 2–4. But I will first offer a brief survey of Second Temple literature in this regard.[3]

---

1. In Biblical Hebrew there is no term for mediator.
2. See Coats 1988; H. Cohen 2010.
3. See Hafemann 1990; VanderKam and Boesenberg 2013; Boesenberg 2013.

Texts from the Second Temple period reveal a complex picture of the ways in which Moses' role was conceived. Some apocryphal, pseudepigraphical, and Jewish-Hellenistic texts (*Jubilees*;[4] Baruch;[5] Maccabees;[6] *Testament of Moses*;[7] Ben Sira[8]; *4 Ezra*;[9] Pseudo-Philo's *LAB*[10]) emphasize Moses as mediator. Lierman[11] shows that the New Testament splits into two main streams, one of which saw Moses principally as a transmitter of the Law, and the other as its creator. The rabbis (*y. Meg.* 74d; *Exod. Rab.* 3.6) view Moses as a mediator as well.[12] They cannot relate the title 'lawgiver' to Moses since in their eyes it is unique to God only.

However, in other texts Moses is presented as a lawgiver. Aristobulus refers to Moses as 'our lawgiver' (8.10.4)[13] and the same direction can be found in Philo (*Mos.* 2.3). Eupolemus writes that Moses first wrote laws for the Jews (*Praep. ev.* 9.26.1). Aristeas follows the same path, describing Moses as νομοθέτης (131, 139, 148, 312).

Philo identifies Moses' role as a lawgiver as part of his prophetic tasks (see *Congr.* 132; *Virt.* 51; *Spec. Laws* 2.104). However, in *Mos.* 2.166 Philo sees Moses as an intermediary: he states that Moses acted as a 'mediator (μεσίτης[14]) and reconciler' between sinful Israel and God. In the Temple Scroll, Moses' status as lawgiver is entirely absent. Indeed, Moses' role as mediator of law is bypassed in order to create an unmediated divine revelation of law.[15]

Turning to Josephus, in some occurrences Josephus seems to present Moses as the lawgiver.[16] In the preface of *Antiquities* (1.18) he refers to 'our lawgiver (νομοθέτης) Moyses'. νομοθέτης appears also in *Ant.* 1.95, 240; 2.6, 18, 20, 23, 24; 3.180, 266, 268, 287, 320; 4.13, 150, 156; *Ag. Ap.* 2.75, 145, 154, 156, 161, 165, 169, 173, 209, 257, 286.[17] In *Ant.* 4.319

4. *Jub.* 1.19, 23.
5. Bar. 1.20; 2.28.
6. 2 Macc. 7.30.
7. *Test. Mos.* 1.14; 3.10-14. See Lierman 2004: 38–9.
8. Ben Sira 45.3, 5.
9. *4 Ezra* 9.30-31; 14.3-6.
10. *LAB* 11.2; 12.4.
11. Lierman 2004: 124–74.
12. Lierman 2004: 50 n. 91. Cf. Hafemann 1990: 88 n. 1.
13. For Moses as lawgiver, see Meeks 1966: 107, 112–13, 130, 132–3, 171–2.
14. This word does not appear in the LXX (aside from Job 9.33). Josephus uses the term in a non-religious context (*Ant.* 7.193; 16.24, 118).
15. Jassen 2007: 61, 234–7.
16. *Ag. Ap.* 2.160. See Kasher 1997: 2:446; Lierman 2004: 124, 136–9; Barclay 2007: 259 n. 620. Feldman 1998a: 374–442; Gager 1972: 25–112.
17. See Feldman 1998a: 98; Spilsbury 1998: 101.

Josephus writes: 'for even a human lawgiver, when his laws are violated and laid down in vain, is a dreadful enemy. Do not put to the test a God who is angry because of laws that are disregarded, which He Himself, who originated them, gave to you.'

In other places, however, Josephus argues for the divine origin of the law: *Ant.* 3.88-101, 222-23, 286; 4.197, 295, 318-19. Though the term μεσίτης does not appear in Josephus with relation to Moses, he is in fact attributing mediation to him in these references.[18]

Conclusion

In this chapter I have dealt with Josephus' view of Moses as a lawgiver and mediator. His position on this issue is ambivalent, as shown from references throughout his works. Josephus' ambivalence is already reflected in the Hebrew Bible and continues in apocryphal, pseudepigraphical, Jewish-Hellenistic texts, the Qumran scrolls, and rabbinic midrashim. Some texts seem to adopt an either/or view, others seem to blend two views, while still others seek to present Moses in unique ways. These two pictures of Moses as lawgiver and mediator continued to be discussed and debated among medieval commentators as well.[19]

---

18. Perhaps the absence of this term in Josephus led Feldman (1998a) to mention only the depiction of Moses as lawgiver in Josephus. The same hold true for VanderKam and Boesenberg 2013: 150–3.

19. See Viezel 2014.

8

Was Josephus Influenced by Roman Law?

In recent years scholars have emphasized that Josephus was a Roman citizen and well-integrated in Roman society.[1] They argue that he was influenced by Roman literature and culture, and is claimed to have intended his books for Roman audiences.[2] Mason notes that the views expressed towards Greek culture in *Life* 40–42 are similar to those found in Roman literature.[3] He observes several characteristically Roman concepts, images, and values assumed in *Antiquities*.[4] Josephus' scorn for Greek ways and the presence of certain literary motifs overlaps with famous Roman accounts.[5] In a second article, Mason demonstrates Josephus' participation in many of the language games current in the elite circles of Flavian Rome. He identifies Josephus' use of figured speech and irony.[6]

Gruen[7] compares Josephus to Polybius. They share similar life experiences and both include criticisms of Rome's brutality. Ward claimed that Josephus' vocabulary and syntax were influenced heavily by Latin.[8]

---

1. See the literature cited in Barclay 2007: 362. Goodman 1994: 335 emphasizes that Josephus might have regarded himself as in some sense Roman. See also Niehoff 2016.
2. Cotton and Eck 2005 argue that there is no positive evidence for any connection between Josephus and the Roman élite. For a different approach, see den Hollander 2014.
3. Mason 2001. Cf. Goodman 1994: 334.
4. Mason 2003: 568.
5. Mason 2003: 589.
6. Mason 2009: 69–102.
7. Gruen 2011.
8. Ward 2007.

More than seventy years ago, Boaz Cohen wrote that Josephus interprets Jewish law in a manner that brings it into harmony with Roman rule.[9] According to Cohen, when there is no biblical or rabbinic source for Josephus' retelling, it must be assigned to Roman influence. He compares Roman and Jewish law in his collection of articles (published in 1966). Some of the laws have direct analogies in rabbinic law (e.g., betrothal, divorce, oath) while others do not. He refers to Josephus only in a few places throughout his works. Cohen's view was preceded by Weyl and has won acceptance among more recent scholars.[10] Jackson has suggested that Josephus' aim in accommodating Jewish to Roman law may have been to smooth his way with his Roman audience.[11]

The question addressed in this chapter is whether Josephus was indeed influenced by Roman law. I will revisit the methodology of finding analogies between Josephus and Roman law and will offer my input on several biblical laws rewritten in Josephus' works and try to uncover their origins.

In the following, I will examine several cases discussed by scholars with regard to biblical laws in Josephus' writings and possibly related Roman laws.

Cohen, commenting on Josephus' statement (*Ant.* 4.272) that if a thief is unable to defray the penalty imposed upon him is to become the slave of the aggrieved party, notes that there is no parallel in either the Bible or the Talmud but that there is in Roman law. The latter draws a distinction between killing a burglar by night and by day as does the author of the Collatio[12] (VII.1) several centuries later.

The *lex talionis* (*Ant.* 4.280) is another case where some scholars regard Josephus' retelling of the biblical law as being in accord with Roman law.[13] It is claimed that Josephus was influenced by the Twelve Tablets (*Lex Duodecium Tabularum*) from the fifth century BCE (VIII.2): 'Si membrum rup<s>it, ni cum eo pacit, talio esto' ('If anyone has broken

---

9. Cohen 1945: 1:117–25. On pp. 117–21 Cohen deals with *Ant.* 3.282; 4.271–72.

10. Weyl 1900; Daube 1992 (collection of his earlier papers); Jackson 1975; Halbertal 1997; Pearce 2000; Loader 2011.

11. Jackson 1975: 242. Cf. Goodman 1994: 335.

12. Cohen 1945. *Collatio Legum Mosaicarum et Romanarum* ('Comparison of Mosaic and Roman law') was written in the fourth century in Italy. See Ribary 2017: 115.

13. B. Cohen 1944; Belkin 1940. Daube (1984: 256) adds: 'he had to make the Biblical injunction palatable to his Roman readers'.

another's limb and does not come to an agreement with him, there shall be retaliation in kind [talio]').[14] According to this opinion, Josephus wanted to show the potential Roman readers of his writings that the distance between Roman law and biblical law is not so great. Others have argued that Josephus may reflect an attitude of some of the conservative priestly judges of his time.[15] Daube[16] completely rejected Josephus' words and believed that they should not be seen as evidence of the existence of this law during the Second Temple period.

Moving to a third case of an alleged Roman influence, Lev. 21.7 forbids priests to marry prostitutes, but Josephus (*Ant.* 3.276) expands this law to include all men in Israel. Loader[17] finds here a Roman influence, where marriage to a prostitute is forbidden. Loader does not mention Roman sources, but McGinn mentions the Augustan marriage law, *lex Iulia et Papia*.[18]

The reader may wonder if that is sufficient to indicate Roman influence. Prostitution was widespread in the Hellenistic period, as can be seen from Ben Sira (9.3-9; 23.22-27), 2 Macc. 6.4, 4Q271 3, and Philo (*Jos.* 43; *Spec. Laws* 3.51).[19]

As for female witnesses, Josephus says: 'Let the testimony of women not be accepted because of the levity and boldness of their gender' (*Ant.* 4.219). Since this reason is not mentioned in tannaitic sources, some argue that Josephus was influenced by Roman conceptions of women rather than any specific Jewish tradition.[20] Pearce cites Juvenal, Quintilian, and other Latin authors by whom Josephus may have been influenced. Indeed, in Roman law, there are cases in which women's evidence could be accepted.[21]

Exodus 21.18-19 deals with injury which occurs in the course of a quarrel. Does the attacker have to compensate the victim only for the

14. Johnson, Coleman-Norton, and Bourne 1961: 11.
15. Finkelstein 1936: 212.
16. Daube 1956: 256.
17. Loader 2011: 324.
18. McGinn 2002.
19. For more sources and bibliography, see Wheeler-Reed, Knust, and Martin 2018.
20. Pearce 2000.
21. See D.28.1.20.6 (Ulpian; Iustiniani Digesta): 'Indeed, a woman will not be able to witness a will, but as an argument that in other cases a woman can be a witness, there is the Julian law on adulteries, which forbids a woman convicted of adultery from being produced as a witness or giving testimony'. See Evans Grubbs 2002: 71.

time he has spent ill in bed or also for the period of recovery? This was disputed by the rabbis in *b. B. Qam.* 85a. Josephus (*Ant.* 4.277) rewrites this law as follows:

> In a fight where there is no iron weapon, if someone is struck and dies on the spot, let him be avenged and let the one who has struck him suffer the same. If he is carried to his home and after being ill for several days then dies, let the one who struck him be free from punishment. If, however, he has been saved but has incurred much expense, let him [the one who struck him] pay for all that he has spent during the time of his confinement to bed and all that he has given to the physicians.

Josephus understands the compensation for the victim to include only the time when he rested. The physician's fee is also mentioned in Targ. Onkelos, the LXX, the Vulgate, and in rabbinic literature (*b. B. Qam.* 85a; *b. Ketub.* 52b).

According to Greengus,[22] Josephus here distinguishes between 'stone or fist', which are both mentioned in Exod. 21.18, and the use of a weapon, which is not mentioned there. Josephus may have relied upon Roman law, where according to the *lex Cornelia* (67 BCE), the use of a weapon was in itself grounds for a charge of homicide.

Josephus adds with regard to the 'first tithe' to the priests the gratitude that the poor will feel for those who leave behind sheaves and grapes (*Ant.* 4.230-32). While the MT (Lev. 19.9; Deut. 24.19) mentions only the divine reward, Josephus adds motivation for the farmers to help the poor. At first glance, Josephus seems influenced by Cicero and Seneca. Seneca expects the poor to express gratitude, and that this satisfies the giver to do what is necessary; he calls such giving a social act (*socialis res*; *De Beneficiis* 3.8.3; 4.10.5, 11.1; 5.11.5). However, the 'needy' in their works 'are respectable citizens, and not the most desperate members of their society'.[23]

Methodological Problems

Comparing Josephus' rewriting of biblical laws to Roman laws creates several methodological problems. Jackson published a programmatic paper in 1981 pointing out the problems of comparing Jewish law and

---

22. Greengus 2011: 162 n. 91. See already Weyl 1900: 67.
23. Parkin 2006.

Roman law.[24] He questions rabbinical familiarity with Roman law and calls for caution in the comparative study of ancient legal cultures. He points out that the evidence for influence is inconclusive and that it is mostly in form rather than content. As far as Josephus is concerned, Jackson did argue that certain changes are due to Roman influence upon him. Though the case may be different with regard to Josephus – he was in Rome for several decades while most of the rabbis were not – some of his notes on methodology hold true for Josephus as well.

The assumption that Josephus knew Latin is questioned by some scholars. Weitzman[25] writes: 'we do not know whether Josephus could even read Latin'. To this Glucker[26] adds that with regard to Greek, Josephus admits that he had assistants who helped him with the language (*War* 1.3; *Ag. Ap.* 1.50). If Josephus had to employ assistants for Greek, why should we suppose he knew Latin?

Moreover, it is very problematic to assume, as Boaz Cohen and Daube do, that if there is nothing in either the Bible or in rabbinic literature supporting Josephus' changes he must have therefore been influenced by Roman law. There are other possibilities for such deviations: Josephus may have used his interpretive skills or practice in order to understand the laws; we should improve our reading of the Hebrew Bible, where different interpretive possibilities are available; or Josephus may preserve an ancient halakha. Indeed, Feldman[27] notes that Josephus nowhere indicates that he had studied or admired Roman law and that he insists on the unique excellence of Jewish law (*Ant.* 1.22-23; *Ag. Ap.* 2.163).[28]

To this we may add that scholars have to fully exploit internal sources before moving to external sources of influence. Likewise, there is always the possibility that the Jews and the Romans developed these practices independently. A comparison of Hammurabi's Code to the biblical laws is illustrative in this respect. It is insufficient to show that in both judicial systems there are laws pertaining to damages caused by a goring ox. David Wright showed that the parallels are much more substantial: the

---

24. Jackson (1981: 170) asks: 'who would have knowledge of Roman law? How deep a knowledge would they possess? Of what kind of Roman law would such knowledge consist?' Ranon Katzoff (2019: 155–69; originally published in 2003) argues that rabbinic law draws from Greek rather than Roman law.
25. Weitzman 2009: 933. Cf. Koskenniemi 2019: 170.
26. Glucker 1998: 108.
27. Feldman 1988: 517.
28. Feldman 1988: 517.

ideas, the sequence, and even the wording of many provisions were taken directly from the Laws of Hammurabi.[29]

We can assume borrowing only if the element is not interpreted organically within a particular religion. Ancient Near Eastern law may have also been a factor.

Scholars focus generally upon similarities, but sometimes the differences are more significant. In some instances, the links between two cultures may be ones of resistance and polemic. And if there is an influence, was Josephus being swayed by oral or written sources? Was the influence direct or indirect? Was it consistent or coincidental? Conscious or unconscious? Is it necessarily borrowing or are both cultures using the lingua franca independently?

Scholars have faced these methodological difficulties and have tried to deal with them in various ways – primarily through the search for evidence, directly and indirectly, for the existence of influence, or by attempting to set reasonable standards to prove that the similarities are due to influence rather than the result of parallel development.

Barclay[30] adds that at least in some cases Josephus relies on earlier Jewish tradition and that 'it is difficult to gauge how much he has molded that tradition into a particularly "Roman" form'. It is hard to say whether, or to what extent, Josephus deliberately 'Romanized' his portrait of Jewish culture.

Barclay wrote his words of caution regarding *Against Apion*, but they are even more relevant with regard to *Antiquities*; one cannot be confident that the additions Josephus enters into his retelling have been Romanized. The non-mention of certain ideas and practices in the Bible or in rabbinic sources is simply insufficient. We must also perform an in-depth search into biblical scholarship, so that we can be sure that no such practices or laws were extant in both the Bible and the ancient Near East.

The burden of proof lies on the researcher who makes a claim for such influences: it is not enough to show that certain Roman authors were mentioned by Josephus. One has to point to lexical, literary, thematic, and structural similarities. One has to show that Josephus as an author referred to the Roman works deliberately, rather than simply pointing to such similarities from a reader's point of view.

---

29. D.P. Wright 2009.
30. Barclay 2007.

Conclusion

Despite the reasonable assumption that, being in Rome, Josephus must have been influenced by the Roman legal tradition, the evidence to support this supposition is meager and cannot lead to a clear-cut conclusion. Scholars have doubts whether Josephus knew Latin, but even if we prove that he did, we still have to demonstrate that he was influenced by Latin rather than Hellenistic sources. Since the methodology of the scholars suggesting such an influence is flawed, we will have to relegate Josephus' changes to biblical laws to exegesis or internal traditions that he may have been acquainted with.

Conclusions

This book has analyzed Josephus' rewriting techniques of the biblical laws found in the Pentateuch, namely in the books of Exodus to Deuteronomy. My main source was *Antiquities* 3–4, yet other Josephan sources, as well as other Second Temple sources, were also consulted. To all these sources I have added a comparison of Josephus with modern commentaries either mentioning Josephus specifically as a legitimate writer on certain laws or as proof that his insights were shared by modern scholars without explicitly mentioning him.

My assumption was that Josephus is an interpreter, seeking to mediate the complex content of the Torah to his readers (pagan or Jewish) through additions and changes to the text. He avoids repetitions and contradictions and resolves them in various ways. His *Vorlage* was essentially close to the MT, with small parts resembling the LXX.

In Chapters 1–4 of this book I analyzed his rewriting of the laws themselves, while in Chapter 5–8 I dealt with general issues pertaining to his rewriting of these laws. Josephus is aware of the topics of 'reasons for the commandments', supplying explanations that were followed in later generations. He is also cognizant of the vexing problem of the placing and organization of the laws. He attempts to reorganize the laws scattered throughout the Torah and offers his understanding of their proper organization, which at times has literary merit, while at other times is difficult to follow.

Josephus' writings are not an ideal source for researching the development of the halakha.[1] In rewriting biblical laws there are many cases where we see Josephus in agreement with tannaitic sources. Yet there are other instances in which he deviates from these sources. This study recommends that Josephus' writings should be accessed with more

---

1. Cf. Dohrmann 2013: 71, concerning Philo and Josephus: 'neither sets legality at the center of his project, nor does either believe that the grander project – communicating what is Jewish or, perhaps more accurately, what is Israel and Torah – means speaking the law. In their distinct ways, what these two authors present is a narrativization of the law, not the legalization of the narrative.'

emphasis on Josephus' own interpretations. Comparative study with the rabbinic sources is important on one hand, but on the other hand it may lead to unrealistic expectations.

Josephus' writings are very different from rabbinic literature. He has only one opinion with regard to each law, while rabbinic literature contains ongoing debate. He is not authoritative, like the rabbis, who viewed their exegesis as a source of binding obligation. If we define Josephus' endeavor as seeking to make Scripture more readable for his intended audience, be it pagan or Jewish, then his project seems successful, albeit not perfect. Josephus had to deal with a unique law book, containing repetitions, inconsistencies, and contradictions. This law book, the Torah, does not give the spirit of the law and the principles lying behind it. In several cases, one cannot even be sure that he or she is dealing with a law at all. Josephus tried to supply such clarity to his readers.

Some of the changes that Josephus entered into his rewriting of the biblical laws are motivated by apologetic concerns, but they are the minority. Most changes derive from either an exegetical problem in Scripture or from a tradition that Josephus shared with other Second Temple authors. While earlier scholars compared Josephus with rabbinic sources and disregarded the Bible itself, I have always started with the biblical record. This enabled me to determine whether the features entered into the text were Josephus' own additions or if they were derived from the Bible.

As for Roman influence upon Josephus, it was shown that the methodology of finding such influences is flawed and needs to be further revised in order to show more convincingly that Josephus was influenced by his Roman milieu. At the moment, internal factors for the changes he enters into the biblical text should be preferred.

The negative assessment of Josephus in previous studies should give way to a more positive stance towards one of the earliest commentators of the Hebrew Bible. Further research should focus more on the exegetical traits of Josephus rather than on his apologetic motives.

Bibliography

Albeck, Ch. (1930), *Das Buch der Jubiläen und die Halacha*, Berlin: Siegfried Scholem.
Allen, O. W. (1997), *The Death of Herod: The Narrative and Theological Function of Retribution in Luke–Acts*, Atlanta: Scholars Press.
Altman, A. (2012), *Tracing the Earliest Recorded Concepts of International Law: The Ancient Near East (2500–330 BC)*, Leiden: Martinus Nijhoff.
Altshuler, D. (1977), 'Descriptions in Josephus's Antiquities of the Mosaic Constitution', PhD diss., Hebrew Union College.
Altshuler, D. (1978–79), 'The Treatise ΠΕΡΙ ΕΘΩΝ ΚΑΙ ΑΙΤΙΩΝ "On Customs and Causes" by Flavius Josephus', *JQR*, 69: 226–32.
Altshuler, D. (1982–83), 'On the Classification of Judaic Laws in the "Antiquities" of Josephus and the Temple Scroll of Qumran', *AJSR*, 7/8: 1–14.
Amihay, A. (2017), *Theory and Practice in Essene Law*, New York: Oxford University Press.
Amit, Y. (2000), *Hidden Polemics in Biblical Narrative*, trans. J. Chipman, BibInt 25, Leiden: Brill.
Amram, D. W. (1911–12), 'Retaliation and Compensation', *JQR*, 2: 191–211.
Aptowitzer, V. (1924), 'Observations on the Criminal Law of the Jews', *JQR*, 15: 55–118.
Archer, L. J. (1990), *Her Price Is Beyond Rubies: The Jewish Woman in Graeco-Roman Palestine*, Sheffield: JSOT.
Ashley, T. R. (1993), *The Book of Numbers*, NICOT, Grand Rapids, MI: Eerdmans.
Ashmon, S. A. (2012), *Birth Annunciations in the Hebrew Bible and Ancient Near East*, Lewiston, NY: Edwin Mellen Press.
Attridge, H. W. (1976), *The Interpretation of Biblical History in the Antiquitates Judaicae of Flavius Josephus*, Harvard Dissertations in Religion 7, Missoula: Scholars Press.
Avioz, M. (2009), 'An Eye for an Eye according to Josephus', *Beit Mikra* 54: 97–108 (Hebrew).
Avioz, M. (2011), 'Josephus' Portrait of Michal', *JSQ*, 18: 1–18.
Avioz, M. (2014), 'Death, Burial and Mourning in Josephus' Writings', *Cathedra* 152 (2014): 7–36 (Hebrew).
Avioz, M. (2015), *Josephus' Interpretation of the Books of Samuel*, London/New York: Bloomsbury.
Avioz, M. (forthcoming a), 'Retelling the David and Bathsheba Narrative in Josephus' Antiquities', in M. Zawanowska (ed.), *Warrior, Poet, Prophet and King: The Character of David in Judaism, Christianity and Islam*, Tübingen: Mohr Siebeck.
Avioz, M. (forthcoming b), 'The Septuagint in Josephus's Writings', in M. Meiser and F. Wilk (eds), *Handbuch zur Septuaginta. Handbook of the Septuagint, LXX.H: Wirkungsgeschichte*, vol. 6, Munich, Gütersloher Verlagshaus.

Baker, D. L. (2009), *Tight Fists or Open Hands: Wealth and Poverty in Old Testament Law*, Grand Rapids, MI: Eerdmans.

Baker, D. L. (2011), 'The Fifth Commandment in Context', in J. A. Aitken et al. (eds), *On Stone and Scroll: Essays in Honour of Graham Ivor Davies*, 253–67, Berlin: de Gruyter.

Balberg, M., and S. Chavel. (2017), 'The Polymorphous Pesah: Ritual Between Origins and Reenactment', *JAJ*, 8: 292–343.

Balla, P. (2005), *The Child–Parent Relationship in the New Testament and Its Environment*, Peabody, MA: Hendrickson.

Bar-Ilan, M. (1982), 'Polemics Between Sages and Priests Towards the End of the Days of the Second Temple', PhD diss., Bar-Ilan University (Hebrew).

Bar-Kochva, B. (1996), *Pseudo-Hecataeus on the Jews Legitimizing the Jewish Diaspora*, Berkeley: University of California Press.

Bar-Kochva, B. (1997), 'On the Festival of Purim and Some of the Sukkot Practices in the Period of the Second Temple and Afterwards', *Zion*, 62: 387–402 (Hebrew).

Barclay, J. M. G. (2007), *Against Apion: Translation and Commentary*, Flavius Josephus. Translation and Commentary, vol. 10, ed. S. Mason, Leiden/Boston: Brill.

Bartos, M., and B. M. Levinson (2013), '"This Is the Manner of the Remission": Implicit Legal Exegesis in 11QMelchizedek as a Response to the Formation of the Torah', *JBL*, 132: 351–71.

Batsch, Chr. (2011), 'Le Système Sacrificiel de Flavius Josèphe au Livre III des Antiquités Juives (Ant. 3.224-236)', in J. Pastor et al. (eds), *Flavius Josephus: Interpretation and History*, 39–51, Leiden: Brill.

Baumgarten, J. M. (1957), 'On the Testimony of Women in 1QSa', *JBL*, 76: 266–9.

Baumgarten, J. M. (1977), *Studies in Qumran Law*, Leiden: Brill.

Baumgarten, J. M. (2006), 'The Law and the Spirit of the Law at Qumran', in J. H. Charlesworth (ed.), *The Bible and the Dead Sea Scrolls: The Second Princeton Symposium on Judaism and Christian Origins. Vol. 2, The Dead Sea Scrolls and the Qumran Community*, 93–105, Waco, TX: Baylor University Press.

Begg, C. T. (2000), *Josephus' Story of the Later Monarchy (AJ 9,1–10,185)*, BETL 145, Leuven: Peeters/Leuven University Press.

Begg, C. T. (2004), 'The Levites in Josephus', *HUCA*, 75: 1–22.

Begg, C. T. (2007), 'Josephus' and Philo's Retelling of Numbers 31 Compared', *ETL*, 83: 81–106.

Begg, C. T. (2009), 'The Death of Nadab and Abihu According to Josephus', *Liber Annuus*, 59: 155–67.

Begg, C. T. (2012), 'Yom Kippur in Josephus', in T. Hieke and T. Nicklas (eds), *The Day of Atonement: Its Interpretations in Early Jewish and Christian Traditions*, 97–120, Leiden: Brill.

Belkin, S. (1936), *The Alexandrian Halakah in Apologetic Literature of the First Century C. E.*, Philadelphia: JPS.

Belkin, S. (1940), *Philo and the Oral Law: The Philonic Interpretation of Biblical Law in Relation to the Palestinian Halakah*, Cambridge, MA: Harvard University Press; London: Humphrey Milford.

Belkin, S. (1970), 'Levirate and Agnate Marriage in Rabbinic and Cognate Literature', *JQR*, 60: 275–329.

Bellefontaine, E. (1979), 'Deuteronomy 21:18-21: Reviewing the Case of the Rebellious Son', *JSOT*, 13: 13–31.

Ben-Eliyahu, E. (2019), *Identity and Territory: Jewish Perceptions of Space in Antiquity*, Oakland: California University Press.

Berkowitz, B. A. (2006), *Execution and Invention: Death Penalty Discourse in Early Rabbinic and Christian Cultures*, New York: Oxford University Press.

Bernstein, M. J. (2013), *Reading and Re-reading Scripture at Qumran*, 2 vols, Leiden: Brill.

Bibb, B. D. (2009), *Ritual Words and Narrative Worlds in the Book of Leviticus*, LHBOTS 480, New York/London: T&T Clark.

Birenboim, H. (2003), '"For all who transgress His word are impure": Sin and Impurity in the Qumran Scrolls', *Zion*, 68: 359–66 (Hebrew).

Blidstein, J. (1976), *Honor Thy Father and Mother: Filial Responsibility in Jewish Law and Ethics*, New York: Ktav.

Boesenberg, D. (2013), 'Moses in Luke–Acts', PhD diss, University of Notre Dame.

Bons, E. (2013), 'Marriage and Family in Flavius Josephus's Contra Apionem (II, § 199–206) against its Hellenistic Background', in E. Passaro (ed.), *Deuterocanonical and Cognate Literature Yearbook*, 455–66, Berlin: de Gruyter.

Borchardt, F. (2015), 'Sabbath Observance, Sabbath Innovation: The Hasmoneans and Their Legacy as Interpreters of the Law', *JSJ*, 46: 159–81.

Brichto, H. C. (1975), 'The Case of the Sotah and a Reconsideration of Biblical Law', *HUCA*, 46: 55–70.

Briggs, R. S. (2009), 'Reading the Sotah Text (Numbers 5:11-31): Holiness and a Hermeneutic Fit for Suspicion', *BibInt*, 17: 288–319.

Brin, G. (1994), *Studies in Biblical Law: From the Hebrew Bible to the Dead Sea Scrolls*, JSOTSup 172, Sheffield: JSOT Press.

Brooke, A. E., and N. McLean, eds (1909), *The Old Testament in Greek: According to the Text of Codex Vaticanus. Vol. I, Part 2: Exodus and Leviticus*, Cambridge: Cambridge University Press.

Brooke, A. E., and N. McLean, eds (1911), *The Old Testament in Greek: According to the Text of Codex Vaticanus, Vol. I, Part 3: Numbers and Deuteronomy*, Cambridge: Cambridge University Press.

Broshi, M. (2009), 'Ways of Life in Qumran', in M. Kister (ed.), *The Qumran Scrolls and their World*, vol. 1, 25–48 Jerusalem: Yad Ben Zvi (Hebrew).

Bruno, C. R. (2013), *'God Is One': The Function of 'Eis ho Theos' as a Ground for Gentile Inclusion in Paul's Letters*, LNTS 497, London: Bloomsbury T. & T. Clark.

Burke, T. J. (2003), *Family Matters: A Socio-Historical Study of Kinship Metaphors in 1 Thessalonians*, JSNTSup 247, New York: T. & T. Clark.

Burnside, J. (2002), *The Signs of Sin: Seriousness of Offence in Biblical Law*, JSOTSup 364, Sheffield: Sheffield Academic.

Carden, M. (2004), *Sodomy: A History of a Christian Biblical Myth*, London: Equinox.

Cassuto, U. (1967), *A Commentary on the Book of Exodus*, trans. Israel Abrahams, Jerusalem: Magnes.

Cassuto, U. (1973), 'The Sequence and Arrangement of Biblical Sections', in *Biblical and Oriental Studies. Vol. 1, Bible*, 1–6, trans. Israel Abrahams, Jerusalem: Magnes.

Castelli, S. (2001), 'Antiquities 3–4 and Against Apion 2:145ff.: Different Approaches to the Law', in J. U. Kalms (ed.), *Internationales Josephus-Kolloquium, Amsterdam 2000*, 151–69, Münster: LIT.

Castelli, S. (2018), 'Murder and Murder Prohibition in Josephus', in C. De Vos and H. Löhr (eds), *"You Shall Not Kill": The Prohibition to Killing in Ancient Religions and Cultures*, , 159–72, Göttingen: Vandenhoeck & Ruprecht.

Chapman, D. W. (2008), *Ancient Jewish and Christian Perceptions of Crucifixion*, WUNT 2/244, Tübingen: Mohr Siebeck.

Chepey, S. D. (2005), *Nazirites in Late Second Temple Judaism: A Survey of Ancient Jewish Writings, the New Testament, Archaeological Evidence, and Other Writings from Late Antiquity*, Leiden: Brill.

Chirichigno, G. C. (1993), *Debt-Slavery in Israel and the Ancient Near East*, Sheffield: JSOT.

Choi, B. (2018), 'Leviticus and Its Reception in the Dead Sea Scrolls from Qumran', PhD diss., University of Manchester.

Christopher, D. (2018), *The Appropriation of Passover in Luke–Acts*, WUNT 2/476, Tübingen: Mohr Siebeck.

Coats, G. W. (1988), *Moses: Heroic Man, Man of God*, JSOTSup 57, Sheffield: Sheffield Academic.

Coffin. F. J. (1900), 'The Third Commandment', *JBL*, 19: 166–88.

Cohen, B. (1944), 'The Relationship of Jewish to Roman Law', *JQR*, 34: 267–80.

Cohen, B. (1945), 'Civil Bondage in Jewish and Roman Law', in S. Lieberman et al. (eds), *Louis Ginzberg: Jubilee Volume on the Occasion of his Seventieth Birthday*, 1:117–25, English Section, New York: American Academy for Jewish Research.

Cohen, B. (1966), *Jewish and Roman Law – A Comparative Study*, 2 vols, New York: Jewish Theological Seminary of America.

Cohen, C. M. (2009), 'The Ancient Critical Misunderstanding of Exodus 21:22-25 and Its Implications for the Current Debate on Abortion', in N. Sacher Fox et al. (eds), *Mishneh Todah: Studies in Deuteronomy and Its Cultural Environment in Honor of Jeffrey H. Tigay*, 437–58, Winona Lake, IN: Eisenbrauns.

Cohen, H. (2010), 'Moses the Man of God: The Bible's Ambivalence Towards Him', in M. Hallamish et al. (eds), *Moses the Man – Master of the Prophets in the Light of Interpretation Throughout the Ages*, 53–78, Ramat Gan: Bar Ilan University Press (Hebrew).

Cohen, M. (1996), *Mikra'ot Gedolot Haketer: Leviticus*, ed. M. Cohen, Ramat Gan: Bar-Ilan University Press.

Cohen, M. (2011), *Mikra'ot Gedolot Haketer: Numbers*, ed. M. Cohen, Ramat Gan: Bar-Ilan University Press.

Cohen, M. (2013a), *Mikra'ot Gedolot Haketer: Exodus*, ed. M. Cohen, Ramat Gan: Bar-Ilan University Press.

Cohen, M. (2013b), *Mikra'ot gedolot Haketer: Numbers*, ed. M. Cohen, Ramat Gan: Bar-Ilan University Press.

Cohen, S. J. D. (1999), *The Beginnings of Jewishness: Boundaries, Varieties, Uncertainties*, Berkeley: University of California Press.

Cohen, S. J. D. (2002), *Josephus in Galilee and Rome: His Vita and Development as a Historian*, 2nd ed., Leiden: Brill.

Cohen, S. J. D. (2007), 'The Judaean Legal Tradition and the Halakhah of the Mishnah', in C. E. Fonrobert and M. S. Jaffee (eds), *The Cambridge Companion to the Talmud and Rabbinic Literature*, 121–47, Cambridge: Cambridge University Press.

Cohn, Y. (2008), *Tangled Up in Text: Tefillin and the Ancient World*, Providence, RI: Brown Judaic Studies.

Colautti, F. M. (2002), *Passover in the Works of Josephus*, JSJSup 75, Leiden: Brill.

Collins J. J. (1997), *Jewish Wisdom in the Hellenistic Age*, Louisville, KY: Westminster John Knox.

Colson, F. H. (1939), *Philo*, LCL 7, Cambridge, MA: Harvard University Press.

Cook, L. S. (2011), *On the Question of the 'Cessation of Prophecy' in Ancient Judaism*, TSAJ 145, Tübingen: Mohr Siebeck.
Cotton, H. M., and W. Eck. (2005), 'Josephus' Roman Audience: Josephus and the Roman Elites', in J. Edmondson et al. (eds), *Flavius Josephus and Flavian Rome*, 37–52, Oxford: Oxford University Press.
Cowan, J. W. (2019), *Writings of Luke and the Jewish Roots of the Christian Way: An Examination of the Aims of the First Christian Historian in the Light of Ancient Politics, Ethnography, and Historiography*, London: Bloomsbury T&T Clark.
Crawford, S. W. (2005), 'Reading Deuteronomy in the Second Temple Period', in K. de Troyer and A. Lange (eds), *Reading the Present in the Qumran Library: The Perception of the Contemporary by Means of Scriptural Interpretations*, 127–40, Atlanta, GA: SBL.
Daube, D. (1956), *Forms of Roman Legislation*, Oxford: Clarendon.
Daube, D. (1984), *The New Testament and Rabbinic Judaism*, reprint, Salem, NH: Ayer; originally published in 1956.
Daube, D. (1986), *Witnesses in Bible and Talmud*, Oxford: Oxford Centre for Postgraduate Hebrew Studies.
Daube, D. (1992), *Collected Works of David Daube*, vol. 1, ed. C. M. Carmichael, Berkeley: Robbins Collection.
Davies, E. W. (1999), 'Walking in God's Ways: The Concept of Imitatio Dei in the Old Testament', in E. Ball (ed.), *In Search of True Wisdom: Essays in Old Testament Interpretation in Honour of Ronald E. Clements*, 99–115, JSOTSup 300, Sheffield: Sheffield Academic.
Davila, J. R. (2005), *The Provenance of the Pseudepigrapha*, Leiden: Brill.
Den Hollander, W. (2014), *Josephus, the Emperors, and the City of Rome: From Hostage to Historian*, Leiden: Brill.
DeRouchie, J. S. (2013), 'Counting the Ten: An Investigation into the Numbering of the Decalogue', in J. S. DeRouchie et al. (eds), *For Our Good Always: Studies on the Message and Influence of Deuteronomy in Honor of Daniel I. Block*, 93–125, Winona Lake, IN: Eisenbrauns.
Diaz Araujo, M. (2017), 'The Sins of the First Woman: Eve Traditions in Second Temple Literature with Special Regard to the Life of Adam and Eve', in E. Schuller and M. T. Wacker (eds), *Early Jewish Writings*, 91–112, Atlanta: SBL.
Dimant, D., and D. W. Parry (eds). (2015), *Dead Sea Scrolls Handbook*, Leiden/Boston: Brill.
Dixon, S. (2015), *The Roman Mother*, London: Routledge.
Doering, L. (1999), *Schabbat: Sabbathalacha und -praxis im antiken Judentum und Urchristentum*, Tübingen: Mohr Siebeck.
Dohrmann, N. B. (2013), 'Law and Imperial Idioms: Rabbinic Legalism in a Roman World', in N. B. Dohrmann and A. Y. Reed (eds), *Jews, Christians and the Roman Empire: The Poetics of Power in Late Antiquity*, 63–78, Philadelphia: University of Pennsylvania Press.
Douglas, M. (1993), *In the Wilderness, the Doctrine of Defilement in the Book of Numbers*, JSOTSup 158, Sheffield: JSOT.
Dozeman, T. B., C. A. Evans, and J. N. Lohr, eds (2014), *The Book of Exodus: Composition, Reception, and Interpretation*, Leiden: Brill.
Drawnel, H. (2004), *An Aramaic Wisdom Text from Qumran: A New Interpretation of the Levi Document*, JSJSup 86, Leiden: Brill.

Duling, D. C. (1985), 'The Eleazar Miracle and Solomon's Magical Wisdom in Flavius Josephus's Antiquitates Judaicae 8.42-49', *HTR*, 78: 1–25.

Durham, J. I. (1987), *Exodus*, WBC, Waco, TX: Word.

Elgvin, T. (2003), 'Qumran and the Roots of the Rosh Hashanah Liturgy', in E. Chazon (ed.), *Liturgical Perspectives: Prayer and Poetry in Light of the Dead Sea Scrolls*, 49–67, Leiden: Brill.

Evans Grubbs, J. (2002), *Women and the Law in the Roman Empire: A Sourcebook on Marriage, Divorce and Widowhood*, London/New York: Routledge.

Feldman, L. H. (1984), *Josephus and Modern Scholarship (1937–1980)*, Berlin: de Gruyter.

Feldman, L. H. (1988), 'Use, Authority, and Exegesis of Mikra in the Writings of Josephus', in Martin J. Mulder and Harry Sysling (eds), *Mikra: Text, Translation, Reading and Interpretation of the Hebrew Bible in Ancient Judaism and Early Christianity*, 455–518, CRINT 2/1, Assen: Van Gorcum.

Feldman, L. H. (1989), 'A Selective Critical Bibliography of Josephus', in L. H. Feldman and G. Hata (eds), *Josephus, the Bible, and History*, 330–448, Detroit: Wayne State University Press.

Feldman, L. H. (1993), *Jew and Gentile in the Ancient World: Attitudes and Interactions from Alexander to Justinian*, Princeton: Princeton University Press.

Feldman, L. H. (1997), 'Torah and Greek Culture in Josephus', *Torah U-Madda Journal*, 7: 41–85.

Feldman, L. H. (1998a), *Josephus's Interpretation of the Bible*, Berkeley: University of California Press.

Feldman, L. H. (1998b), *Studies in Josephus' Rewritten Bible*, Leiden: Brill

Feldman, L. H. (2000), *Judean Antiquities 1–4: Translation and Commentary*, ed. S. Mason, Leiden: Brill.

Feldman, L. H. (2006), *Judaism and Hellenism Reconsidered*, JSJSup107, Leiden: Brill.

Feldman, L. H. (2007), 'The Case of the Blasphemer (Lev. 24:10-16) according to Philo and Josephus', in L. LiDonnici and A. Lieber (eds), *Heavenly Tablets: Interpretation, Identity and Tradition in Ancient Judaism*, 213–26, Leiden: Brill.

Feldman, L. H. (2008), 'Josephus' View of the Amalekites', in K. E. Pomykala (ed.), *Israel in the Wilderness: Interpretations of the Biblical Narratives in Jewish and Christian Traditions*, 89–115, Themes in Biblical Narrative 10, Leiden: Brill.

Finkelstein, L. (1930), 'Some Examples of the Maccabean Halaka', *JBL*, 49: 20–42.

Finkelstein, L. (1936), 'An Eye for an Eye', *The Menorah Journal*, 24: 207–18.

Fine, S. (1999), 'Non-Jews in the Synagogues of Palestine: Rabbinic and Archaeological Perspectives', in S. Fine (ed.), *Jews, Christians and Polytheists in the Ancient Synagogue: Cultural Interaction During the Greco-Roman Period*, 224–41, London: Routledge.

Flatto, D. (2010), 'Between Royal Absolutism and an. Independent Judiciary: The Evolution of Separation of Powers in Biblical, Second. Temple and Rabbinic Texts', PhD diss., Harvard University.

Forsling, J. (2013), *Composite Artistry in the Book of Numbers: A Study in Biblical Narrative Conventions*, Studia Theologica Holmiensa, Abo: Abo Akademi University Press.

Fraade, S. (2011), *Legal Fictions: Studies of Law and Narrative in the Discursive Worlds of Ancient Jewish Sectarians and Sages*, Leiden: Brill.

Frevel, Ch. et al., eds (2005), *Die Zehn Worte: Der Dekalog als Testfall der Pentateuchkritik*, Questiones Disputatae 212, Freiburg: Herder.

Friedman, R. E. (2012), 'The "Sotah": Why Is this Case Different from All Other Cases?', in I. Provan and M. J. Boda (eds), *Let Us Go Up to Zion: Essays in Honour of H. G. M. Williamson on the Occasion of His Sixty-Fifth Birthday*, 372–82, Leiden: Brill.

Frymer-Kensky, T. (1998), 'Virginity in the Bible', in V. H. Matthews et al. (eds), *Gender and Law in the Hebrew Bible and the Ancient Near East*, 79–96, Sheffield: Sheffield Academic.

Gager, J. G. (1972), *Moses in Greco-Roman Paganism*, Nashville: Abingdon.

Gagnon, R. A. G. (2001), *The Bible and Homosexual Practice: Texts and Hermeneutics*, Nashville: Abingdon.

Gallant, R. P. (1988), 'Josephus' Expositions of Biblical Law: An Internal Analysis', PhD diss., Yale University.

Gane, R. E. (2016), 'Innovation in the Suspected Adulteress Ritual (Num 5:11-31)', in N. McDonald (ed.), *Ritual Innovation in the Hebrew Bible and Early Judaism*, 113–27, BZAW 468, Berlin: de Gruyter.

Gärtner, J., and B. Schmitz, eds (2016), *Exodus: Rezeptionen in deuterokanonischer und frühjüdischer Literatur*, Berlin/Boston: de Gruyter.

Gerber, C. (1997), *Ein Bild des Judentums für Nichtjuden von Flavius Josephus: Untersuchungen zu seiner Schrift Contra Apionem*, AGJU 40, Leiden: Brill.

Gibbs, J., and L. H. Feldman (1986), 'Josephus' Vocabulary for Slavery', *JQR*, 76: 281–310.

Gilmour, R. (2015), *Juxtaposition and the Elisha Cycle*, LBHOTS 594, New York/London: Bloomsbury.

Gilat, Y. D. (1995), 'Does the Jubilee Year Cancel Debts?', *Tarbiz*, 64: 229–36 (Hebrew).

Glucker, J. (1998), 'Arieh Kasher's Translation and Commentary on Josephus' "Against Apion"', *Zion*, 63: 89–123 (Hebrew).

Goldenberg, D. (1978), 'The Halakhah in Josephus and in Tannaitic Literature: A Comparative Study', PhD diss., Dropsie University.

Goldenberg, D. (1987), 'Antiquities IV, 277 and 288, Compared with Early Rabbinic Law', in L. H. Feldman and G. Hata (eds), *Josephus, Judaism and Christianity*, 198–211, Leiden: Brill.

Goodblatt, D. M. (1994), *The Monarchic Principle: Studies in Jewish Self-Government in Antiquity*, Tübingen: Mohr Siebeck.

Goodfriend, E. A. (1992), 'Prostitution', *ABD* 5: 505–10.

Goodman, M. (1994), 'Josephus as Roman Citizen', in F. Parente and J. Sievers (eds), *Josephus and the History of the Greco-Roman Period*, 329–38, Leiden: Brill.

Gorman, M. J. (1998), *Abortion & the Early Church: Christian, Jewish & Pagan Attitudes in the Greco-Roman World*, Eugene, OR: Wipf & Stock.

Gottlieb, I. B. (2009), *Order in the Bible: The Arrangement of the Torah in Rabbinic and Medieval Jewish Commentary*, Jerusalem: Magnes (Hebrew).

Greenberg, M. (1990), 'The Decalogue Tradition Critically Examined', in B.-Z. Segal (ed.), *The Ten Commandments in History and Tradition*, 279–312, Jerusalem: Magnes.

Greenfield, J. C., M. E. Stone and E. Eshel (2004), *The Aramaic Levi Document*, Leiden/Boston: Brill.

Greengus, S. (2011), *Laws in the Bible and in Early Rabbinic Collections: The Legal Legacy of the Ancient Near East*, Eugene, OR: Cascade.

Gruber, M. (1982), 'Changing the Name *aseret ha-debarim*', *Beit Mikra*, 27: 16–21 (Hebrew).

Gruen, E. S. (2011), 'Polybius and Josephus on Rome', in J. Pastor et al. (eds), *Flavius Josephus: Interpretation and History*, 149–62, Leiden: Brill.

Grushcow, L. (2006), *Writing the Wayward Wife: Rabbinic Interpretations of Sotah*, Leiden: Brill.
Gurtner, D. M. (2013), *Exodus: A Commentary on the Greek Text of Codex Vaticanus*, Septuagint Commentary Series, Leiden/Boston: Brill.
Gunkel, H. (1998), *Introduction to the Psalms: The Genres of the Religious Lyric of Israel*, completed by J. Begrich, trans. J. D. Nogalski, Macon: Mercer University Press.
Hadas-Lebel, M. (1993), 'Les mariages mixtes dans la famille d'Hérode et la Halakha prétalmudique sur la patrilinéarité', *REJ*, 152: 397–404.
Hafemann, S. J. (1990), 'Moses in the Apocrypha and Pseudepigrapha: A Survey', *JSP*, 7: 79–104.
Halbertal, M. (1997), *Interpretative Revolutions in the Making: Values as Interpretative Considerations in Midrashei Halakhah*, Jerusalem: Magnes (Hebrew).
Halevy, E. E. (1967–68), 'The Oath', *Tarbiz*, 37: 24–29 (Hebrew).
Hanneken, T. R. (2015), 'Moses Has His Interpreters: Understanding the Legal Exegesis in Acts 15 from the Precedent in Jubilees', *CBQ*, 77: 686–706.
Harrington, H. K. (1996), 'Interpreting Leviticus in the Second Temple Period: Struggling with Ambiguity', in J. F. A. Sawyer (ed.), *Reading Leviticus: Responses to Mary Douglas*, 214–29, Sheffield: Sheffield Academic.
Hartley, J. E. (1992), *Leviticus*, WBC 4, Dallas: Word.
Harvey, G. (1998), 'Synagogues of the Hebrews: "Good Jews" in the Diaspora', in S. Jones and S. Pearce (eds), *Jewish Local Patriotism and Self-Identification in the Graeco-Roman Period*, 132–47, JSPSup 31, Sheffield: Sheffield Academic.
Hayes, C. (2015), *What's Divine about Divine Law? Early Perspectives*, Princeton: Princeton University Press.
Heger, P. (1999), *The Three Biblical Altar Laws*, BZAW 279, Berlin: de Gruyter.
Heinemann, Y. (1940), 'Josephus' Method in the Presentation of Jewish Antiquities', *Zion*, 5: 180–203 (Hebrew).
Heinemann, Y. (2008), *The Reasons for the Commandments in Jewish Thought: From the Bible to the Renaissance*, trans. L. Levin, Boston: Academic Studies Press; Hebrew Original 1953.
Hempel, C. (2017), 'Wisdom and Law in the Hebrew Bible and at Qumran', *JSJ*, 48: 155–81.
Henshke, D. (1990–91), 'Four Bailees?', *Shenaton ha-Mishpat ha-Ivri*, 16–17: 145–218 (Hebrew).
Henshke, D. (2007), *Festival Joy in Tannaitic Discourse*, Jerusalem: Magnes (Hebrew).
Herman, M. (2016), 'Systematizing God's Law: Rabbanite Jurisprudence in the Islamic World from the Tenth to the Thirteenth Centuries', PhD diss., University of Pennsylvania.
Hezser, C. (2005), *Jewish Slavery in Antiquity*, Oxford: Oxford University Press.
Hiebert, R. J. V. (1994), 'Deuteronomy 22:28-29 and Its Premishnaic Interpretations', *CBQ*, 56: 203–20.
Himbaza, I. (2004), *Le Décalogue et l'histoire du texte. Etudes des formes textuelles du Décalogue et leurs implications dans l'histoire du texte de l'Ancien Testament*, Orbis biblicus et orientalis 207, Fribourg: Academic; Göttingen: Vandenhoeck & Ruprecht.
Houtman, C. (1984), 'Another Look at Forbidden Mixtures', *VT*, 34: 226–8.
Houtman, C. (2000), *Exodus, vol. 3*, HCOT, Leuven: Peeters.
Ilan, T. (2017), 'Flavius Josephus and Biblical Women', in E. Schuller and M. T. Wacker (eds), *Early Jewish Writings*, 167–85, Atlanta: SBL.

Instone-Brewer, D. (2002), *Divorce and Remarriage in the Bible: The Social and Literary Context*, Grand Rapids: Eerdmans.
Isser, S. (1990), 'Two Traditions: The Law of Exodus 21: 22-23 Revisited', *CBQ*, 32: 30–45.
Jackson, B. S. (1972), *Theft in Early Jewish Law*, Oxford: Clarendon.
Jackson, B. S. (1974), 'The Goring Ox Again', *Journal of Juristic Papyrology*, 18: 55–93.
Jackson, B. S. (1975), *Essays in Jewish and Comparative Legal History*, Leiden: Brill.
Jackson, B. S. (1981), 'On the Problem of Roman Influence on the Halakah and Normative Self-Definition in Judaism', in E. P. Sanders et al. (eds), *Jewish and Christian Self-Definition: Aspects of Judaism in the Graeco-Roman Period*, vol. 2, 157–203, Philadelphia: Fortress.
Jackson, B. S. (2006), *Wisdom-Laws: A Study of the Mishpatim of Exodus 21:1–22:16*, Oxford: Oxford University Press.
Jassen, A. (2007), *Mediating the Divine: Prophecy and Revelation in the Dead Sea Scrolls and Second Temple Judaism*, STDJ 68, Leiden: Brill.
Jassen, A. (2014), *Scripture and Law in the Dead Sea Scrolls*, New York: Cambridge University Press.
Jastram, N. (2000), 'Numbers, Book of', in L. H. Schiffman and J. C. VanderKam (eds), *Encyclopedia of the Dead Sea Scrolls*, 2:615–19, 2 vols, New York: Oxford University Press.
Jewell, P. (2009), 'Flavius Josephus' Terminology of Magic: Accommodating Jewish Magic to a Roman Audience', *Journal for the Academic Study of Magic*, 5: 8–40.
Johns, L. (2004), *The Lamb Christology of the Apocalypse of John: An Investigation into Its Origins and Rhetorical Force*, WUNT 2/167, Tübingen: Mohr Siebeck.
Johnson, A. C., P. Robinson Coleman-Norton, and F. C. Bourne (1961), *Ancient Roman Statutes*, The Corpus of Roman Law II, Austin: University of Texas Press.
Jonquière, T. (2007), *Prayer in Josephus*, Ancient Judaism and Christianity 70, Leiden: Brill.
Kasher, A. (1996), *Flavius Josephus: Against Apion*, 2 vols, Jerusalem: Zalman Shazar Center (Hebrew).
Katzoff, R. (2019), *On Jews in the Roman World: Collected Studies*, Tübingen: Mohr Siebeck.
Kazen, T. (2010), *Jesus and Purity Halakhah: Was Jesus Indifferent to Impurity?*, Coniectanea Biblica, New Testament Series 38, Winona Lake, IN: Eisenbrauns.
Kee, H. C. (1983–85), 'Testaments of the Twelve Patriarchs', in J. H. Charlesworth (ed.), *The Old Testament Pseudepigrapha*, 775–828, Garden City, NY: Doubleday.
Kellogg, S. H. (1906), *The Book of Leviticus*, The Expositor's Bible, London: Hodder & Stoughton.
Keun, L. J. (1993), 'The Theological Concept of Divine Ownership of the Land in the Hebrew Bible', PhD diss., Boston University.
Kochman, M. (1987), *Leviticus*, in B. A. Levine et al. (eds), *The World of the Bible*, Ramat Gan: Revivim (Hebrew).
Kohler, K. (1931), 'The Halakik Portions in Josephus' Antiquities (IV, 8, 5-43)', in *Studies, Addresses, and Personal Papers*, 69–85, New York: Bloch.
Koskenniemi, E. (2019), *Greek Writers and Philosophers in Philo and Josephus: A Study of Their Secular Education and Educational Ideals*, Studies in Philo of Alexandria 9, Leiden/Boston: Brill.
Kottek, S. S. (1993), *Medicine and Hygiene in the Works of Flavius Josephus*, Leiden: Brill.

Kraemer, D. (2007), *Jewish Eating and Identity through the Ages*, London: Routledge.
Kugel, J. L. (1993), 'Levi's Elevation to the Priesthood in Second Temple Writings', *HTR*, 86: 1–64.
Kugel, J. L. (1998), *Traditions of the Bible: A Guide to the Bible as It Was at the Start of the Common Era*, Cambridge, MA: Harvard University Press.
Kugler, R. A. (2000), 'The Priesthood at Qumran', in P. W. Flint and J. VanderKam (eds), *The Dead Sea Scrolls after Fifty Years: A Comprehensive Assessment*, 2:93–116, 2 vols, Leiden/Boston: Brill.
Lachs, S. T. (1988), 'Why Was the "Amen" Response Interdicted in the Temple?', *JSJ*, 19: 230–40.
La Barge, K. F. (2009), 'A Biological Consideration for the Extended Period of Impurity after the Birth of a Daughter in Ancient Israel', in E. A. McCabe (ed.), *Women in the Biblical World: A Survey of Old and New Testament Perspectives*, 21–30, Lanham, MD: University Press of America.
Lange, A., and M. Weigold (2011), *Biblical Quotations and Allusions in Second Temple Jewish Literature*, Göttingen: Vandenhoeck & Ruprecht.
Lauterbach, J. Z., and D. Stern, eds (2004), *Mekhilta de-Rabbi Ishmael: A Critical Edition, Based on the Manuscripts and Early Editions*, 2nd ed., Philadelphia: Jewish Publication Society.
Lavee, M. (2013), 'The Noahide Laws: The Building Blocks of a Rabbinic Conceptual Framework in Qumran and the Book of Acts', *Meghillot*, 10: 73–114 (Hebrew).
Lawrence, J. D. (2006), *Washing in Water: Trajectories of Ritual Bathing in the Hebrew Bible and Second Temple Literature*, Atlanta: SBL.
Lee, M. M. (2015), *Body, Dress, and Identity in Ancient Greece*, Cambridge: Cambridge University Press.
Lee, W. W. (2008), 'The Conceptual Coherence of Numbers 5,1–10,10', in T. Römer (ed.), *The Books of Leviticus and Numbers*, 473–89, Leuven: Peeters.
Levine, B. A. (1989), *Leviticus*, JPS Torah Commentary, Philadelphia: Jewish Publication Society of America.
Levine, B. A. (1993), *Numbers 1–20*, AB 4A, New York: Doubleday.
Levine, D. B. (1993), 'Hubris in Josephus' Jewish Antiquities 1–4', *HUCA*, 64: 51–87.
Levinson, B. M. (1994), 'The Case for Revision and Interpolation within the Biblical Legal Corpora', in B. M. Levinson (ed.), *Theory and Method in Biblical and Cuneiform Law: Revision, Interpolation and Development*, 37–59, Sheffield: Sheffield Academic.
Licht, J. (1971), 'Kilayim', in *Encyclopedia Mikrait* IV, 104–5, Jerusalem: Bialik Institute (Hebrew).
Licht, J. (1985–95), *Commentary on the Book of Numbers*, 3 vols, Jerusalem: Magnes (Hebrew).
Liddell, H. G., and R. Scott. (1996), *A Greek–English Lexicon*, 9th ed., Oxford: Clarendon.
Liebman, T. (2002), 'The Jewish Exegetical History of Deuteronomy 22:5: Required Gender Separation or Prohibited Cross-Dressing?', MA thesis, Montreal: Department of Jewish Studies, McGill University.
Lierman, J. (2004), *The New Testament Moses: Christian Perceptions of Moses and Israel in the Setting of Jewish Religion*, WUNT 2/173, Tübingen: Mohr Siebeck.
Lim, T. H. (2007), 'Deuteronomy in the Judaism of the Second Temple Period', in S. Moyise and Maarten J. J. Menken (eds), *Deuteronomy in the New Testament: The New Testament and the Scriptures of Israel*, 6–26, LNTS 358, London/New York: T&T Clark.

Lincicum, D. (2010), *Paul and the Early Jewish Encounter with Deuteronomy*, WUNT 2/284, Tübingen: Mohr Siebeck.
Loader, W. (2011), *Philo, Josephus, and the Testaments on Sexuality: Attitudes towards Sexuality in the Writings of Philo and Josephus and in the Testaments of the Twelve Patriarchs*, Grand Rapids, MI/Cambridge: Eerdmans.
Maimonides, M. (1956), *The Guide for the Perplexed*, trans. M. Friedländer, New York: Dover.
Magness, J. (2011), *Stone and Dung, Oil and Spit: Jewish Daily Life in the Time of Jesus*, Grand Rapids, MI: Eerdmans.
Mason, S. (2001b), *Life of Josephus*, in *Flavius Josephus: Translation and Commentary*, ed. S. Mason, Leiden: Brill.
Mason, S. (2003), 'Flavius Josephus in Flavian Rome: Reading On and Between the Lines', in A. J. Boyle and W. J. Dominik (eds), *Flavian Rome: Culture, Text, Image*, 559–89, Leiden: Brill.
Mason, S. (2009), *Josephus, Judea and Christian Origins: Methods and Categories*, Peabody, MT: Hendrickson.
McDonough, S. M. (1999), *YHWH at Patmos: Rev. 1–4 in its Hellenistic and Early Jewish Setting*, WUNT 2/107, Tübingen: Mohr Siebeck.
McGinn, T. A. (2002), 'The Augustan Marriage Legislation and Social Practice: Elite Endogamy versus Male "Marrying Down"', in J. J. Aubert and B. Sirks (eds), *Speculum Iuris: Roman Law as a Rejection of Social and Economic Life in Antiquity*, 46–93, Ann Arbor, MI: University of Michigan Press.
McKay, H. A. (1994), *Sabbath and Synagogue. The Question of Sabbath Worship in Ancient Judaism*, Religions in the Graeco-Roman World 122, Leiden: Brill.
Meeks, W. (1967), *The Prophet-King: Moses Traditions and the Johannine Christology*, NovTSup 14, Leiden: Brill.
Meshorer, Y. (1982), *Ancient Jewish Coinage*, 2 vols, New York: Amphora.
Metso, S. (2012), 'Evidence from the Qumran Scrolls for the Scribal Transmission of Leviticus', in J. S. Kloppenborg and J. H. Newman (eds), *Editing the Bible: Assessing the Task Past and Present*, 67–80, Atlanta: SBL.
Metso, S. (2014), 'The Character of Leviticus Traditions at Qumran', in T. M. Law et al. (eds), *In the Footsteps of Sherlock Holmes: Studies in the Biblical Text in Honour of Anneli Aejmelaeus*, 645–58, CBET 72, Leuven: Peeters.
Metso, S., and E. Ulrich. (2003), 'The Old Greek Translation of Leviticus', in R. Rendtorff and R. A. Kugler (eds), *The Book of Leviticus: Composition and Reception*, 247–68, VTSup 93, Leiden: Brill.
Milgrom, J. (1974), 'Function of the *hattat* Sacrifice', *Tarbiz*, 40: 1–8 (Hebrew).
Milgrom, J. (1990), *Numbers*, The JPS Torah Commentary, Philadelphia: The Jewish Publication Society.
Milgrom, J. (1991), *Leviticus 1–16*, AB 3, New York: Doubleday.
Milgrom, J. (1993), *Numbers*, Olam Hatanach; Tel Aviv: Davidson-Atai (Hebrew).
Milgrom, J. (1995), '4QThrAl: An Unpublished Fragment on Purities', in D. Dimant and L. H. Schiffman (eds), *Time to Prepare the Way in the Wilderness*, 59–68, STDJ 16, Leiden: Brill.
Milgrom J. (1997), *The Book of Numbers*, Olam HaTanach, Tel Aviv, Davidson-Attai (Hebrew).
Milgrom, J. (2000), *Leviticus 17–22*, AB 3, New York: Doubleday.
Milgrom, J. (2001), *Leviticus 23–27*, AB 3, New York: Doubleday.

Miller, Y. (2019), 'Phinehas' Priestly Zeal and the Violence of Contested Identities', *JSQ*, 26: 117–45.

Nakman, D. (2004), 'The Halakhah in the Writings of Josephus', PhD diss., Bar-Ilan University (Hebrew).

Nakman, D. (2009), 'Tefillin and Mezuzot at Qumran', in M. Kister (ed.), *The Qumran Scrolls and Their World*, 2 vols, 1:143–55, Jerusalem: Yad Izhak Ben-Zvi.

Nakman, D. (2016), 'Josephus and Halacha', in H. H. Chapman and Z. Rodgers (eds), *A Companion to Josephus*, 282–92, Chichester, West Sussex, UK: Wiley-Blackwell.

Neusner, J. (1975), *Between Time and Eternity: The Essentials of Judaism*, California: Dickenson Publishing.

Niehoff, M. (2016), 'Josephus and Philo in Rome', in H. H. Chapman and Z. Rodgers (eds), *A Companion to Josephus*, 135–46, Chichester, West Sussex, UK: Wiley-Blackwell.

Niese, B. (1887–95), *Flavii Iosephi opera: Edidit et apparatu critico instruxit*, 7 vols, Berlin: Weidmann.

Noam, V. (2003), *Megillat Taanit: Versions, Interpretation, History*, Jerusalem: Yad Ben-Zvi (Hebrew).

Noam, V. (2010), 'Creative Interpretation and Integrative Interpretation in Qumran', in A. D. Roitman et al. (eds), *The Dead Sea Scrolls and Contemporary Culture: Proceedings of the International Conference held at the Israel Museum, Jerusalem (July 6–8, 2008)*, 363–76, STDJ 93, Leiden: Brill.

Noam, V. (2011a), 'Josephus and Early Halakhah: The Exclusion of Impure Persons from Holy Precincts', in A. M. Maeir et al. (eds), *'Go Out and Study the Land' (Judges 18:2): Archaeological, Historical and Textual Studies in Honor of Hanan Eshel*, 133–46, Leiden: Brill.

Noam, V. (2011b), 'Embryonic Legal Midrash in the Qumran Scrolls', in N. Dávid et al. (eds), *The Hebrew Bible in Light of the Dead Sea Scrolls*, 237–62, FRLANT 239, Göttingen: Vandenhoeck & Ruprecht.

Nodet, E. (1990–95), *Flavius Josephe: Les Antiquites Juives, 2 vols: Livres I à V*, Paris: Cerf.

Nodet, E. (1997), 'Josephus and the Pentateuch', *JSJ*, 28: 154–94.

Norton, J. D. H. (2011), *Contours in the Text: Textual Variation in the Writings of Paul, Josephus, and the Yaḥad*, LNTS 430, London: T &T Clark.

Novick, T. (2008), 'Law and Loss: Response to Catastrophe in Numbers 15', *HTR*, 101: 1–14.

Olitzki, M. (1885), *Flavius Josephus und die Halacha*, Berlin: Druck. Itzkowski.

Olson, D. T. (1985), *The Death of the Old and the Birth of the New: The Framework of the Book of Numbers and the Pentateuch*, Chico, CA: Scholars Press.

Olyan, S. M. (1998), 'What Do Shaving Rites Accomplish and What Do They Signal in Biblical Ritual Contexts?', *JBL*, 117: 611–22.

Oppenheimer, A. (1977), *The 'Am Ha-aretz: A Study in the Social History of the Jewish People in the Hellenistic-Roman Period*, Leiden: Brill.

Ortlund, D. C. (2012), *Zeal without Knowledge: The Concept of Zeal in Romans 10, Galatians 1, and Philippians 3*, LNTS 472, London: T&T Clark.

Pakkala, J. (2004), *Ezra the Scribe: The Development of Ezra 7–10 and Neh 8*, BZAW 347, Berlin: de Gruyter.

Park, S. (2008), *Pentecost and Sinai*, LHBOTS 342, New York/London: T&T Clark.

Parkin, A. (2006), '"You Do Him No Service": An Exploration of Pagan Almsgiving', in M. Atkins and R. Osborne (eds), *Poverty in the Roman World*, 60–82, New York: Cambridge University Press.

Paul, S. M. (1970), *Studies in the Book of the Covenant in the Light of Cuneiform and Biblical Law*, VTSup 18, Leiden: E. J. Brill.

Pearce, S. (1995), 'Flavius Josephus as Interpreter of Biblical Law: The Council of Seven and the Levitical Servants in Jewish Antiquities 4.214', *Heythrop Journal*, 36: 477–92.

Pearce, S. (1999), 'Josephus and the Witness Laws of Deuteronomy', in J. Kalms (ed.), *Internationales Josephus-Kolloquium: Aarhus 1999*, 122–34, Münster: LIT.

Pearce, S. (2000), 'Josephus and the Witness Laws of Deuteronomy', in J. Kalms (ed.), *Internationales Josephus-Kolloquium Aarhus 1999*, 122–34, Münster: LIT.

Pearce, S. (2013), *The Words of Moses: Studies in the Reception of Deuteronomy in the Second Temple Period*, TSAJ 152, Tübingen: Mohr Siebeck.

Petersen, N. (2009), 'An Analysis of Two Early LXX Manuscripts from Qumran: 4QLXXNum and 4QLXXLev-a in the Light of Previous Studies', *BBR*, 19: 481–510.

Phillips, A. (1970), *Ancient Israel's Criminal Law*, Oxford: Oxford University Press.

Phua, R. L. S. (2005), *Idolatry and Authority: A Study of 1 Corinthians 8.1–11.1 in the Light of the Jewish Diaspora*, London/New York: T. & T. Clark.

Pietersma, A., and B. G. Wright, eds (2007), *A New English Translation of the Septuagint*, New York: Oxford University Press.

Pressler, C. (1993), *The View of Women Found in the Deuteronomic Family Laws*, BZAW 216, Berlin: de Gruyter.

Propp, W. H. C. (2006), *Exodus 19–40*, AB 2A, New York: Doubleday.

Qimron, E. (2010), *The Dead Sea Scrolls: The Hebrew Writings*, 2 vols, Between Bible and Mishnah, Jerusalem: Yad Ben-Zvi Press (Hebrew).

Reeder, C. A. (2012), *The Enemy in the Household: Family Violence in Deuteronomy and Beyond*, Grand Rapids, MI: Baker Academic.

Regev, E. (1996a), 'The Controversy Regarding the Eating of the Cereal Offering of the Well-Being Sacrifices and the Thanksgiving Cakes in 4QMMT, the Temple Scroll, and the Scholion to Megillat Ta'anit', *Tarbiz*, 65: 375–88 (Hebrew).

Regev, E. (1996b), 'Ritual Baths of Jewish Groups and Sects in the Second Temple Period', *Cathedra*, 79: 3–21 (Hebrew).

Regev, E. (2005), *The Sadducees and Their Halakhah*, Jerusalem: Yad Ben-Zvi (Hebrew).

Regev, E., and D. Nakman (2002), 'Josephus and the Halakhah of the Pharisees, the Sadducees, and Qumran', *Zion*, 67: 401–33 (Hebrew).

Reinhartz, A., and K. Shier (2012), 'Josephus on Children and Childhood', *Studies in Religion*, 41: 364–75.

Revel, B. (1923–24), 'Some Anti-Traditional Laws of Josephus', *JQR*, 14: 293–301.

Reventlow, H. G., and Y. Hoffman, eds (2011), *The Decalogue in Jewish and Christian Tradition*, New York/London: T&T Clark.

Ribary, M. (2017), 'Literary Signals for Legal Abstraction in the Talmud Yerushalmi and the Justinianic Legal Corpus', PhD diss., University of Manchester.

Ritter, B. (1879), *Philo und die Halacha: eine vergleichende Studie unter steter Berücksichtigung des Josephus*, Leipzig, J. C. Hinrichs.

Robertson, S. D. (1991), 'The Account of the Ancient Israelite Tabernacle and First Priesthood in the "Jewish Antiquities" of Flavius Josephus', PhD diss., Annenberg Research Institute.

Rooker, M. F. (2010), *The Ten Commandments: Ethics for the Twenty-First Century*, New American Commentary Studies in Bible and Theology, Nashville: Broadman & Holman.

Rosenblum, J. (2016), *The Jewish Dietary Laws in the Ancient World*, New York: Cambridge University Press.

Rosen-Zvi, I. (2012), *The Mishnaic Sotah Ritual: Temple, Gender and Midrash*, Leiden: Brill.
Rubenstein, J. L. (1994), 'The Sadducees and the Water Libation', *JQR*, 84: 417–44.
Rubenstein, J. L. (1995), *The History of Sukkot in the Second Temple and Rabbinic Periods*, Atlanta: Scholars Press.
Ruwe, A. (2003), 'The Structure of the Book of Leviticus in the Narrative Outline of the Priestly Sinai Story (Exod 19:1–Num 10:10*)', in R. Rendtorff and R. A. Kugler (eds), *The Book of Leviticus: Composition and Reception*, 55–78, Leiden/Boston: Brill.
Safrai, Sh. (1987), 'Halakha', in *The Literature of the Sages, First Part: Oral Torah, Halakha, Mishna, Tosefta, Talmud, External Tractates*, 121–210, CRINT II.3.1, Assen: Van Gorcum.
Safrai, Z. (2018), *Seeking Out the Land: Land of Israel Traditions in Ancient Jewish, Christian and Samaritan Literature (200 BCE–400 CE)*, Leiden: Brill.
Salvesen, A. (1991), *Symmachus in the Pentateuch*, Journal of Semitic Studies Monograph 15, Manchester: University of Manchester Press.
Sarna, N. (1991), *Exodus*, JPS Torah Commentary, Philadelphia/New York: Jewish Publication Society.
Sasson, J. M. (2014), 'Another Look at the Tenth Commandment', in J. L. Berquist and A. Hunt (eds), *Focusing Biblical Studies: The Crucial Nature of the Persian and Hellenistic Periods: Essays in Honor of Douglas A. Knight*, 3–18, London: Bloomsbury.
Satlow, M. L. (2001), *Jewish Marriage in Antiquity*, Princeton: Princeton University Press.
Saulnier, S. (2009), 'Jub 49:1-14 and the (Absent) Second Passover: How (and Why) to Do Away with an Unwanted Festival', *Henoch*, 31: 42–8.
Saulnier, S. (2012), *Calendrical Variations in Second Temple Judaism: New Perspectives on the 'Date of the Last Supper' Debate*, Leiden/Boston: Brill.
Schalit, A. (1944–63), *Josephus' Jewish Antiquities with a Translation from the Greek: Introduction, Commentary, Maps, and Illustrations*, 3 vols, Jerusalem: Bialik Institute (Hebrew).
Schiff, D. (2002), *Abortion in Judaism*, Cambridge: Cambridge University Press.
Schiffman, L. H. (1975), *The Halakhah at Qumran*, Studies in Judaism in Late Antiquity 16, Leiden: Brill.
Schiffman, L. H. (1983), *Sectarian Law in the Dead Sea Scrolls, Courts, Testimony, and the Penal Code*, Brown Judaic Studies 33, Chico, CA: Scholars Press.
Schiffman, L. H. (2008), *The Courtyards of the House of the Lord: Studies in the Temple Scroll*, STDJ 75, Leiden/Boston: Brill.
Schiffman, L. H. (2009), 'Halakhic Terminology in the Dead Sea Scrolls', *Revue de Qumrân*, 24: 115–33.
Schiffman, L. H. (2018), 'Second Temple Period Rationales for the Torah's Commandments', *Diné Israel*, 32: 55–76.
Schremer, A. (2003), *Male and Female He Created Them: Jewish Marriage in the Late Second Temple, Mishnah, and Talmud Periods*, Jerusalem: Zalman Shazar Center (Hebrew).
Schwartz, D. R. (1990), *Agrippa I: The Last King of Judaea*, TSAJ 23, Tübingen: Mohr Siebeck.
Schwartz, D. R. (1992), *Studies in the Jewish Background of Christianity*, WUNT 60, Tübingen: Mohr Siebeck.
Schwartz, J. (2004), 'Dogs in Jewish Society in the Second Temple Period and in the Time of the Mishnah and Talmud', *JJS* 55: 246–77.

Schwartz, J. (2014), 'Sacrifice without the Rabbis: Ritual and Sacrifice in the Second Temple Period according to Contemporary Sources', in A. Houtman et al. (eds), *The Actuality of Sacrifice: Past and Present*, 123–49, Leiden/Boston: Brill.

Scullion, J. P. (1990), 'A Traditio-Historical Study of the Day of Atonement', PhD diss., Catholic University of America.

Segal, B. Z., ed. (1986), *The Ten Commandments in History and Tradition*, Jerusalem: Magnes (Hebrew).

Segal, J. B. (1963), *The Hebrew Passover from the Earliest Times to A.D. 70*, London: Oxford University Press.

Sharon, N. (2012), 'Setting the Stage: The Effects of the Roman Conquest and the Loss of Sovereignty', in D. R. Schwartz and Z. Weiss (eds), *Was 70 CE a Watershed in Jewish History? On Jews and Judaism before and after the Destruction of the Second Temple*, 415–45, Leiden: Brill.

Shemesh, A. (1998), '4Q271.3: A Key to Sectarian Matrimonial Law', *JJS*, 49: 244–63.

Shemesh, A. (2009), *Halakhah in the Making: The Development of Jewish Law from Qumran to the Rabbis*, Oakland: University of California Press.

Shemesh, A. (2010), 'Halakhah Between the Dead Sea Scrolls and Rabbinic Literature', in T. H. Lim and J. J. Collins (eds), *The Oxford Handbook of the Dead Sea Scrolls*, 595–616, Oxford: Oxford University Press.

Shinan, A., and Y. Zakovitch (2015), 'Why Is "A" Placed Next to "B"? Juxtaposition in the Bible and Beyond', in M. Kister et al. (eds), *Tradition, Transmission, and Transformation from Second Temple Literature through Judaism and Christianity in Late Antiquity*, 322–42, STDJ 113, Leiden: Brill.

Siggelkow-Berner, B. (2011), *Die jüdischen Feste im Bellum Judaicum des Flavius Josephus*, WUNT 2/306, Tübingen: Mohr Siebeck.

Ska, J. L. (2006), *Introduction to Reading the Pentateuch*, Winona Lake, IN: Eisenbrauns.

Solevag, A. R. (2013), *Birthing Salvation: Gender and Class in Early Christian Childbearing Discourse*, Leiden/Boston: Brill.

Spilsbury, P. (1996), '"Contra Apionem" and "Antiquitates Judaicae": Points of Contact', in L. H. Feldman and J. R. Levison (eds), *Josephus' 'Contra Apionem': Studies in Its Character and Context with a Latin Concordance to the Portion Missing in Greek*, 348–68, Leiden: Brill.

Spilsbury, P. (1998), *The Image of the Jew in Flavius Josephus' Paraphrase of the Bible*, TSAJ 69, Tübingen: Mohr Siebeck.

Spilsbury, P. (2014), 'Exodus in Josephus', in T. B. Dozeman et al. (eds), *The Book of Exodus: Composition, Reception, and Interpretation*, 465–84, Leiden/Boston: Brill.

Sprinkle, J. M. (1993), 'The Interpretation of Exodus 21.22-25 (Lex Talionis) and Abortion', *WTJ*, 55: 233–53.

Sprinkle, J. M. (1994), *The Book of the Covenant: A Literary Approach*, JSOTSup 174, Sheffield: JSOT Press.

Stackert, J. (2007), *Rewriting the Torah: Literary Revision in Deuteronomy and the Holiness Legislation*, FAT 52, Tübingen: Mohr Siebeck.

Stemberger, G. (2005), 'Leviticus in Sifra', in J. Neusner and A. J. Avery Peck (eds), *Encyclopedia of Midrash*, 429–47, Leiden: Brill.

Sterling, G. E. (1992), *Historiography & Self-Definition: Josephos [sic!], Luke–Acts, & Apologetic Historiography*, NovTSup 64, Leiden: Brill.

Sterling, G. E. (2018), 'When Silence is Golden: The Omission of the Golden Calf Story in Josephus', in E. F. Mason and E. F. Lupieri (eds), *Golden Calf Traditions in Early Judaism, Christianity, and Islam*, 87–96, Leiden: Brill.

Stern, D. (1998), 'The Captive Woman: Hellenization, Greco-Roman Erotic Narrative, and Rabbinic Literature', *Poetics Today*, 19: 91–127.

Stern, S. (2002), 'Jewish Calendar Reckoning in the Graeco-Roman Cities', in J. R. Bartlett (ed.), *Jews in the Hellenistic and Roman Cities*, 107–16, New York: Routledge.

Stevenson, G. (2001), *Power and Place: Temple and Identity in the Book of Revelation*, BZNW 107, Berlin: de Gruyter.

Stökl Ben Ezra, D. (2002), 'The Christian Exegesis of the Scapegoat between Jews and Pagans', in A. I. Baumgarten (ed.), *Sacrifice in Religious Experience*, 207–32, Studies in the History of Religions 93, Leiden: Brill.

Stökl Ben Ezra, D. (2003), *The Impact of Yom Kippur on Early Christianity: The Day of Atonement from Second Temple Judaism to the Fifth Century*, WUNT 163, Tübingen: Mohr Siebeck.

Stol, M. (2000), *Birth in Babylonia and the Bible: Its Mediterranean Setting*, Cuneiform Monographs 14, Groningen: Styx.

Stol, M. (2009), 'Embryology in Babylonia and the Bible', in V. R. Sasson and J. M. Law (eds), *Imagining the Fetus: The Unborn in Myth, Religion, and Culture*, 137–56, Oxford: Oxford University Press.

Sussmann, Y. (1989–90), 'The History of Halakhah and the Dead Sea Scrolls: Preliminary Observations on Miqsat Ma'ase ha-Torah (4QMMT)', *Tarbiz*, 59: 11–66 (Hebrew).

Svebakken, H. (2012), *Philo of Alexandria's Exposition of the Tenth Commandment*, Atlanta: SBL.

Tabory, J. (1995), *Jewish Festivals in the Time of the Mishnah and Talmud*, Jerusalem: Magnes (Hebrew).

Teeter, D. A. (2014), *Scribal Laws: Exegetical Variation in the Textual Transmission of Biblical Law in the Late Second Temple Period*, Tubingen: Mohr Siebeck.

Termini, C. (2004), 'Taxonomy of Biblical Laws and ΦΙΛΟΤΕΧΝΙΑ in Philo of Alexandria: A Comparison with Josephus and Cicero', *SPhiloA*, 16: 1–29.

Thackeray, H. St. John et al., ed. and trans. (1926–56), *Josephus*, LCL, 9 vols, Cambridge, MA: Harvard University Press.

Thelle, R. I. (2012), *Approaches to the Chosen Place: Accessing a Biblical Concept*, LHBOTS 564, London: T&T Clark.

Tigay, J. H. (2016), *Deuteronomy, with Introduction and Commentary*, 2 vols, Mikra Leyisrael; Tel Aviv: Am Oved; Jerusalem: Magnes (Hebrew).

Tilford, N. L. (2013), '"After the Ways of Women": The Aged Virgin in Philo's Transformation of the Philosophical Soul', *SPhiloA*, 25: 17–39.

Tomson, P. J. (1990), *Paul and the Jewish Law: Halakha in the Letters of the Apostle to the Gentiles*, CRINT, Minneapolis: Fortress.

Tomson, P. J. (2002), 'Les systèmes de halakha du "Contre Apion" et des "Antiquités"', in F. Siegert and J. U. Kalms (eds), *Internationales Josephus-Kolloquium, Paris 2001*, 189–220, Münster: LIT.

Tomson, P. J. (2019), *Studies on Jews and Christians in the First and Second Centuries*, WUNT 418, Tübingen: Mohr Siebeck.

Toorn, K. van der (1994), *From Her Cradle to Her Grave: The Role of Religion in the Life of the Israelite and Babylonian Woman*, Sheffield: JSOT.

Tov, E. (2001), *Textual Criticism of the Hebrew Bible*, 2nd rev. ed., Minneapolis: Augsburg Fortress.

Tov, E. (2018), 'The Septuagint of Numbers as a Harmonizing Text', in M. Meiser et al. (eds), *Die Septuaginta – Geschichte, Wirkung, Relevanz: 6. Internationale Fachtagung veranstaltet von Septuaginta Deutsch (LXX.D), Wuppertal 21-24 Juli 2016*, 181–201, WUNT 405, Tubingen: Mohr Siebeck.

Towers, S. C. (2014), 'An Analysis of Philo's Exegesis of the Sotah Ritual', *Women in Judaism*, 11: 1–24.

Tsai, D. Y. (2014), *Human Rights in Deuteronomy with Special Focus on Slave Laws*, BZAW 464, Berlin: de Gruyter.

Tsevat, M. (1970), 'The Connection Between Šemitta and Mount Sinai', in S. Abramsky et al. (eds), *Shmuel Yeivin Jubilee Volume*, 283–8, Jerusalem: Israel Society for Biblical Research (Hebrew).

Ulrich, E. (2002), 'The Text of the Hebrew Scriptures at the Time of Hillel and Jesus', in A. Lemaire (ed.), *Congress Volume: Basel 2001*, 85–108, VTSup 92, Leiden: Brill.

Ulrich, E. (2010), *The Biblical Qumran Scrolls: Transcriptions and Textual Variants*, VTSup 134, Leiden: Brill.

Urbach, E. E. (1960), 'Halakhot Regarding Slavery as a Source for the Social History of the Second Temple and the Talmudic Period', *Zion*, 25: 141–89 (Hebrew).

Van der Horst, P. W. (2014), *Studies in Ancient Judaism and Early Christianity*, Leiden: Brill.

VanderKam, J. C. (2012), 'Exegesis of Pentateuchal Legislation in Jubilees and Related Texts Found at Qumran', in A. Moriya and G. Hata (eds), *Pentateuchal Traditions in the Late Second Temple Period: Proceedings of the International Workshop in Tokyo, August 28–31, 2007*, 176–200, Leiden: Brill.

VanderKam, J. C. (2018), *Jubilees: A Commentary*, 2 vols, Hermeneia, Minneapolis: Fortress.

VanderKam, J. C., and D. Boesenberg (2013), 'Moses in Second Temple Jewish Texts', in J. Charlesworth and D. Bock (eds), *Parables of Enoch: A Paradigm Shift*, 124–58, T&T Clark Jewish and Christian Texts Series 11, London/New York: Bloomsbury.

Vermes, G. (1982), 'A Summary of the Law by Flavius Josephus', *NovT*, 24: 289–303.

Viezel, E. (2014), 'Moses' Role in Writing the Torah: The History of Jewish Fundamental Tenet', *Journal for the Study of Religions and Ideologies*, 39: 3–44.

Vogelzang, M. E., and W. J. van Bekkum (1986), 'Meaning and Symbolism of Clothing in Ancient Near Eastern Texts', in H. L. J. Vanstiphout (ed.), *Scripta Signa Vocis: Studies about Scripts, Scriptures, Scribes and Languages in the Near East, Presented to J. H. Hospers by his Pupils, Colleagues and Friends*, 265–84, Groningen: E. Forsten.

Voitila, A. (2015), 'Leviticus', in J. A. Aitken (ed.), *T&T Clark Companion to the Septuagint*, 43–57, London: T&T Clark.

Von Ehrenkrook, J. (2011), *Sculpting Idolatry in Flavian Rome: (An)Iconic Rhetoric in the Writings of Flavius Josephus*, Atlanta: SBL.

Waaler, E. (2008), *The Shema and the First Commandment in First Corinthians: An Intertextual Approach to Paul's Re-reading of Deuteronomy*, WUNT 253, Tübingen: Mohr Siebeck.

Wadler, S. (2018), 'Genesis and Halakhah: An Analysis of the Relationship Between Genesis and Law in the Second Temple and Early Rabbinic Periods', PhD diss., University of Notre Dame.

Ward, J. S. (2007), 'Roman Greek: Latinisms in the Greek of Flavius Josephus', *CQ*, 57: 632–49.

Wassen, C. (2005), *Women in the Damascus Document*, Academia Biblica 21, Atlanta: SBL; Leiden: Brill.
Waters, G. (2006), *The End of Deuteronomy in the Epistles of Paul*, WUNT 2/221, Tübingen: Mohr Siebeck.
Watts, J. W. (2013), *Leviticus 1–10*, HCOT, Leuven: Peeters.
Weinfeld, M. (2001), *The Decalogue and the Recitation of 'Shema': The Development of the Confessions*, Tel Aviv: Hakibbutz Hameuchad (Hebrew).
Weisberg, D. E. (2009), *Levirate Marriage and the Family in Ancient Judaism*, Waltham: Brandeis University Press.
Weiss, H. (1998), 'The Sabbath in the Writings of Josephus', *JSJ*, 29: 363–90.
Weitzman, S. (2009), 'Mimic Jews and Jewish Mimics in Antiquity: A Non-Girardian Approach to Mimetic Rivalry', *JAAR*, 77: 922–40.
Wells, B. (2004), *The Law of Testimony in the Pentateuchal Codes*, Wiesbaden: Harrassowitz.
Wells, B. (2005), 'Sex, Lies, and Virginal Rape: The Slandered Bride and False Accusation in Deuteronomy', *JBL*, 124: 41–72.
Wenham, J. (1979), *The Book of Leviticus*, NICOT, Grand Rapids: Eerdmans.
Werman, C. (1995), 'The Rules of Consuming and Covering Blood in Priestly and Rabbinic Law', *Revue de Qumran*, 16: 621–36.
Werman, C., and A. Shemesh (2009), 'The Halakhah in the Dead Sea Scrolls', in M. Kister (ed.), *Qumran Scrolls and Their World*, 2:409–33, 2 vols, Jerusalem: Yad Ben Zvi (Hebrew).
Werman, C., and A. Shemesh. (2011), *Revealing the Hidden: Exegeses and Halakha in the Qumran Scrolls*, Jerusalem: Mosad Bialik (Hebrew).
Wevers, J. W. (1998), *Notes on the Greek Text of Numbers*, SCS 46, Atlanta: Scholars Press.
Weyl, H. (1900), *Die jüdischen Strafgesetze bei Flavius Josephus in ihren Verhaltnis zu Schrift und Halacha*, Berlin: Itzkowski.
Wheeler-Reed, D., J. W. Knust, and D. B. Martin (2018), 'Can a Man Commit πορνεία with His Wife?', *JBL*, 137: 383–98.
Willis, T. M. (2009), *Leviticus*, AOTC, Nashville: Abingdon.
Wilson, B. E. (2015), *Unmanly Men: Refigurations of Masculinity in Luke–Acts*, Oxford: Oxford University Press.
Winston, D. (1979), *The Wisdom of Solomon*, AB 43, Garden City: Doubleday.
Wright, B. G. (2008), *Praise Israel for Wisdom and Instruction: Essays on Ben Sira and Wisdom, the Letter of Aristeas and the Septuagint*, JSJSup 131, Leiden/Boston: Brill.
Wright, B. G. (2015), *The Letter of Aristeas: 'Aristeas to Philocrates' or 'On the Translation of the Law of the Jews'*, Berlin/Boston: de Gruyter.
Wright, D. P. (1987), 'Deuteronomy 21:1–9 as a Rite of Elimination', *CBQ*, 49: 387–403.
Wright, D. P. (2009), *Inventing God's Law: How the Covenant Code of the Bible Used and Revised the Laws of Hammurabi*, Oxford/New York: Oxford University Press.
Zevit, Z. (1976), 'The Egla Ritual of Deuteronomy 21:1–9', *JBL*, 95: 377–90
Zlotnick, Z. H. (2002), *Dinah's Daughters: Gender and Judaism from the Hebrew Bible to Late Antiquity*, Philadelphia: University of Pennsylvania Press.

Index of References

Hebrew Bible/Old Testament

Genesis
4	21
8	52
9.4	49
9.6	21
14	86
19	53
22	20, 86
28.20-21	63
29.34	65
34	65, 69
35.22	52
38	99

Exodus
1.1–15.21	10
3.16	91
4.6	70, 122
5.17	68
12	10-14
12.1	11
12.10	13
12.14	13
12.17	13
12.42	13
12.43-44	12
13	11
13.1-10	14
13.2	80
13.9	10, 14, 125
13.11-16	14
13.12-13	10
13.13	80
13.16	14, 125
15.22–18.27	10
16	10, 11
16.23	11
17	113
17.8-16	85, 113
18.13-27	129
19–40	10
19.1	36
19.19	129
19.24	129
20	10, 11, 15, 84
20.1	15
20.3-5	17
20.3	15, 17
20.4-6	17
20.5-6	111
20.5	111
20.6	18
20.12	15, 19, 102
20.13-16	15
20.13-15	16
20.13	23
20.14	23
20.17	23
20.20	86
20.22	31
20.23	31
20.26	31
20.26	31
20.29	32
20.30	32
20.31	32
20.36	32
21–24	11
21–23	117
21	11, 25, 84
21.1	117
21.2-6	24
21.2	25
21.7-11	24, 26
21.12-17	26
21.12-14	80
21.13-14	11
21.14-17	56
21.16	22, 26
21.17	26, 30
21.18-27	26
21.18-19	26, 134
21.18	135
21.20-21	24, 26, 27
21.22-23	27
21.22	28
21.23-25	56
21.24	10
21.26-27	24, 26
21.28-36	31
21.32	24
21.33	110
21.37–22.3	28
21.37	28
22	84, 99, 107
22.1-3	22
22.1-2	28
22.2	24
22.3	28
22.4-5	29
22.6-14	29
22.6-7	29
22.9-12	29
22.15-16	98
22.24-26	11, 107

Exodus (cont.)		3.13	39	12.2-8	51
22.24	124	3.16-17	39	13–15	35, 50
22.30	50	4–5	40	13–14	50, 69
23–34	129	4.1–5.13	37	13.46	50
23	29	4.22-26	34	14.3	50
23.4-5	29	4.27-30	40	14.4	118
23.11	124	4.31-35	40	14.6	118
23.13	45	5	34	14.7	118
23.16	47	5.14-26	37	14.9	69
23.17	87	5.20-26	33	14.16	118
23.19	12	5.20-26	61	14.27	118
24.2	107	5.59	45	14.51	118
25–40	10, 11, 35, 36	6	64	15.19	51
		6.1-7	33, 34	16	43, 44
25–31	10	6.1-4	37	16.3	45
25.23-30	47	6.2-6	37	16.7-10	43
25.30	19	6.7-11	37	16.7-9	43
28	34	6.12-23	34	16.11-19	44
28.30	34	6.12-16	34, 48	16.11-14	44
29	34	6.14-23	41	16.14	44
30.17-21	68	6.17-23	37	16.15	44
32–34	7, 69, 122	6.19-23	34	16.20-22	43
32	65	7.1-10	37	16.25	44
33.11	129	7.11-34	37	16.27	44
34.20	80	7.11-16	41	17.1–27.34	34
34.23-24	87	7.12	39	17.10-16	34, 49
34.26	12	7.22-27	34, 49	17.15	50
34.28	16	7.23	50	18	52
35–40	10	7.24	50	18.6-17	52
35.13	47	7.25	50	18.16	99
39.36	47	7.28-34	39	18.21	37
		7.35-36	37	18.22	52
Leviticus		8–9	34	19	20, 22, 37, 84, 93, 94
1–9	36	8	34		
1–7	36	8.1–10.20	34	19.9-10	93, 94
1	34	8.8	34	19.9	135
1.1–7.38	34	10.1-7	34	19.11	22
1.3-17	37	10.8-11	35	19.14	107
1.14-17	39	10.9-10	94	19.16	37
2.1-16	37	10.14-15	39	19.17-18	37
2.1-3	34, 41	11	49	19.19	56, 126
3	34	11.1–16.34	34	19.20-22	24
3.1-17	37	11.24-47	49	19.23-25	57
3.2	39, 40	11.36	68	19.26-31	37
3.3-4	50	11.39-40	34	19.29	97
3.8	39, 40	12–15	118	19.32	37
3.12-16	40	12	35, 118	19.33-34	37

20	52	25.40	25	5.14	72		
20.10-21	35	25.42	24	5.15	72		
20.10-12	22	25.43	24	5.16	74		
20.10	118	25.44-45	24	5.17	72		
20.21	99	25.47-5	24	5.18	71, 74		
21–22	53	26	37	5.19	74		
21	54, 84	27	36, 37, 55	5.21	73, 74		
21.1-15	35	27.1-8	55	5.22	74		
21.5	97	27.2-8	55	5.23	72		
21.7	53, 97, 134	27.9-14	55	5.25	74		
		27.13	55	5.27	70		
21.16-23	35	27.14-16	55	5.30	74		
21.18-20	54	27.16-25	55	5.31	70		
21.21	111	27.19	55	6	60, 76		
21.22-24	111	27.26-27	55	6.1-21	76		
22	37	27.27	55, 80	6.9	65		
22.17-25	35	27.30-33	55, 93	6.18	76		
22.24	112	27.30-31	93	6.22-27	61		
22.27-30	34	27.32	55	7	34, 37		
22.28-29	41			7.1–8.26	66		
22.28	41	*Numbers*		7.1-89	59		
22.29-30	41	1–8	66	8	60, 64–6		
23	37, 46	1–4	60	8.5-26	64–6		
23.5-14	12	1–2	63	8.7	69		
23.12	13	1.1–4.49	59	8.8	68		
23.15-21	46	1.1-4	63	8.9	69		
23.17	47	1.1	117	8.13	67		
23.22	94	2	64	8.16-19	64		
23.23-25	42, 43	3	60, 64, 66	8.17	69		
23.26-32	43	3.5–4.49	66	9	60, 129		
23.33-43	45	3.5-13	66	9.1–10.10	66		
23.40	46	3.5-10	64	9.1–9.14	59		
24	56, 63, 129	3.11-13	64	9.1-14	61		
		3.13	69	9.1-5	61		
24.5-9	34, 47	3.40-51	64	9.1	117		
24.7	48	5	70	9.6-14	59		
24.8	19, 48	5.1–8.4	66	10.1-10	59		
24.17-21	56	5.1–6.27	66	10.2	64		
24.19-20	84, 109	5.1-4	59	10.10	36		
24.19	107	5.2	68	10.11-28	59		
25	35, 36, 54	5.5-10	59, 61	10.29–14.45	59		
25.1-55	54	5.7-12	67	12	122		
25.1	124	5.11–6.24	59	12.8	129		
25.6	24	5.11-31	60, 117	12.10	70		
25.8-22	54	5.11-30	70	14	129		
25.35-38	11	5.12	70	15	37, 41, 60, 63		
25.39-42	24	5.13	70				

Numbers (cont.)		28–29	60	5.17-19	16		
15.1-41	59	28	37	5.17	15, 23		
15.1-16	40	28.1–30.1	59	6	84		
15.3	76	28.3-10	19	6.4-9	14		
15.4-10	60, 78	28.16-25	12	6.4	17, 24		
15.4	34	28.26-31	46	6.8	14, 125		
15.7	40	28.26	47	7.1-2	84		
15.8	76	29	42	7.2-5	85		
15.20-21	76	29.1-6	42, 43	7.16	85		
15.32-36	60, 63	29.7-11	43	7.25-26	85		
15.38-39	62	29.8-11	45	10.4	16		
16–17	65, 69	29.8-9	45	10.18-19	110		
16.1–17.26	59	29.8	43	11	84		
16.32-36	59	29.11	43	11.13-21	14		
17.27–19.22	59	29.12-38	45	11.16	85		
18	60	30	60, 63	11.18	14, 125		
18.11	39	30.2-17	59	11.28	85		
18.12	93	31	6, 60	12–26	83		
18.15	80	31.1-34	59	12	49, 84, 86, 87		
18.20-32	93	32.1-42	59				
18.21-32	93, 94	33.1-56	59	12.2-3	85		
18.25-32	93	34.1–35.34	59	12.12	24, 89		
19	60, 65, 68, 78, 118	35	11, 60, 80, 85, 118	12.16	49		
				12.18	24		
19.1-13	35, 50	35.9–36.12	59	12.23	49		
19.4	118	36	60, 79	12.30-31	85		
19.6	118	36.1-13	99	13	85, 114		
19.11-12	78	36.1-4	79	13.1-15	85		
19.18	118			13.2-6	114		
19.19	118	*Deuteronomy*		13.7-12	114		
19.21	118	1–11	83	13.13-18	114		
20.1–21.9	59	1.14	123	14	34, 49, 84, 93		
20	118	1.16	110				
20.29	101	2.22-24	63	14.21	12, 110		
21.2	63	4	11, 80, 83	14.22-29	94		
21.10-20	59	4.4-41	80	14.22-27	87, 93		
21.21-31	59	4.13	16	14.28-29	93, 94		
21.32-35	59	4.15-35	85	14.29	110		
22.1–28.18	59	5	15, 83	15	25		
22.4	91	5.6-10	85	15.12-18	54		
25	60	5.6	15	15.12	25		
25.19–26.65	59	5.7	15	15.13-14	25		
27	60, 79, 129	5.9	111	15.15	25		
		5.13	89, 110	15.19-23	93		
27.1-11	59, 99	5.14	123	16	45, 84		
27.12-23	59	5.16	19, 102	16.1-17	85		
28–39	60	5.17-20	15	16.9-12	46		

Reference	Page(s)
16.11	24, 110
16.13-16	45
16.14	24, 110
16.16	46, 87
16.18–17.13	88
16.18-20	88
16.21–17.1	88
16.21-22	85
17	84, 92
17.2-7	88
17.2-3	85
17.8-13	88
17.14-20	92
18	85
18.4	93
18.9-14	85
19	11, 80, 84
19.1-13	85
19.1-12	80
19.11-13	91
19.14	84, 93
19.15-21	89
19.15	71
19.16-19	23
19.21	84, 107
20–21	112
20	85
20.1-9	112
20.10	112
20.17-18	85
20.19	113
21–22	84
21	84, 118
21.1-10	90
21.1-9	4
21.8	91
21.10-23	118
21.10-14	24, 100
21.10	90
21.11	118
21.12-13	101
21.15-17	98
21.15	118
21.18-21	101
21.18	118
21.20	125
21.22-23	105, 106, 119
21.22	56
21.23	106
22–25	96
22	29, 84, 85, 99
22.1-3	29
22.5	113
22.6-7	86
22.8	110
22.9-11	126
22.11	56, 57
22.12	62
22.13-29	98
22.13-21	97
22.15	98
22.22-23	22
22.22	97
22.23-24	98
22.28-29	98, 99
23–24	84
23	84, 85
23.1-25	95
23.2-26	95
23.2	111
23.4	85
23.8	110
23.9	85
23.10-15	112
23.15-16	24
23.19	87
23.20-21	11, 124
23.25-26	95
24–25	84
24	84, 85, 93, 94
24.1	99
24.5	112
24.7	22
24.10-13	11, 106, 125
24.10	107
24.14-15	110
24.14	110
24.16	110
24.17	110
24.19-22	93, 94
24.19-21	110
24.19	135
25	113
25.1-5	99
25.4	95
25.5-10	99
25.5-6	127
25.7-10	100
25.17-19	113
25.17	85, 113
26	84, 93, 96
26.1-12	94
26.1-11	96
26.11-13	110
26.12-15	93, 96
26.12	93, 95, 96
27–34	85
27–28	83
27	84, 87
27.4-6	86
27.14	107
27.15-26	74
27.15	85
27.18	107
27.19	110
28	37
28.36	85
28.43	110
28.52	89
28.55	89
29.10	110
29.17-18	85
29.25	85
30.17	85
31	83, 84, 88, 113
31.9-13	88
31.10-13	84
31.12	110
31.16-20	85
32	83
33	83
34	83
34.8	101

Joshua

4.2	86
7.20-21	23
7.24-25	111
20	80
23.2	91

Judges

5	8
11	63
13.5	76
19	53, 65, 66
21	63

Ruth

4	99, 100

1 Samuel

1.11	63
8	92
9.3-4	66
14.31-35	49
15.15	111
15.33	77
17	7

2 Samuel

15.8	63
21.8-9	111
21.19	7

1 Kings

1.36	74
1.49	27
1.50-52	11
2.28	11, 27
3.16-28	89
18.31-32	86
21	23
22.38	97

2 Kings

5.17	86
14	111
14.6	110

1 Chronicles

15.2	69
16.36	74

2 Chronicles

19.11	89
25.4	110
30	61
30.3	61

Nehemiah

5.13	74
7–8	42
8	88
8.1-12	88
8.6	74

Psalms

15.5	125
18	41
30	41
32	41
34	41
37.26	125
40	41
41	41
41.14	74
66	41
72.19	74
81.5	43
89.53	74
92	41
112.5	125
116	41
118	41
138	41

Proverbs

1.8	102
8.33	102
19.27	102
20.25	63

Ecclesiastes

5.3-5	63

Isaiah

1.13-14	19
4.6	45
56.2-7	19
58.13	19
65.16	74
66.23	19

Jeremiah

11.5	74
17.19-27	19
28.6	74

Ezekiel

18.8	125
18.17	125
20.12-24	19
22.8	19
22.26	19
23.38	19
44.24	19
45.17	19
46.1-5	19
46.12	19

Hosea

2.13	19

Amos

7.17	97
8.5	19

Jonah

1.16	63
4.5	45

NEW TESTAMENT

Matthew

5.38-42	109
9.20	62
23.5	62

Mark

6.20	62

Index of References

Luke		
17.12-19	51	

Acts		
21.15-27	76	

1 Corinthians		
9.9	95	

1 Timothy		
5.18	95	

APOCRYPHA

Ecclesiasticus	
9.3-9	134
23.22-27	134
45.3	130
45.5	130

Baruch	
1.20	130
2.28	130

2 Maccabees	
6.4	134
7.30	130

Tobit	
1.6	55
1.7-8	95
1.7	96
8.8	74

Wisdom of Solomon	
7.2	76
11.16	109

Ecclesiasticus	
3.3-7	20
3.5	20
22.3	75
23.10	18
25.26	99
50.14-15	41

2 Maccabees	
1.10	91
4.44	91
7.27	75
11.27	91

PSEUDEPIGRAPHA

4 Ezra	
9.30-31	130
14.3-6	130

3 Maccabees	
7.23	74
18.24	74

Jubilees	
1.19	130
1.23	130
2.17-33	63
4.31	109
7.5	41
13.25-26	55
14.1	46
14.10	46
14.20	46
15.1	46
16.3	46
21.7	41
30.17-20	69
32.11	95, 96

Letter of Aristeas	
128-29	49
131	130
139	130
142-57	49
148	130
158	62
228	20
310	88
312	130

Liber Antiquitatum Biblicarum	
11.2	130
11.12	90
12.4	130
16.1	62
44.10	22

Sibylline Oracles	
593-94	20

Testament of Joseph	
3.7	75

Testament of Moses	
1.14	130
3.10-14	130

Testament of Naphtali	
3.3-4	53

DEAD SEA SCROLLS

11Q19	
60.3-4	57
66, ll. 8-11	98

11QMelch	
ll. 2-3	55

11QT	
8.9-10	48
9–12	41
25.14-16	45
34.11-14	41
45.11-12	51
45.12-14	54
56.17-18	92
60.2-4	55, 57
63.5	91

1QM	
7.4	54

4Q266	
12, 4-9	97
5 ii 1-3	88

4Q270	
3 ii 12-19	94
4, 12-21	97
col. 4 l. 3	71
frag. 2 col. ii	55

4Q271	97	*Ḥagigah*		*Nedarim*	
3	134	1.1	87	2.1	63
		2.4	47		
4Q274				*Parah*	
Frg. 1 Col. i 1-4	51	*Ḥullin*		1.2	39
		8.1	12	1.3	39
4Q96				3.5	78
col. II, ll. 11	86	*Kil'ayim*			
col. III, l. 1	86	9.1	57	*Pe'ah*	
				1.1	20
4QMMT		*Mo'ed Qaṭan*			
13.62-63	57	3.4	62	*Pesaḥim*	
B64-72	51			7.3	87
		Ma'aśer Šeni		10	12
CD		4.3-5	57		
4.2021	92	5.1-5	57	*Roš Haššanah*	
		5.6	95	1.2	47
TARGUMS				1.8	89
Ps.-Jonathan		*Makkot*			
Deut. 26.1-13	95	1.6	90	*Sanhedrin*	
		2.1	81	1.1	112
MISHNAH		3.10	98	3.3	89
Abot				6.4	56
2.14	120	*Megillah*		8.1	102
		2.5-6	96	8.2	103
Baba Mesi'a				8.3	103
2	29	*Menaḥot*			
7.8	30	3.7	62	*Soṭah*	
9.13	106, 126	4.5	48	1.1-2	71
		5.1	48	2.4	72
Baba Qamma		6.1-2	41	7.8	88
4.9	32	6.2	41	9.6	91
8.1	108	10.3	46		
83a	108	11.1	48	*Sukkah*	
		11.2	48	3.4	45, 46
Bekorot				4.4-5	45
1	80	*Middot*		4.9	41
		3.3	31	5.1-4	45
Bikkurim		3.4	87		
3.9	96			*Yebamot*	
		Miqwa'ot		4.7	100
Eduyyot		1.7-8	68	12.3	100
4.10	62				
		Nazir		*Yoma*	
Giṭin		1.3	77	7.3	45
9.10	99				

Zebaḥim		*Sanhedrin*		*Berakot*	
5.3	40	67a	30	6.10	62
5.8	55	56b	50	*Pe'ah*	
		59a	49	2.13	94
BABYLONIAN TALMUD		71a	102, 103		
Baba Meṣiʿa		8.4	104	*Pesaḥim*	
21-33a	29			4.15	13
87b	95	*Šabbat*			
92b	95	110b	111	*Zebaḥim*	
				5.3	41
Baba Qamma		*Soṭah*			
7.1	29	2a	118	**MIDRASH**	
15b	110	26a	75	*Exodus Rabbah*	
85a	26, 27, 135			3.6	130
		Zebaḥim			
		91b	78	*Bam. Rabbah*	
Berakot				12.15	67, 69
44a	96	**JERUSALEM TALMUD**			
		Berakot		*Leviticus Rabbah*	
Kettubot		1.5 3c	16	7.3	33
52b	27, 135				
		Megillah		*Mekhilta Kaspa*	
Moʿed Qaṭan		74d	130	4	87
28a	118				
		Niddah		*Mekhilta Mishpatim*	
Makkot		1.3, 49b	75	8	28
23b-24a	6				
		Roš Haššanah		*Mekhilta Nezikin*	
Megillah		58d-59a	55	2	25
26a	89			12	29
		Šebuʿot			
Menaḥot		2.7	94	*Mekhilta Pesikta*	
34b-35a	14	5b	93	1-3	11
40b	62	34a	94		
45b	47	39c	55	*Mekhilta Pisha*	
65b	47			18	80
		Šeqalim			
Qidduši̇n		6.1	16	*Mekhilta de R. Ishmael, Jethro*	
21b	101			11	31
30a	20	*Sanhedrin*			
30b	104	7.19	30	*Mekhilta de R. Ishmael, Nezik.*	
		7.25	30	17	99
Roš Haššanah					
8a	43	**TOSEFTA**			
12b	94	*Baba Qamma*			
29b	42	7.11	29		

Mekhilta de R. Ishmael,
Yithro, Bahodesh 8 #
Exod. 20.12-14   16

Numbers Rabbah
11.2   61

Sifra
Tzav
3.3   48
7.10   40
19.23   75

Mezora
2.2   51

Emor
18.19   48

Sifre
Bamidbar
128   68

Devarim
15   89
63   93
76   49
96a   87
107   87
143   87
190   112
211   101
218   102
221   56
226   113
237   98
289   100
302   96
357   77

Numbers
7.12   71
25   77
64   117
106-107   78
107   40, 41
115   62

119   55
123   78
134   79

Sotah
17b   72

PHILO
De Abrahame
133-136   53

De congressu eruditionis
gratia
132   130

De decalogo
10.36   16
50   16
154   16
157   18
165-66   20

In Flaccum
10, 74   91

Hypothetica
7.1-2   22
7.7   111
11.14-17   90

De Iosepho
43   134

Quaestiones et
solutiones in Exodum
1.1   11

Quaestiones et
solutiones in Genesin
4.154   97

De Somniis
2.184   112

De specialibus legibus
1.9.52   110
1.29   69

1.67   86
1.70   87
1.101-102   97
1.127   80
1.135   80
1.141   55
1.162-256   38
1.175   41, 48
1.188   45
1.200   75
1.212   39
1.224   39
1.226   52
1.240   40
1.243   40
1.247-54   76
1.255-56   48
1.268   78
1.325   112
2.28   13
2.104   130
2.156   13
2.158   13
2.170-73   69
2.188   43
2.215-22   96
2.226-27   20
2.232   105
2.249-51   63
2.261   20
2.344   112
2.1262   46
3.8   16
3.27.148-49   110
3.30   99
3.32-36   102
3.39   53
3.51   134
3.53-55   70
3.54   73
3.55   72
3.65-71   98
3.105-107   27
3.108-19   28
3.123   81
3.145   32
3.164-68   111

3.181-83	109	1.207-209	22	3.92	18, 19, 21–3
3.195	109	1.222	20		
3.251	77	1.224	86	3.93	16, 117
4.11-12	29	1.174	114	3.94	17, 120
4.34	30	1.214	120	3.100-218	117
4.41.226-29	113	1.240	130	3.100-203	11
4.98	55	2–4	129	3.101	16
4.137-39	15	2.5-6	114	3.138	16
175	48	2.6	130	3.143	19
		2.18	130	3.152	31
De virtutibus		2.20	130	3.180	130
20.102-103	110	2.23	130	3.188-92	34
51	130	2.24	130	3.188-286	33
90–94	94	2.41-44	22	3.189	38
95	55, 96	2.176	8	3.198	68
110-15	101	2.194	22	3.199-301	2
111	101	2.201–3.203	10	3.200-203	34
125-30	41	2.207	22	3.204-207	34
142	41	2.215-17	22	3.204	38
143-44	12	2.237-39	88	3.205	17, 37, 67, 120
		2.251	88		
De vita Mosis		2.260	88	3.208-11	34, 35
2.3	130	2.276	22	3.212-13	34
2.43	62	2.311-19	12	3.214-18	
2.208	18	2.311-14	12	3.218	120
2.209-20	63	2.311-13	11	3.219-23	34
2.224-33	61	2.311	11	3.219	38
2.237	62	2.312	13	3.220-22	37
		2.313	13	3.221	39
JOSEPHUS		2.316-19	12	3.222-23	80, 131
Antiquities		2.318	11	3.223	17, 37
1–11	9, 12	2.319	88	3.224-86	2
1–4	110	3–4	59, 60	3.224-57	37, 57, 66
1.14	83	3.10.3 §243	44	3.224-25	38
1.18	130	3.17	13	3.224	34, 38
1.22-23	104, 136	3.20-32	40	3.225-27	34
1.25	17, 120	3.22	39	3.226-29	39
1.29	17, 120	3.39-61	114	3.226	39
1.33	18, 123	3.67-75	2	3.228-29	34, 39
1.95	130	3.87	24	3.228	39
1.102	21, 49	3.88-101	80, 131	3.229	39
1.136	83	3.90-286	2	3.230-32	38
1.155-56	17	3.89	24	3.230	52, 120
1.155	17	3.90	16, 23, 24	3.231	40
1.164-65	22	3.91-92	11, 26	3.232-34	34
1.180	86	3.91	17, 18, 24	3.232	38, 61
1.200	53			3.233-34	40

Josephus, *Ant.* (cont.)		3.259	34, 49, 120	3.474-75	22
3.233	40			4	35
3.234	37, 41, 60, 78	3.260	34, 49	4.13	24, 130
		3.261-69	118	4.14-66	69
3.235-36	41	3.261-64	35, 50, 69	4.67-75	60, 93
3.235	34	3.261-62	50	4.67-69	65
3.236	34	3.261	51	4.70-71	11
3.237-49	60	3.262	51, 78	4.71-73	55
3.237-48	37	3.264	51	4.71	55, 80
3.237	19	3.265-69	51	4.72	76
3.238	38	3.265-68	35, 51, 69	4.73	37, 55, 60
3.239-40	38	3.266	130	4.78-81	78
3.239	42, 43	3.268	130	4.78	11
3.240-54	85	3.269	35, 51, 58	4.79-81	60, 78, 118
3.240-43	43	3.270-79	58		
3.240-41	44	3.270-73	60, 70	4.81	68
3.240	11	3.270	73, 118	4.150	130
3.241-42	44	3.271	73, 75	4.156	130
3.241	38, 43	3.273	38, 72, 75	4.165	60
3.242-43	44	3.274-75	35, 52	4.172-73	11, 21, 60, 80
3.243	44	3.274	21, 52		
3.244-47	45	3.275	52	4.172	81, 85
3.244	45	3.276-79	53	4.174-75	60, 79
3.245	45, 46	3.276-77	35	4.176-331	84
3.246	38	3.276	53, 134	4.184	117
3.247	38	3.278-79	35	4.194	117
3.248-51	12	3.279	54	4.196-301	2, 33
3.248-49	12	3.280-86	58	4.197	35, 66, 80, 84, 131
3.248	11, 13	3.280-85	35, 54		
3.249	38	3.281-86	54	4.198	37, 117, 120
3.250-51	46	3.281	18, 123		
3.250	38, 46	3.282	133	4.200-300	84
3.251	39	3.286	35, 36, 80, 131	4.200-201	84, 86
3.252-53	46			4.201	17, 31
3.252	47	3.287-94	60, 63	4.202	56, 98
3.253	38, 47	3.287	64, 67, 130	4.203-204	84, 87
3.254	46			4.205	84, 87
3.255-56	34, 47	3.288	64	4.206	84, 87, 88
3.255	19, 47	3.289	64	4.208	56
3.256	41, 48	3.290	64, 65	4.209-11	84, 88
3.257	34, 48, 120	3.291	64	4.212-13	11, 14, 84
		3.294	61	4.213	125
3.258-68	57	3.294b	60	4.214-18	84, 88, 91
3.258	60, 64, 66, 68	3.316	13	4.218	98
		3.317	13	4.219	23, 71, 84, 89, 134
3.259-73	66	3.318	110		
		3.320	130	4.220-22	84, 90, 98

4.223-24	84, 92	4.277	26, 135	6.129	114
4.223	117	4.278	27, 28	6.131-55	114
4.224	98	4.279	30	6.310	117
4.225	84, 93	4.280	107, 133	6.336	114
4.226-27	57	4.281-82	31	6.356-67	114
4.227	57	4.284	110	6.371-72	114
4.228	126	4.285-88	84	6.423	13
4.230-32	135	4.286-87	110	7.1-6	114
4.230	117	4.288	110	7.84	11
4.231-43	84, 87, 93	4.287	30	7.130-61	22
4.231-34	95	4.289	85, 110	7.130	23
4.233	95	4.290-91	85, 111	7.193	130
4.234-37	95	4.290	111	7.196	63
4.242-43	96	4.292-301	85	7.357	74
4.242	96	4.292	117	7.361	27
4.244-59	84, 96	4.295	80, 131	7.367	66
4.244	21, 25, 97	4.296-300	112	7.369	8
4.245	97	4.296	112	8.13	27
4.246-48	98	4.298	112	8.100	45
4.249-50	98	4.301	113	8.104	16
4.251	98	4.302-304	117	8.176	66
4.252	98	4.302-33	85	8.191-93	86
4.253	99	4.302	117, 120	8.191	86
4.254-56	99	4.304	113	8.195	17
4.254	127	4.310	114	8.343	17
4.255-56	98	4.318-19	80, 131	8.355-62	23
4.257-59	100	4.319	130	9.188-98	114
4.260-65	84	4.304	16, 85	9.209	63
4.260-64	20, 101	4.305-308	37	9.242	8
4.263	102	4.310	85	9.263	68
4.265	105, 106	4.324	91	10.35-36	85
4.266	11, 124	5.7-8	53	10.43	68
4.267-70	84, 106, 125	5.33-44	23, 111	10.61	85
		5.97	17	10.104	85
4.268	106	5.210	114	10.264-67	61
4.269-85	11	5.112	17	10.70-72	61
4.270	126	5.169	63	10.186	111
4.271-87	117	5.278	76, 77	11–20	83
4.271-72	133	5.285	76	11.109	87
4.271	22, 26	5.335	100	11.152	8
4.272	28, 133	5.347	76, 77	11.155	42
4.273	25	6.35	117	11.182	93
4.274-75	84	6.44	117	11.209	114
4.274	29	6.46	66	11.211	114
4.276	107	6.83	117	11.277	114
4.277-84	84, 107	6.120	50	11.338	54
4.277-83	110	6.121	50	11.343	54

Josephus, *Ant.* (cont.)		20.181	93	2.208	22
12–20	13	20.200	98	2.209	130
12.4	18	20.206-207	93	2.210	37, 110
12.138	91	20.206	22	2.213	86
12.274	18	20.214	22	2.215-17	85
12.358	23	20.216-18	66	2.215	22
12.378	54	20.259	83	2.216	22
13.252	18, 46, 47	20.268	120	2.238-54	17
13.257-58	110			2.257	37, 130
13.294	22	*Against Apion*		2.261	37
13.318-19	110	1.35	53	2.273	53
13.343	54	1.50	136	2.286	130
13.372	46	1.92	120	188	93
14.4-5	81	1.200-204	39		
14.19-20	81	1.212	18	*Life*	
14.21	12, 13	1.219-320	51	12	93
14.63	18	1.281	50	15	93
14.202-206	54	1.282	69	17–21	81
14.245	93	2.20-27	123	40–42	132
14.334-35	81	2.27	123	149	30, 110
14.339	81	2.75	130	414	97
14.366	54	2.80-81	80	426-27	99
14.476	54	2.137	49	429	25
14.477	81	2.141	49		
14.480	81	2.145-296	117	*War*	
15.7	54	2.145-295	2	1.3	136
15.50	45	2.145	130	1.10	93
15.147	68	2.154	130	1.25	93
15.254-55	110	2.156	130	1.31	93
15.371	120	2.160	130	1.39	54
15.265	91	2.161	130	1.149	81
16.24	130	2.163	104, 136	1.253	47
16.43	19	2.165	130	1.269	54
16.118	130	2.169	130	1.477	92
16.194-95	97	2.171-74	122	1.584-90	90
17.14	92	2.173-74	49	1.656	73
17.42	23	2.173	130	2.135	18, 23
17.64-65	90	2.174	18	2.313	76, 77
17.93	90	2.190-92	17	2.456	18
18.21	26	2.193	86	2.487	93
18.82	110	2.199-203	97	2.570-71	89
18.255	90	2.199	102	4.131	93
18.318	18	2.201	21, 90	4.151	81
18.359	18	2.202	21, 28, 102	4.203-204	81
19.278	93			4.264	113
20.17	110	2.206	20, 98, 102	4.561	113
20.106	12			4.626	85

5.225	31
5.523	113
6.248	81
6.299	47
6.312	85
6.423	2
6.425-26	61
6.425	87
6.426-27	2

CLASSICAL AND ANCIENT CHRISTIAN LITERATURE

Aristobulus
8.10.4	130

Collatio
VII.1	133
VIII.2	133

Digesta
D.28.1.20.6	134

Dio Chrysostom
Discourses
32.3	25

Dio
Roman History
55.27.3	91

Diogenes Laertius
7.120	20

Dionysius of Halicarnassus
Roman Antiquities
2.74	93

Eusebius
Praeparatio evangelica
8.7.12-13	88
9.26.1	130

Herodotus
Histories
8.105-106	112
9.107	68

Maimonides
Guide
III, 40	91
III, 39, 340	124

Seneca
De beneficiis
3.8.3	94, 135
4.10.5	94, 135
4.11.1	135
5.11.5	94, 135
11.1	94

OTHER SOURCES
Pseudo-Phoclydes
l. 8	20

INDEX OF AUTHORS

Albeck, Ch. 5
Allen, O. W. 73
Altman, A. 112
Altshuler, D. 2, 37, 40, 47, 50, 85, 100, 120, 127
Amihay, A. 2, 3
Amit, Y. 19
Amram, D. W. 109
Aptowitzer, V. 28
Archer, L. J. 75
Ashley, T. R. 59, 67, 73, 74
Ashmon, S. A. 75
Attridge, H. W. 126
Avioz, M. 1, 2, 6, 23, 74, 92, 97, 109, 111

Baker, D. L. 20, 29, 93
Balberg, M. 13
Balla, P. 20
Bar-Ilan, M. 13, 42
Bar-Kochva, B. 39
Barclay, J. M. G. 2, 17, 22, 80, 86, 102, 110, 130, 132, 137
Bartos, M. 55
Batsch, Chr. 38
Baumgarten, J. M. 65, 90, 96
Begg, C. T. 4, 35, 60, 65, 111
Bekkum, W. J. van 62
Belkin, S. 4, 22, 43, 79, 133
Bellefontaine, E. 103
Ben-Eliyahu, E. 83
Berkowitz, B. A. 81
Bernstein, M. J. 6, 58, 105, 106
Bibb, B. D. 36
Birenboim, H. 65
Blidstein, J. 20
Boesenberg, D. 129, 131
Bons, E. 111
Borchardt, F. 19
Bourne, F. C. 134

Brichto, H. C. 72
Briggs, R. S. 73
Brin, G. 80
Brooke, A. E. 8
Broshi, M. 67
Bruno, C. R. 17
Burke, T. J. 20
Burnside, J. 104

Carden, M. 53
Cassuto, U. 28, 31, 116
Castelli, S. 21, 93
Chapman, D. W. 56, 106
Chavel, S. 13
Chepey, S. D. 76
Chirichigno, G. C. 24
Choi, B. 33
Christopher, D. 12
Coats, G. W. 129
Coffin, F. J. 18
Cohen, B. 133
Cohen, C. M. 28
Cohen, H. 129
Cohen, M. 8
Cohen, S. J. D. 7, 62, 67
Cohn, Y. 14, 15
Colautti, F. M. 12–14, 61
Collins, J. J. 20
Cook, L. S. 85
Cotton, H. M. 132
Cowan, J. W. 117
Crawford, S. W. 83

Daube, D. 90, 133, 134
Davies, E. W. 18, 123
Davila, J. R. 34
DeRouchie, J. S. 15-17
Den Hollander, W. 19, 132
Diaz Araujo, M. 23

Index of Authors

Dimant, D. 8, 41, 51, 55, 57, 61, 86, 90, 94, 97, 99
Dixon, S. 102
Doering, L. 18, 19
Dohrmann, N. B. 139
Douglas, M. 66
Dozeman, T. B. 10
Drawnel, H. 68, 76
Duling, D. C. 74
Durham, J. I. 20

Eck, W. 132
Edwards, D. R. 999
Elgvin, T. 42
Eshel, E. 68
Evans Grubbs, J. 134
Evans, C. A. 10

Feldman, L. H. 3, 4, 14, 18, 25, 31, 32, 38, 39, 46, 47, 50, 53, 54, 56, 61-63, 67, 69, 72, 77, 79, 80, 85, 87, 91, 93, 95, 104, 106, 108, 112, 114, 117, 118, 130, 136
Fine, S. 88
Finkelstein, L. 95, 134
Flatto, D. 92
Forsling, J. 59
Fraade, S. 4, 88
Frevel, Ch. 15, 29
Friedman, R. E. 71
Frymer-Kensky, T. 97

Gager, J. G. 130
Gagnon, R. A. G. 52
Gallant, R. P. 27, 51, 66, 116, 117, 122, 125
Gane, R. E. 74
Gärtner, J. 10
Gerber, C. 2
Gibbs, J. 25
Gilat, Y. D. 55
Gilmour, R. 116
Glucker, J. 136
Goldenberg, D. 3, 5, 27, 56, 69, 104, 125
Goodblatt, D. M. 91
Goodfriend, E. A. 97
Goodman, M. 132
Gorman, M. J. 21
Gottlieb, I. B. 116

Greenberg, M. 20
Greenfield, J. C. 68
Greengus, S. 135
Gruber, M. 16
Gruen, E. S. 132
Grushcow, L. 71-4
Gunkel, H. 41
Gurtner, D. M. 16

Hadas-Lebel, M. 5
Hafemann, S. J. 129, 130
Halbertal, M. 70, 71, 104, 133
Halevy, E. E. 23
Hanneken, T. R. 49
Harrington, H. K. 33
Hartley, J. E. 20
Harvey, G. 25
Hayes, C. 120
Heger, P. 31
Heinemann, Y. 120, 121, 123
Henshke, D. 30, 96
Herman, M. 6, 63
Hezser, C. 25, 97
Hiebert, R. J. V. 99
Himbaza, I. 24
Hoffman, Y. 15
Houtman, C. 22, 29, 90, 127

Ilan, T. 90
Instone-Brewer, D. 99
Isser, S. 28

Jackson, B. S. 22, 30, 32, 133, 136
Jassen, A. 2, 3, 130
Jastram, N. 59
Jewell, P. 74
Johns, L. 39
Johnson, A. C. 134
Jonquière, T. 63, 74

Kasher, A. 2, 22, 108, 130
Katzoff, R. 136
Kazen, T. 51
Kee, H. C. 75
Kellogg, S. H. 36
Keun, L. J. 124
Knust, J. W. 134
Kochman, M. 124
Kohler, K. 3

Koskenniemi, E. 136
Kottek, S. S. 73
Kraemer, D. 12
Kugel, J. L. 20, 69
Kugler, R. A. 68

La Barge, K. F. 52
Lachs, S. T. 74
Lange, A. 33
Lauterbach, J. Z. 25, 28, 29
Lavee, M. 50
Lawrence, J. D. 65, 67
Lee, M. M. 25, 66
Levine, B. A. 50, 64, 65, 71, 78
Levine, D. B. 59, 88
Levinson, B. M. 28, 55
Licht, J. 65, 69, 127
Liddell, H. G. 46
Liebman, T. 113
Lierman, J. 80, 130
Lim, T. H. 83, 84
Lincicum, D. 83, 112
Loader, W. 21, 23, 52, 133, 134
Lohr, J. N. 10

Magness, J. 62
Martin, D. B. 134
Mason, S. 5, 97, 132
McDonough, S. M. 18, 72
McGinn, T. A. 134
McKay, H. A. 19
McLean, N. 8
Meeks, W. 130
Meshorer, Y. 64
Metso, S. 33, 35
Milgrom, J. 33, 36, 39, 41, 43, 48, 50, 51, 54, 55, 59, 65, 67–9, 71–4, 107, 123
Miller, Y. 60

Nakman, D. 3–5, 8, 12, 15, 24, 27, 39, 47, 48, 54–6, 67, 69, 76, 78, 84, 90, 93, 98
Neusner, J. 108
Niehoff, M. 132
Noam, V. 3, 41, 47, 50, 57, 109
Nodet, E. 13, 14
Norton, J. D. H. 39
Novick, T. 63

Olitzki, M. 42, 69, 80, 95
Olson, D. T. 59
Olyan, S. M. 65
Oppenheimer, A. 62
Ortlund, D. C. 73

Pakkala, J. 88
Park, S. 46
Parkin, A. 94, 135
Parry, D. W. 8, 51, 55, 57, 61, 86, 90, 94, 97, 99
Paul, S. M. 28
Pearce, S. 89, 90, 122, 133, 134
Petersen, N. 71
Phillips, A. 28
Phua, R. L. S. 17
Pietersma, A. 75
Pressler, C. 100, 127
Propp, W. H. C. 31

Qimron, E. 71

Reeder, C. A. 20
Regev, E. 40, 65, 78, 109
Reinhartz, A. 111
Revel, B. 58
Reventlow, H. G. 15
Ribary, M. 133
Ritter, B. 2, 80
Robertson, S. D. 11
Robinson Coleman-Norton, P. 11, 134
Rooker, M. F. 18
Rosen-Zvi, I. 70, 73, 75
Rosenblum, J. 49
Rubenstein, J. L. 40, 45, 46
Ruwe, A. 36

Safrai, Sh. 1, 54
Salvesen, A. 71
Sarna, N. 20, 26, 31
Sasson, J. M. 23
Satlow, M. L. 92, 127
Saulnier, S. 61
Schalit, A. 5, 24, 38, 54
Schiff, D. 28
Schiffman, L. H. 2, 3, 5, 52, 55, 74, 83, 98, 120, 127
Schmitz, B. 10
Schremer, A. 92, 97

Schwartz, D. R. 78, 88, 89
Schwartz, J. 3, 88
Scott, R. 46
Scullion, J. P. 43, 45
Segal, B. Z. 15
Segal, J. B.
Sharon, N. 91
Shemesh, A. 3, 12, 14, 57, 62, 95, 97
Shier, K. 111
Shinan, A. 116
Siggelkow-Berner, B. 13
Ska, J. L. 10, 59
Solevag, A. R. 75
Spilsbury, P. 7, 12, 17, 24, 52, 130
Sprinkle, J. M. 27, 31
Stackert, J. 93
Stemberger, G. 33
Sterling, G. E. 7, 35, 52
Stern, D. 25, 28, 29, 101
Stern, S. 11
Stevenson, G. 81
Stökl Ben Ezra, D. 44, 45
Stol, M. 75
Stone, M. E. 68
Sussmann, Y. 1
Svebakken, H. 23

Tabory, J. 61
Teeter, D. A. 1, 80
Termini, C. 6
Thackeray, H. St. John 53, 73
Thelle, R. I. 86
Tigay, J. H. 57, 98–101, 106, 125, 126
Tilford, N. L. 90
Tomson, P. J. 1, 83
Toorn, K. van der 30
Tov, E. 15, 59
Towers, S. C. 70
Tsai, D. Y. 107
Tsevat, M. 123

Ulrich, E. 8, 33, 59, 70, 76, 83
Urbach, E. E. 25

Van der Horst, P. W. 12
VanderKam, J. C. 61, 109, 129, 131
Vermes, G. 85
Viezel, E. 131
Vogelzang, M. E. 62
Voitila, A. 33
Von Ehrenkrook, J. 8, 17

Waaler, E. 24
Wadler, S. 2
Ward, J. S. 132
Wassen, C. 71, 90, 97, 102
Waters, G. 85
Watts, J. W. 34
Weinfeld, M. 20, 24
Weigold, M. 33
Weisberg, D. E. 100
Weiss, H. 19
Weitzman, S. 136
Wells, B. 89, 98
Wenham, J. 34
Werman, C. 3, 12, 14, 49, 57, 62, 95
Wevers, J. W. 32, 59, 72
Weyl, H. 27, 30, 104, 133, 135
Wheeler-Reed, D. 134
Willis, T. M. 33
Wilson, B. E. 112, 113
Winston, D. 109
Wright, B. G. 25, 62, 75
Wright, D. P. 30, 91, 137

Zakovitch, Y. 116
Zevit, Z. 91
Zlotnick, Z. H. 73

www.ingramcontent.com/pod-product-compliance
Lightning Source LLC
Chambersburg PA
CBHW070640300426
44111CB00013B/2186